T0301309

The Governance of Network Industries

STUDIES IN EVOLUTIONARY POLITICAL ECONOMY

Studies in Evolutionary Political Economy is a new series sponsored by the European Association for Evolutionary Political Economy. The series contains original, thematic works that challenge existing perspectives in economics, offering new and exciting views on topical issues. It will undoubtedly promote a better understanding of new developments in economics.

Titles in the series include:

Understanding the Dynamics of a Knowledge Economy
Edited by Wilfred Dolfsma and Luc Soete

Advances in Evolutionary Institutional Economics
Evolutionary Mechanisms, Non-Knowledge and Strategy
Edited by Hardy Hanappi and Wolfram Elsner

Varieties of Capitalism and New Institutional Deals
Regulation, Welfare and the New Economy
Edited by Wolfram Elsner and Hardy Hanappi

The Governance of Network Industries
Institutions, Technology and Policy in Reregulated Infrastructures
Edited by Rolf W. Künneke, John Groenewegen and Jean-François Auger

The Governance of Network Industries

Institutions, Technology and Policy in Reregulated Infrastructures

Edited by

Rolf W. Künneke

Delft University of Technology, the Netherlands

John Groenewegen

Delft University of Technology, the Netherlands

Jean-François Auger

Delft University of Technology, the Netherlands

STUDIES IN EVOLUTIONARY POLITICAL ECONOMY

Edward Elgar

Cheltenham, UK • Northampton, MA, USA

Published by
Edward Elgar Publishing Limited
The Lypiatts
15 Lansdown Road
Cheltenham
Glos GL50 2JA
UK

Edward Elgar Publishing, Inc.
William Pratt House
9 Dewey Court
Northampton
Massachusetts 01060
USA

A catalogue record for this book
is available from the British Library

Library of Congress Control Number: 2009930862

Mixed Sources
Product group from well-managed
forests and other controlled sources
www.fsc.org Cert no. SA-COC-1565
© 1996 Forest Stewardship Council

ISBN 978 1 84720 117 1

Printed and bound by MPG Books Group, UK

Contents

PART III   POLICIES

Figures

Tables

Contributors

Mónica Altamirano, a doctoral candidate, works at the Energy and Industry section, Delft University of Technology, Delft, the Netherlands. She studies economic and institutional dimensions of road procurement strategies from a comparative perspective. She also researches on the impact of new contracting practices on opportunistic behavior by making use of simulation games. She is part of the program Flexible Infrastructures of the Next Generation Infrastructures Foundation.

Jean-François Auger specializes in the economic history of infrastructures. He researches the governance of large sociotechnical systems in Europe and North America since the mid-eighteenth century. He occupies the position of Assistant Professor in the Economics of Infrastructures at Delft University of Technology, Delft, the Netherlands. In addition he assumes the position of editor-in-chief of the *Network Industries Quarterly* and co-manages the subprogram on critical infrastructures of the Next Generation Infrastructures Foundation. Auger graduated with a doctoral degree in the history of technology from the University of Quebec at Montreal, and carried out postdoctoral researches at Louis-Pasteur University and Delft University of Technology.

Peer Ederer is a globally active expert for innovation and growth. For companies, he coaches innovation teams on how to achieve new business models, and advises top management on the strategic role of innovation for their business. On the macrolevel, he specializes on the contribution of human capital to the economic growth function of a society. In this capacity, he has presented to various policy-making circles, such as the Economic Policy Committee of the European Union, the World Bank and several prime ministerial government think-tanks. In Germany, he has published several award-winning books on the connection between human capital and long-term economic success. At Zeppelin University, Germany, he heads the Innovation and Growth Academy. At Wageningen University, the Netherlands, he is Scientific Director of the European Food and Agribusiness Seminar. The energy industry has been a long-time focus of his activities. Currently he is particularly active in promoting wind energy in Africa.

Matthias Finger is Chair and Professor of Management of Network Industries, as well as Dean of the School of Continuing Education, at the Swiss Federal Institute of Technology, Lausanne, Switzerland. He is interested in issues of liberalization, deregulation, globalization and reregulation. He has written extensively about the institutional aspects of global economic and environmental change. Among his publications, he has written *The Earth Brokers: Power, Politics, and World Development*, with Pratap Chatterjee (London, Routledge, 1994), *Water Privatization: Transnational Corporations and the Re-Regulation of the Global Water Industry*, with Jeremy Allouche (London: SPON Press, 2001) and *Limits to Privatization: Report to the Club of Rome*, with Ernst U. von Weizsäcker and Oran Young (London: Earthscan, 2005). Finger worked as an assistant professor at Syracuse University and as an associate professor at Columbia University. He received doctoral degrees in political science and adult education, both from the University of Geneva.

Fabienne Fortanier is Assistant Professor of International Business and Sustainable Development, Amsterdam Business School, University of Amsterdam, the Netherlands. In addition, she works as a senior statistical researcher in the International Economic Relationship Programme at Statistics Netherlands.

Jean-Michel Glachant holds the Loyola de Palacio Chair in European Energy Policy at the European University Institute, Florence, Italy. He was formerly Professor in Economic Science at the University Paris-Sud–Jean Monnet. His researches deal with competition and reforms in the electricity sector, the European policy in network industries and the advent of a European internal market. He has recently edited *Electricity Reform in Europe: Towards a Single Energy Market* with F. Lévêque (Cheltenham: Edward Elgar, 2009).

John Groenewegen has been Professor of Economics of Infrastructures, at Delft University of Technology, Delft, the Netherlands since 2007. In 1999 he was appointed as Full Professor of Institutional Economics at Erasmus University. In the same year he was also appointed at the University of Utrecht to the Chair of Comparative Institutional Analysis. He is General Secretary of the European Association for Evolutionary Political Economy and President of the Association of Political and Institutional Economics. He is past president of the American Association for Evolutionary Economics. He recently edited *Teaching Pluralism in Economics* (Cheltenham: Edward Elgar, 2007).

Vic Hayes is a senior research fellow at the Faculty of Technology, Policy and Management, Delft University of Technology, Delft, the

Netherlands. In 1974 he joined National Cash Registers (NCR) in the Netherlands and co-established and chaired the Institute of Electrical and Electronics Engineers (IEEE) 802.11 Standards Working Group for wireless local area networks. He successfully mobilized the industry to support the World Radio Conference 2003 on the allocation of 455 MHz of spectrum on a license-exempt basis. He is the recipient of eight awards, including the *The Economist* Innovation Award 2004, the Dutch Vosko Trophy, the IEEE Hans Karlsson Award and the IEEE Steinmetz Award. Vic received a degree in electrical engineering from the Hogere Technische School Amsterdam in 1961.

Marija Ilić is a professor in the Departments of Electrical and Computer Engineering and Engineering Public Policy, Carnegie Mellon University, Pittsburgh, Pennsylvania. She is also an honorary chaired professor for control of future electricity network operations, Faculty of Technology, Policy and Management, Delft University of Technology, Delft, the Netherlands. Her areas of research include electric power systems modeling; design of monitoring, control and pricing algorithms for electric power systems; and modeling and control of economic and technical interactions in dynamical systems with applications to competitive systems. She has co-authored and edited several books in the area of electric power systems and electricity restructuring. She recently edited *Engineering Electricity Services of the Future* with colleagues (Berlin: Springer, forthcoming).

Mariann Jelinek is the Richard C. Kraemer Professor of Strategy in the Mason School of Business, College of William and Mary, Virginia, and Visiting International Professor of Strategy and Entrepreneurship at Eindhoven University of Technology, Eindhoven, the Netherlands. She received a doctoral degree from the University of California at Berkeley and another from the Graduate School of Business at Harvard. She has published six books and more than fifty articles on innovation, strategic change and technology. She was director of the programme Innovation and Organization Change at the National Science Foundation from 1999 to 2001.

Martin de Jong is Associate Professor at the Faculty of Technology, Policy and Management, Delft University of Technology, Delft, the Netherlands, and a visiting professor at the National Centre for Technology, Policy and Management, Harbin Institute of Technology, Harbin, China. He lectures and publishes on cross-national institutional comparison, cross-cultural management, transport infrastructure policy, strategic actor behavior in liberalized utility industries and the influence of policy analysis studies on political decision-making.

Rolf W. Künneke is Associate Professor in Economics of Infrastructures at the Faculty of Technology, Policy and Management at Delft University of Technology, Delft, the Netherlands. He holds a master's degree in economics from the University of Dortmund, Germany, and received his doctoral degree from Twente University, the Netherlands, on the effects of privatization of Dutch energy companies. He has a long record of research on the restructuring of infrastructure industries, with a special focus on the energy sector. His recent research has been on innovations in energy networks; institutional reform, regulation and privatization, ownership unbundling; the co-evolution between institutions and technology in infrastructures; and national reforms in European gas.

Wolter Lemstra is a senior research fellow at the Faculty of Technology, Policy and Management, Delft University of Technology, Delft, a senior lecturer at the Strategy Academy, Rotterdam, both in the Netherlands, and a faculty member of the e-Governance Master's program at École polytechnique fédérale, Lausanne, Switzerland. He links his academic interests to 25 years of experience in the telecom sector, most recently as vice-president at Lucent Technologies. He received an engineering degree, *cum laude*, in electrical engineering from Delft University of Technology in 1978. In 2006, he received a doctoral degree in technology, policy and management from the same university.

Malcolm Matson, a graduate of the Universities of Nottingham and Harvard, is a broadband pioneer and has been an entrepreneur since the 1980s. He founded COLT telecom, Europe's first all-fiber telecommunications network. The originator and long-time advocate of the concept of open public local access networks (OPLAN), he is the founder and director of Open Planet, which is working with cities and communities around the world to fund and develop their own OPLANs. He is also the founder and president of the OPLAN Foundation, an international not-for-profit educational foundation promoting the OPLAN concept. Finally he is an associate researcher at the SMARTlab, London.

Claude Ménard, Professor of Economics at the University of Paris (Panthéon–Sorbonne), has published extensively in international journals. He is co-editor of the *Journal of Economic Behavior and Organization*. On the board of several international journals, he is editor of the series 'Advances in New Institutional Analysis' at Edward Elgar. His main interests are the economics of organization, the economics of regulation and the reform of public utilities. His most recent books are *The International Library of New Institutional Economics* (Cheltenham: Edward Elgar, 2005), *Handbook of New Institutional Economics*, co-edited with Mary Shirley

(Dordrecht: Springer, 2005) and *Regulation, Deregulation, Re-regulation: Institutional Perspectives*, co-edited with Michel Ghertman (Cheltenham: Edward Elgar, 2009).

Alexandra Rotileanu holds a degree in political science from the University of Bucharest, Romania, and a degree in international management from the University of Nijmegen, the Netherlands. After working as a research associate at Strategy Academy, in Rotterdam, she joined the Ministry of Economy and Finance of Romania, where she specialized in structural funds management. She is currently covering the field of cohesion policy at the Permanent Representation of Romania to the European Union, in Brussels. Her research interests include the provision of public goods, the development of public–private partnerships, cohesion policy implementation tools and best practices, and the prospective studies on the European Union.

Marianne van der Steen, an expert in the field of innovation and scientific entrepreneurship, is a senior research associate at Twente University, Enschede, the Netherlands. She was previously an assistant professor at Delft University of Technology. From 1999 to 2004, she was a senior policy advisor at the Dutch Ministry of Economic Affairs. In addition, she was a project leader for the Organisation for Economic Co-operation and Development (OECD). She notably published *Turning Science into Business* (Paris: OECD, 2003). She received several international awards and grants, among others a research grant from the Dutch Organization for Scientific Research. She served on advisory boards at the OECD, European Commission and was advisor to the European Union Presidency Conference on Investing in Research and Innovation, the Dutch Innovation Platform and the European Parliament. She received a doctoral degree in economics from Twente University.

Frédéric Varone is Professor of Political Science at the University of Geneva, Geneva, Switzerland. His current research interests include comparative public policy on sustainable management of natural resources, regulation of biotechnologies and regulation of financial markets, as well as on program evaluation with qualitative comparative analysis and institutionalization of policy evaluation. He is also interested in public sector reforms, for instance in new public management, liberalization and privatization of public services and public service motivation. He has published articles in the *Journal of European Public Policy*, *Comparative Political Studies*, *Governance*, the *European Journal of Political Research* and the *Journal of Public Policy*.

Casper van der Veen holds a doctoral degree from the Faculty of Economics and Business Studies at the VU University Amsterdam, the Netherlands. His research interests involve corporate-level strategy, headquarter roles, corporate management, strategic decision-making, top-management teams and managerial cognition. Besides his research, he is engaged as senior strategy consultant at Strategy Works, a strategy consulting and coaching firm that facilitates boardroom decision-making and guides companies through processes of strategic renewal. He is also involved as a lecturer with the Strategy Academy, an executive educational institution. He has taught strategic management to executives in various business schools and in-company programs.

Bob de Wit is Professor of Strategic Leadership at the Open University, Rotterdam, the Netherlands, and at Strategy Academy. He holds a doctoral degree and a master's degree in business administration, both from Erasmus University, Rotterdam, and has contributed to nine books including, with Ron Mayer, *Strategy Synthesis: Resolving Strategy Paradoxes to Create Competitive Advantage* (London: Thompson Learning, 2nd edn, 2005), and numerous articles on strategic management. He is co-founder of Rotterdam-based Strategy Works, a consulting, research and training company. He has worked with organizations such as IBM Europe, Lucent Technologies, Delft University of Technology, INGDirect and CapGemini.

1. Challenges for readjusting the governance of network industries

Rolf W. Künneke and John Groenewegen

INTRODUCTION

In the past three decades, infrastructures have been subject to substantial readjustments of governance structures, often labeled as liberalization, privatization or reregulation. This readjustment appeared as a global phenomenon, in countries with different political preferences, ideologies, and stages of economic development. It affected all traditional infrastructure sectors, including communication, energy, transport, water and postal services. Basically this readjustment of governance consists of stronger involvement of private sector initiatives, allowing for competition in certain parts of the value chain, and arms length regulation of governments. Conway and Nicoletti (2006) provide some empirical evidence for these tendencies. Between 1975 and 2003, there was a significant decline of barriers to entry, less price control and a diminishing degree of public ownership. A fundamental change of market structures and industry restructuring, that is, vertical disintegration, is less obvious (see Figure 1.1).

The reform efforts started in the late 1970s. Chile was one of the pioneering countries with its early liberalization of the electricity market (Raineri 2006). The United States, the United Kingdom, Canada, New Zealand and the Scandinavian countries started their liberalization policy in the early and mid 1980s (see Figure 1.2). Evidently all member countries of the Organisation for Economic Co-operation and Development (OECD) are significantly engaged in readjusting the governance of network industries in order to allow for more competition and private sector involvement. The period after 1995 shows an acceleration of these developments.

Along with these institutional changes, technological innovations emerged, most prominently in the field of information and communication technology (ICT). Innovations in this field include wireless telephony, the internet, glass fiber networks and Wi-Fi, allowing for the development of competing communication media and novel services. Besides, ICT

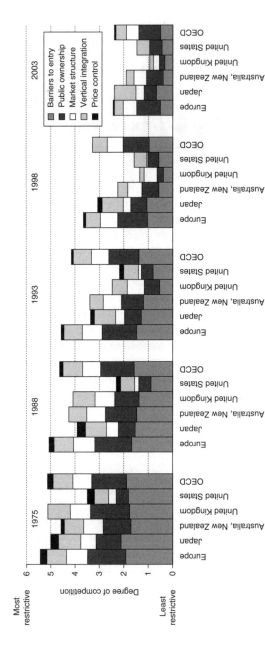

Notes:
1. Regulation is scaled from 0 to 6 from least to most restrictive of competition.
2. The values are calculated as simple averages of the regulatory indicators for seven industries: electricity, gas, road freight, railways, air transport, post and telecommunications.
3. Data for Europe, Australia and New Zealand, and the Organisation for Economic and Co-operation Development are simple cross-country averages.
4. Europe is defined as the European Union with 15 member states.

Source: Conway and Nicoletti (2006, p. 41).

Figure 1.1 Reform in energy, transport and communications according to regulatory area, 1975–2003

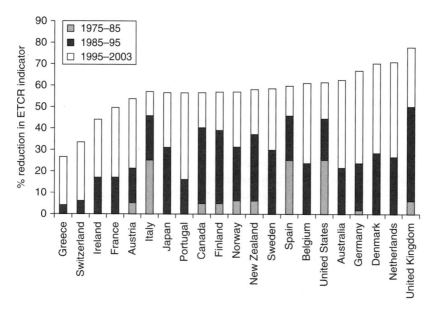

Note: 'The ETCR indicators measure restrictions to competition in seven industries: electricity, gas, air passenger transport, rail transport, road freight, postal services and telecommunications . . . They have been estimated at an annual frequency over the period 1975 to 2003 for 21 OECD countries, based on a number of published sources as well as on replies to the OECD Regulatory Indicators Questionnaire (for the 1998 and 2003 data points)' (Conway and Nicoletti 2006, pp. 8–9).

Source: Conway and Nicoletti (2006, p. 42).

Figure 1.2   *Timing of reforms in energy, transport and communications, 1975–2003*

proved also to be an enabler for other infrastructures in offering openings for more competition and private sector initiative. For instance, nowadays there are opportunities to levy a price on the use of certain parts of the road infrastructure with quite low transaction costs. There is no need any more to install physical barriers to toll roads, in which drivers have to stop and physically pay for the passage. This traditional method of road-pricing does also cause traffic congestion, which adds to transaction costs. Nowadays road-pricing can be accomplished by electronic ports that register all passing vehicles and automatically debit the price from individual accounts. As a consequence of these technological changes private investment is more likely for specific parts of the roads. In the energy sector, many countries decided to install electronic meters even for private households. This enables distant metering and provides price signals to final consumers on an hourly or even minute-by-minute basis. This offers completely new opportunities for the physical balancing of the production and consumption of electricity. While under present conditions consumers pay an average price independent from local or temporary congestion, electronic metering provides opportunities for flexible prices and hence incentives to mitigate the electricity consumption accordingly. This increases the efficiency of electricity systems, for instance by lowering the necessary standby electricity production reserve capacity that is only used to satisfy peak demand.

These institutional and technological changes were accompanied by shifting political and social preferences. Network industries are no longer perceived as public utilities but increasingly as commercially oriented firms that offer their services for commercial prices. The paternalism of governments with respect to the secure and affordable provision of essential public utilities is replaced by a perception of empowered citizens and consumers. They are willing and able to make their own choices on the emerging markets for infrastructure services.

However it would be naive to assume that network industries can only be commercially driven. Public values and national interests are at the core of these industries and often demand public involvement and governmental interference. Infrastructures provide basic services that belong to the fundamental needs of modern societies. Examples of public values include clean drinking water, sound sanitation, reliable energy, dependable communication and secure transportation. Nowadays national interests are, for example, related to the long-term provision of energy sources like natural gas. There seems to be an increasing competition between different parts of the world and countries to acquire access to natural gas and oil. Among others, China's and India's growing economies put an ever increasing claim on the world's energy resources. A similar politically sensitive issue is the access to clean water for drinking and irrigation purposes, especially in parts of the world with a dry climate.

Another reason for political involvement is related to technological features of network industries. These industries typically depend on physical networks that coordinate production processes and access final consumers. However, such networks are often classic examples of natural monopolies. Multiple and competing networks are only profitable in some network industries like postal services, ICT, aviation and maritime shipping. Hence monopolistic networks need to be regulated, even in liberalized infrastructures. To allow competition, a separation between commercial and monopolistic activities (that is, unbundling) is necessary so as to prevent unwarranted strategic behavior. Moreover non-discriminatory access to reasonable tariffs has to be safeguarded. For this reason, new institutional arrangements are established, such as for instance network operators, independent system operators and regulatory offices.[1]

These ongoing readjustments of the governance of network industries are very complex by nature. The introductory examples illustrate that institutional restructuring is closely related to technological innovation and changing political preferences. Although the readjustment of governance structures appears a global phenomenon, there are differences between countries (depending on political preferences) and between industries (depending on technological features).

This book aims to highlight and illustrate some major challenges for readjusting the governance of network industries from a multidisciplinary perspective, including economics, institutions, politics and technology. The central problem of this book can be formulated as follows: what are major challenges for readjusting the governance of network industries in the context of institutional restructuring, technological innovation and changing political preferences?

The remainder of this chapter is structured as follows. The second section presents a framework that specifies the various interrelations between institutions, technology and policy. This framework provides a structure for the different contributions in this book. Accordingly the contributions are presented following the three parts of this volume. The first part addresses some challenges to the institutional design of liberalized network industries. The second part deals with the role of technology. And the third part elaborates on policy issues.

INSTITUTIONS, TECHNOLOGY AND POLICY

Infrastructures are complex sociotechnical systems in which institutions and technology are strongly interwoven. However, the institutional and technological designs of network industries are perceived traditionally as separate disciplines. Engineers dominate technological design, whereas economists, politicians and lawyers are concerned with the institutional design of laws, regulation and contracts. The literature on the coevolution of technology and institutions is an important contribution to bridge this gap.[2]

This research is typically based on an *ex post* historical analysis and applies a long-term perspective, somewhere between 50 and 100 years or even more. Different cycles of industrial development are analyzed, related to different technological breakthroughs. For instance, Perez (2002) identifies five technological revolutions, starting in 1717 with the industrial revolution facilitated by the invention of the steam machine, and ending in 1971 with the introduction of microprocessors marking the beginning

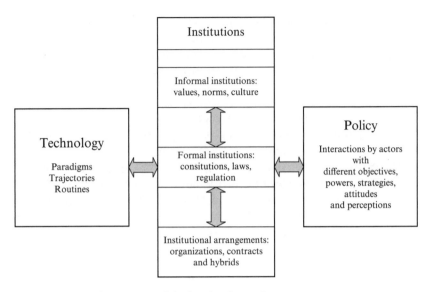

Figure 1.3   A dynamic model of technological, socioeconomic systems

of the age of information and telecommunications. This research helps to appreciate the drivers and barriers for certain revolutionary technological and institutional changes. Yet the significance of these theories for the recent restructuring of network industries is not straightforward. Is this the beginning of a new technological era, or just a further evolution of the age of information and communication? What is the significance of these historical examples for the future technological and institutional development of very specific infrastructures like telecommunications, electricity, water and railroads? Are there any concrete lessons to be learned for policy and industry in these specific sectors? These questions go much further than the above mentioned literature and require a different approach.

Building on a combination of works in institutional economics, we apply a dynamic model of technological, socioeconomic systems (Williamson 1993, 1998; Groenewegen 2007; Künneke 2008). Using a heuristic approach, we identify different elements of technological, socio-economic systems (see Figure 1.3). Institutions are characterized by three layers: first, informal or embedded institutions, like values, norms and culture; secondly, formal institutions, including constitutions, formal laws and regulation; and thirdly, institutional arrangements, for instance contracts, organizations and public–private partnerships. The main indicative criteria to distinguish these layers are the frequency of change and the purpose of the institutions.

At the first layer, informal institutions only change very rarely, like once in 100 or 1000 years. These logical time periods are only illustrative in order to exemplify how fast or slow certain institutions might change. In fact this might be a continuous process with incremental and gradual changes. Values, norms and culture are informal institutions that are deeply rooted in society and inherited through many generations. They are noncalculative and emerge spontaneously. Hence there are very few opportunities to directly influence these informal institutions by direct governmental intervention. At the second layer, formal institutions include formal legal arrangements like the constitution, law and regulations. These institutions serve a certain purpose as they define the rules of the game of political, social and economic activities. Typical rules of the game include the assignment of property rights, the basic rules and institutions of a state and political decision-making, the economic and judiciary organization and the governmental bureaucracy. These formal institutions are typically modified within periods of decades. At the third layer, institutional arrangements are made of contracts, organization and public–private cooperation. This describes the play of the game that enables individual agents to realize their specific objectives. These institutional arrangements are subject to frequent change, typically in a period ranging between one year and a decade.

As indicated by the arrows (in Figure 1.3), these different layers of institutions are related to each other, constituting a certain institutional logic. The game (institutional arrangements) is largely defined by the rules of the game (formal institutions), which in turn depend on the culture, value and norms of society (informal institutions). This explains the top-down arrows between the three boxes. However there might also be an opposite relation. Newly emerging institutional arrangements might force changes of the formal institutions. This might even influence certain norms and values in society. With respect to liberalized infrastructures, there are increasing opportunities for international exchange and economic trade. For instance, cross-border trading of electricity significantly increased under liberalized market conditions. However, legislation was mainly nationally oriented, assuming a local orientation of the electricity business. Though as a consequence of increasing international trade, new needs for national and international regulation of this sector emerged. For instance, interconnection capacity needs to be allocated, and international trade has to be monitored in order to safeguard the technical stability of national grids. As another consequence of the increasing commercial orientation of liberalized infrastructures, they are no longer perceived as public utilities but as commercial firms. This indicates a change of norms and values associated with these industries.

Another element of our dynamic model concerns the policy, which we characterize as purposeful interactions by actors with different objectives, powers, strategies, attitudes and perceptions. Actors create institutions in order to realize their objectives. They try to influence and change institutions if this contributes to their well-being. They do so based on a specific shared mental model. This relates to the intimate relationship between the mental models of actors and institutions (Denzau and North 1994). 'With mental models (internal) individuals interpret the environment, whereas institutions (external) are created by individuals to structure and order the environment' (Groenewegen 2007, p. 10).

Technology is defined as 'the way in which technological artifacts are planned and operated in order to meet human needs' (Künneke 2008). It is organized along paradigms, trajectories and routines. According to Dosi, technological paradigms are defined as 'models or patterns of solutions to selected technological problems, based on selected principles based on natural science or selected material technologies' (Dosi 1982, p. 152). Hence paradigms refer to the way in which technical problems are approached and mitigated in order to meet societal and economic needs. Traditionally infrastructure facilities are perceived as large-scale systems with strong technological complementarities. This resulted in the development of star or tree networks in order to facilitate centralized critical system-wide functions. For instance in electricity, centralized load-balancing between production and consumption is necessary in order to guarantee technical system stability. In transport sectors like railroad and air traffic, centralized traffic control centers are required to prevent accidents. However, since the emergence of the internet, a new paradigm has evolved, which is much more based on diffused functionalities within a web-based network. Consequently, parts of the network might break down without major implication for the rest of the system. Critical control functions are no longer concentrated in very few nodes or links, but are distributed throughout the system. In electricity, consideration is being given to developing smart grids in order to allow for an electricity web (European Commission 2006). These smart grids would perform critical technical functions, like load-balancing, independently from a central coordinator and closer to the final consumers, for instance within a residential neighborhood.

Trajectories are 'the pattern of normal problem solving activity . . . on the ground of a technological paradigm' (Dosi 1982, p. 152). Changes of trajectory are continuous and appear gradually as an optimization of the paradigm according to customers' evolving needs. For instance, high-speed trains are developed in order to shorten travel times and railroads being able to compete with air transport. The mobile telephone indicates a specific trajectory within the paradigm of telephony. These trajectories typically occur on an industry level.

Finally, routines are referred to as 'a collection of procedures which, taken together, result in a predictable and specifiable outcome' (Nelson and Sampat 2001, p. 42). Routines are developed within firms, based on certain trajectories and paradigms. These routines reflect the technical needs of specific production facilities that are established in order to meet specific requirements of final consumers.

Technology is related to institutions' and actors' behavior. For instance, technological paradigms are interrelated with informal institutions like culture, norms and values. This is quite significantly demonstrated by the above mentioned literature on coevolution. For instance, the industrial revolution was not only characterized by a new technological paradigm based on the use of steam power, but also very significant societal changes such as economic industrialization. The development of new technological trajectories needs to be facilitated by changing formal institutions and institutional arrangements. For instance, the introduction of high-speed train connections is only possible if new safety standards are developed and the rules for using the railway tracks are accordingly mitigated. In order to develop new railway tracks, new institutional arrangements like public–private partnerships need to be developed. Finally, technology and actor behavior are related. Actors might get more concerned with environmental pollution. This translates into new preferences and hence technical needs, for instance with respect to the carbon dioxide emissions of airplanes and electricity generators.

This book aims to analyze and illustrate these complex interrelations between institutions, technology and interactions by actors. We intend to contribute to a better understanding of the evolution of technological, socioeconomic systems like network industries. Accordingly, the book is divided into three parts, each taking a different perspective on our model. The first part takes the challenges of the institutional design of liberalized infrastructures as a point of departure. The second part highlights the role of technology as an opportunity or barrier for institutional changes. The third part exemplifies some important policy issues.

INSTITUTIONS

Institutional Arrangements

Why reform infrastructures and with what institutional arrangements? Claude Ménard addresses these questions in the second chapter. He illustrates it for the development of public–private partnerships (PPP) in the water sector. Infrastructure reforms are the result of sector endogenous economic tensions and exogenous political forces. A reform includes several endogenous economic factors. First, water can be unsatisfactorily serviced or insufficiently accessible. For instance, in developing countries there are often problems with respect to the accessibility of clean drinking water. Secondly, a lack of appropriate investments and maintenance can lead to the deterioration of the system and low reliability. In this respect, water leakages are particularly problematic. Thirdly, prices are perceived as too high. Actually the reverse might be the case, since infrastructures are often heavily subsidized, especially drinking water. Lastly, there can be a lack of organizational efficiency. Since infrastructures are characterized by very high sunk investments, and there is political pressure to keep prices low, public providers of infrastructures are tempted to offer services for a tariff that does not cover the total cost price. In the long run this leads to the above mentioned developments, resulting in a financial crisis.

A financial or political crisis often serves as an exogenous factor to force infrastructure reform in order to introduce private interests that might mitigate the above mentioned problems. Since there are always winners and losers, the initiation of a reform depends on swing voters. Hence there is only a short time window to establish the necessary political, economic and technological changes. This is a specific challenge for the institutional design of liberalized infrastructures, since there is incomplete knowledge about the exact characteristics of the reform and there are problems with respect to the credibility of commitments of public authorities.

Against this background, Ménard considers different contractual arrangements to introduce private interests into the water sector. He defines forms of arrangements according to the allocation of property rights. On the one hand, there are the public bureau and the public corporation that correspond to the public form of arrangement. On the other hand, there is the public company as the private form of arrangement. In between, public–private partnerships can be made in the form of a service or management contract, lease and concession. This illustrates the broad range of institutional designs for establishing public–private partnerships in infrastructures. Referring to our above mentioned model, these arrangements are located at the third layer of institutions.

This diversity of arrangements can exist in the same institutional environment of different countries, even within the same infrastructure sector. Equally within the same type of PPPs there are significant differences of contractual arrangements, for instance with respect to price formulas. This illustrates the complex nature of these arrangements and the need to adjust them to the specific requirements and features of infrastructures, technologies and political objectives.

How are choices made? Ménard finds strong support of the transaction cost approach to explain the economics of the various PPPs. Although from a theoretical perspective, PPPs can be expected to alleviate some of the above mentioned problems, empirical studies show a more differentiated picture. There are often problems, for instance, with respect to a lower quality than promised and lack of responsiveness of operators with respect to maintenance and repair. Besides, significant price increases are common. In order to overcome these problems, Ménard argues for a more rigorous application of transaction cost theory, which helps in identifying suitable institutional arrangements. In addition it is also necessary to consider the important role of microinstitutions. These microinstitutions include local and regional bodies—for instance municipalities, regional regulators—the role of local politics, and conflict resolution mechanisms. In Ménard's words: 'This brings into the picture the key role of institutions, which goes far beyond the general level of the political or judiciary system, all the way down to how local or regional authorities are organized and interfere, and how local or regional institutions are shaped and embedded in more global institutions.' In order to better understand the institutional restructuring of network industries and the empirical results, it is necessary to understand all levels of institutions in which they are embedded. In this sense contractual arrangements are a limited tool for reform.

Formal Institutions

Jean-Michel Glachant provides an interesting analysis of the creation of new formal institutions in the restructured electricity industry for the case of retail markets. 'Creating markets in an industry having been monopolized and vertically integrated for decades can be a good test of what makes a market work', according to Glachant. The introduction of competitive wholesale and retail markets in this sector is a remarkable institutional innovation. Glachant adds: 'The competitive reforms of the electricity industry literally consisted of elaborating gigantic and complex architectures for trading on markets—comparable in some ways to architects designing skyscrapers or engineers erecting suspension bridges.'

Glachant's thorough analysis is focused on what it means to create a market for the retail of electricity. What is the nature of this market, what role does it play in the electricity sector, which transactions, property rights and accountabilities are involved? These are the fundamental ingredients for the establishment of formal institutions in the reregulated electricity market with very specific technological characteristics.

Traditionally retailers have the function of adapting products or services delivered by the producers to the needs and expectations of the final customers by adding complementary services. In the case of electricity, these complementary services include transforming electricity from high voltage to low voltage and load-balancing. However, these tasks are typically performed by the system operator without any involvement of retail traders. Accordingly, why is retail of electricity needed in a liberalized market regime? Or would it even be possible to rely only on the wholesale market?

The wholesale market organizes the exchange of rights between producers, traders and consumers, and implements several transactions. Organizing property rights is an important issue, since there is no dedicated point to point delivery of electricity between sellers and buyers. Market parties agree on a future claim to deliver or abstract power from the electricity system. In order to implement these transactions, a complex market design is necessary with respect to the collective management of the common electricity system. This involves the establishment of a system operator, as a third party or mediator facilitating market transactions. This system operator has to manage the collective technical system by aligning the transactions with the technical feasibilities of the system. Since electricity cannot be stored and its use is not completely predicable, physical clearing of demand and supply and financial settlement is necessary. These are the typical tasks of the system operator in order to safeguard the continuity and quality of power supply.

The architecture of the wholesale market is strongly influenced by a shared registration and monitoring system, that is, very particular technological facilities. The system operator has to manage the collective infrastructure in order to accommodate individual transactions. Wholesale traders act as price-makers and aggregators of individual demand. In order to accommodate these functions, a registration system has to be established that monitors the actual contributions of consumers and producer of power according to the initial contractual arrangements. If all individual electricity consumers could be made part of this metering and monitoring system, there would be no need for designing a retail market. However, typically the consumption of individual consumers is only metered in a very rudimentary way, for instance once a year. In this case, proxies or profiles of the electricity consumptions of typical groups of users have to be defined in order to support the collective implementation of individual transactions. Glachant considers various institutional designs to cope with this task. Hence technological differences between residential and industrial users result in different institutional arrangements and different markets.

Glachant's chapter illustrates convincingly the challenges to design new formal institutions for markets in infrastructures. These markets do not emerge autonomously but have to be created as institutional innovations that are adapted to the specific technological features of infrastructures.

Informal Institutions

Mónica Altamirano and Martin de Jong examine the liberalization and privatization of road management in the two different national settings of Finland and Sweden. While analyzing various institutional arrangements in these countries, they point to the importance of national endowments for shaping the development paths and outcomes of these processes. Finland represents a Northern European approach, whereas the Spanish case might be described as the Latin way to liberalization. While both styles are quite different, each is successful in its own way.

Among the various approaches to the restructuring of road management, there seem to be four major trends. A first approach consists of contracting a project for the whole life cycle of the road; a second is to allow freedom of design to contractors, because their performance can be monitored and measured; a third is to finance projects by private investors; and a fourth is to grant road contracts for the longer term.

Finland and Sweden engaged in this restructuring process from different starting positions. Among others, they inherit their specific institutional frameworks. In addition, they have different experiences with market-oriented approaches in road management. Southern European countries like Spain have a tradition of toll levies for the use of certain roads, and the transfer or responsibilities for the funding and management of roads to private sector parties. Northern European countries relied more on direct forms of governmental involvement. These different traditions and sociopolitical preferences are directly related to the informal institutions of these countries, that is, the norms and values, customs and traditions of how to organize certain vital infrastructural services. Altamirano and De Jong illustrate how these informal institutions are revealed in the restructuring process and its outcome.

The Finnish government aimed at enhanced efficiency and less public spending. Although there was some internal opposition, the road authority, Finra, supported the plans for restructuring, since it expected stronger incentives for innovative solutions. Employees of Finra had to get accustomed to a new way of dealing with road management. Essential decision rights of Finra were transferred to the private sector. This established an important cultural shift in the operation and management of roads. In addition, left-wing parties and labor unions initially opposed these plans, since they feared unwarranted employment effects. Road constructors were opposed because they feared unfair competition.

Spain's conservative government had privatization high on the political agenda. The reform of road management was proposed according to the concession model, granting private firms long-term management and exploitation rights. Contractors, concessionaires, banks and consultants were in favor, whereas labor unions opposed these plans. They feared negative employment effects for contracting firms and opposed the private control of public roads.

Nowadays the restructuring of road management is largely accepted in both countries. The results satisfy the main stakeholders. However, there are interesting differences with respect to contracting practices. Finland established a strong competitive environment. The road authority, Finra, emphasizes transparency, a level playing field and efficiency. On the side of the market players, there is a lack of trust as they are reluctant to establish long-term contractual relations. In Spain, however, informal contracts between road authorities and contractors seem to be widely accepted and practiced. There is far less emphasis on transparency, and firms seem to accept more easily that the selection procedures are not always objective. In Spain a contract is not interpreted as the ultimate guidance for future activities, but the beginning of a long-term mutual relationship that needs to be elaborated continuously. The competitive pressures seem to be less developed in Spain as compared to Finland, as there are different cultural and informal approaches how to deal with it.

TECHNOLOGY

Regulatory Practice and the Role of Technology

Matthias Finger and Frédéric Varone reflect on the coevolution of technology and institutions in European network industries. They argue that the present regulatory arrangements are insufficient to take care of the technological specificities of different infrastructure industries. Hence fundamental changes of the regulatory practice are necessary in order to cope with the current challenges in liberalized infrastructures, such as insufficient investments, partial system breakdowns or barriers to innovations. As a general picture, infrastructures in the European Union have traditionally been strongly vertically integrated and owned by public entities. Liberalization was conducted through vertical unbundling; this allows for separating commercial activities from monopolistic, network-related parts of infrastructures. Subsequently, commercial activities are exposed to market competition and, in an ideal situation, the ownership of the related firms is transferred into private hands. Monopolistic network-related activities are perceived as essential facilities which need to be accessible on a nondiscriminatory basis in order to allow for competition in the commercial parts of the sectors. The monopolistic parts of infrastructures are regulated by an independent regulatory authority. These regulators have to ensure different economic, political and technical objectives. Sometimes even the allocation of scarce resources like airspace, water or radio spectrum has to be regulated. This roughly describes Majone's evolution of a European model of regulation (Majone 1990, 1996).

Finger and Varone argue that 'the emergence of the European model of regulating the network industries seems to be to a certain extent—and increasingly so—at odds with the technical and systemic evolution of the network industries'. Therefore the technical specificities of different infrastructure sectors need to be taken into consideration while assessing and designing the institutional arrangements of liberalized markets in these sectors. How and by whom can this be accomplished in the European context? How could the regulatory powers be delegated in order to integrate technological considerations into the regulatory framework?

The European approach of assigning independent regulatory authorities can be interpreted as a trust relationship in which political authorities delegate power to regulated markets, thereby safeguarding public service obligations and supporting the technical reliability of infrastructure systems. Who might be the designated trustee of the European Union to manage the complex sociotechnical infrastructure systems? This results in three scenarios. The first concerns the evolution of European regulators, comparable with the air and rail safety authorities. This sector-specific European regulatory authority is necessary in order to serve the high safety standards in these sectors. From a technical and economic perspective this approach has many advantages. It supports the strong international interconnectedness of these networks and possibly lowers transaction costs for regulators and industry. However, in other infrastructure sectors strong national interests create barriers toward this approach. In the second scenario, self-regulation by market operators might occur if European institutions lack the knowledge and expertise to regulate complex infrastructures. Under these conditions public intervention is mainly concerned with competition policy. An important disadvantage of this scenario is the political control and accountability of infrastructure firms. In the third scenario, differentiated regulations are the result of a gradual bottom-up process. Market operators and national regulators cooperate, even across borders, if this serves their interests. This results in different regulatory arrangements across the European Union, and hence not necessarily in an integrated European market. The assessment of these scenarios in terms of economic and technical performance, and their contribution to various political objectives, constitutes a next step on the research agenda.

Bottom-up Network Modernization

Wolter Lemstra, Vic Hayes and Marianne van der Steen describe the emergence of Wi-Fi networks that started as an innovative product for business use and evolved into the leading platform for private area networking. Nowadays, so called Wi-Fi hotspots provide an alternative for wide area networking. The development of this global network is driven by communities with citizens as the primary investors. This provides an interesting case of bottom-up development and self-regulation of networks.

In the 1980s the development of Wi-Fi networks emerged from a quite specific need of warehouses looking for an alternative way to connect their cash registers to the computer network. The traditional wired network connection was not sufficiently flexible to adjust to different events, like summer or Christmas sales. Fine wooden paneling and marble floors are quite costly to repair after a reorganization of the store. Wireless access was a possible way out; but it was prevented by the very strict radio spectrum regulation. A landmark change occurred in 1985, when the United States Federal Communications Commission (FCC) dedicated certain frequency bands for industrial, scientific and medical use. One of the producers of cash registers, National Cash Registers (NCR), recognized the opportunity to develop wireless cash registers that could serve the above mentioned needs. Hence the development of wireless local area network started as a very specialized niche initiative, driven by outsiders of the traditional ICT business.

In order to develop wireless networks in these unlicensed frequencies, certain norms and standards are needed to safeguard the interoperability and interconnection of different components or systems. By that time, the interfacing protocols were prescribed by the market leader IBM. Since NCR was much more in favor of an open standard, it identified the Institute of Electrical and Electronic Engineers (IEEE) as an appropriate forum to attain this objective. The IEEE is a nonprofit organization which, among others, facilitates the development and accreditation of technical standards through a careful mediation process between major market parties. In 1990 the workgroup IEEE 802.11 was established, chaired by NCR. This turned out to be a decisive step toward a worldwide Wi-Fi standard that allowed the development of a completely new kind of wireless networks.

The case of Wi-Fi networks is an interesting bottom-up approach that is largely based on self-regulation of industry. Newcomers like NCR were initially the driving forces. Although Wi-Fi networks were initially intended for a limited private domain, it turned out that they are also suitable for public domain networking. Hotspots developed in public places such as airports and restaurants. Communities emerged that rolled out local Wi-Fi networks for public access in certain cities or rural areas. This might even be the start of the evolution of innovative network architectures, substituting and finally replacing traditional communication networks.

This chapter provides an appealing interpretation of this case based on evolutionary and institutional economic theory. A major shift in the institutional environment, that is, the FCC decision, triggered the development and application of this new technology. Since this appeared as a niche development, it was not confronted with the vested interests of the incumbent telecommunication operators. These traditional telecommunication operators took another technological trajectory for network modernization. The technological innovation of Wi-Fi networks is certainly not random. It is the result of cumulative advantages in technology and the alignment of certain industry interests that allowed this network modernization. Even the role of one of the initial entrepreneurs like NCR is not to be underestimated. This finally contributed to the modernization of the corporate, private and public networks.

Changing Paradigms in the Electricity Sector

Marija Ilić and Mariann Jelinek provide a profound sociotechnical analysis of shifting paradigms in the electric power industry. Changing institutional and technological conditions create a 'difficult environment', according to them, that demands a fundamentally different approach to that known for the past century. They describe and analyze the potential evolution of the electricity system from a 'rigid, hierarchically controlled entity . . . to a far more dynamic, real-time optimized and information-driven entity of greater long-term robustness and efficiency'.

The present sociotechnical structure of the electricity sector is the result of the available technology, political preferences and social needs of the past decades. Nowadays the industry is confronted with fundamentally different institutional and technological circumstances. The process of deregulation and liberalization created a novel institutional environment. The emphasis is on market competition and leads to a decentralized decision-making process. The government plays a less dominant role in central decision-making with respect to system development. Technological changes include the substantial advancements in ICT, power electronics and turbine technology. Among others, this allows the efficient exploitation of small-scale electricity generators, enhanced control of power flows through the network, and much improved gathering and processing of user-related data. Besides, the political preferences strongly change toward clean production of electricity, in order to reduce carbon dioxide emissions and become less dependent on the traditional fossil fuels. These developments shape the ingredients of a new regulatory and technological paradigm triggering a possible paradigm change. The potential changes encompass all major elements of the sector, including electricity generation, transmission and distribution, supported and intensified by information technologies monitoring and automated switching.

These changes enable a new technological and institutional architecture of the electricity system. It will possibly result in a hybrid system with a large number of distributed generators that are close to the final consumers. A limited number of central generators provide additional services, for instance for large consumers, backup and system stability. Since the current regulatory regime is developed to support centralized electricity production, the above mentioned technological changes need to be accompanied by a regulatory reform that stimulates system innovations and hence the development of next generation electricity networks. In addition, decision-making under uncertainty needs to be taken into consideration, because there is no system-wide coordination of investment as in the traditional electricity system. Under these conditions, there is an eminent role for ICT technology enabling the necessary information needs and facilitating the automated monitoring and switching of the partly independent segments of the electricity system. Ilić and Jelinek argue that only these fundamental technological and institutional changes will accommodate a solution to the difficult problems that characterize the present electricity system.

POLICY

Achieving Public Values by Private Infrastructure Firms

Casper van der Veen et al. ask to what degree private infrastructure firms are dedicated to adhere to certain public values in a restructured market. Regulators and policy-makers are concerned that, under liberalized market conditions, efficiency and profit might be higher on the strategic agenda of firms than public values. The chapter addresses this issue by investigating the strategic behavior of 42 infrastructure firms in four different sectors and five European Union countries.

The authors introduce different polarized strategy perspectives or biases with respect to three different levels of strategic decision-making: corporate-level strategy, network-level strategy and organizational purpose. Corporate-level strategy is concerned with the way in which different businesses are integrated within the boundaries of a firm. There are two opposing possibilities: either as autonomous business units or by centralization through standardization of resources and activities. In the latter case, synergies between different activities are the driving strategic concern, whereas in the former case it is responsiveness to changing market conditions.

Network-level strategy addresses the external relations between firms. The fundamental strategic bias deals with autonomy versus embeddedness. Autonomy offers the advantage that firms can pursue their own objectives without having to compromise with others. However, no firm can act completely independently from others. Advantages to be achieved by cooperation include the realization of economies of scale through the integration of activities, learning effects or lobbying.

The bias of the organizational purpose is between profitability and responsibility. Under competitive market conditions, firms have strong incentives to put profitability high on the strategic agenda. This satisfies shareholders' wishes and contributes to the long-term continuity of the firm. On the other hand, stakeholders, such as consumers and politicians, emphasize social responsibilities and public values, especially in the case of infrastructure firms.

The notion of public value is operationalized into five objectives that are of importance in infrastructures: sustainability, reliability, quality, price and access. These public values are prominent in the current public debate in different sectors, they are observable and they are of a distinctive fundamental nature.

The empirical part of this study departs from several hypotheses between the above mentioned strategic biases and the realization of public values. The chosen infrastructures are telecommunications, electricity, cable and railways in the following five countries: Germany, the Netherlands, Belgium, the United Kingdom and France. The fieldwork is based on desk research and interviews. A quantitative score is developed in order to validate the hypotheses by quantitative methods.

The study includes several interesting results for the understanding of the governance of network industries. First, it is not possible to explain certain strategies of infrastructure firms by referring to their country-specific context or the sector. Second, there is no evidence that the realization of public values can be related to certain sectors or country-specific circumstances. These two findings contradict perceptions that strategies of infrastructure firms might be country- or sector-specific. In addition, the authors found three positive correlations: firms inclined to cooperate create higher public value in term of reliability; those that have a strategy of synergy, in terms of quality; and those that have a strategy of responsibility, in terms of access.

Of course, these findings would certainly have to be validated in other countries and sectors. However, the results are an interesting starting point for discussing further issues addressed in this volume. For instance, as stated by Finger and Varone, is there evidence for the possible evolution of a European model of regulation? Following Altamirano and De Jong, what about the importance of the national embeddedness for infrastructure regulation?

Disruptive Behavior

Malcom Matson, an entrepreneur who has worked for more than 25 years in the ICT sector, shares his observations on the relationship between institutional and technological changes in the telecommunication industry. His observations are based on Carlota Perez's (2002) work, which relates different technical revolutions to ages of infrastructure development, starting with the development of canals, turnpike roads and mail coaches in the industrial revolution, and ending with the age of information technology with global digital telecommunications and ICT-supported networks. Based on this framework Matson states that paradigm-changing technological innovations are always created by outsiders, that is, entrepreneurs who do not belong to the incumbent industry. He adds that incumbent infrastructure industries will never embrace or deploy paradigm-changing innovative technologies. For infrastructure industries left to themselves, the paradigm-changing technology pervades the market and subsumes the previous infrastructure.

Matson exemplifies these statements by a tale of the regulation of disruptive technologies, in which he confronts the ancient technological innovation of steam engines with the modern institutions of sector-specific infrastructure relation. Matson illustrates how the present sector-specific regulation of infrastructures, the lobbying of vested interests, and the doubtful roles of some politicians and policy experts can create barriers for the introduction of these obvious technological advancements.

Matson applies this reasoning to the presently emerging age of information technology. He describes major changes in the topology of telecommunication technology and its potential promises, and points out how disruptive ICT technologies are strangled by sector-specific regulation. This sector-specific regulation protects the interests of incumbent telecommunication operators and allows them to maintain their original business model. Hence disruptive technologies cannot deploy their full benefits to final customers. In Matson's words: 'This absurdity only persists thanks to the fact that governments, public policy-makers and politicians with well-intentioned but misguided intentions to modernize the world have mistakenly taken to looking to yesterday's powerful vested interests to map a smooth, migratory path to the future deployment of these digital disruptive technologies.' According to him, a smooth transition is not an option to gain the full benefits of innovative ICT technologies. However, a breakthrough of these technologies seems inevitable and only a matter of time. There are already hopeful signs, in countries like Estonia, or with respect to certain services like Internet telephony. Matson's recommendation: 'Disruptive technologies do precisely what they say they do—they disrupt. Let them do it!'

CONCLUSIONS

This book illustrates and analyses the complex nature of the restructuring of major infrastructures in energy, ICT, transport and water. The multifaceted interrelations between institutions, technology and policy constitute the leading theme throughout this volume. A multidisciplinary approach is necessary to fully appreciate the process of fundamental change in these sectors and even throughout economic systems as a whole. Several authors emphasize the paradigmatic nature of the changes that occur in these sectors, which is even compared with the significance of the industrial revolution. This book is intended to illustrate the nature of some of these complex relationships and provide insights how to cope with this challenge from an analytical institutional-economic perspective.

NOTES

1. Under most ideal market conditions, system operators and regulators should be completely independent from policy. However, there is a broad scale of possible political involvement in the regulation and operation of networks. For the electricity sector see, for instance, Littlechild (2006).
2. Important contributions include the work of Dosi (1982), Soete (1985), North (1990), Saviotti (1996), Perez (2002), Von Tunzelmann (2003) and Murmann (2003).

REFERENCES

Conway, P. and G. Nicoletti (2006), 'Product market regulation in the non-manufacturing sectors of OECD countries: measurements and highlights', working paper 530, Paris. Economics Department, OECD.

Denzau, A.T. and D.C. North (1994), 'Shared mental models: ideologies and institutions', *Kyklos*, **47**: 3–31.

Dosi, G. (1982), 'Technological paradigms and technological trajectories: a suggested interpretation of the determinants and directions of technical change', *Research Policy*, **11** (1): 147–62.

European Commission (2006), *European Smart Grids Technology Platform: Vision and Strategy for Europe's Electricity Networks of the Future*, Luxemburg: Directorate-General for Research, European Commission.

Groenewegen, J.P.M. (2007), 'On pluralism and interdisciplinarity in economics', in J.P.M. Groenewegen (ed.), *Teaching Pluralism in Economics*, Cheltenham, UK and Northampton, MA, USA: Edward Elgar, pp. 1–21.

Künneke, R.W. (2008), 'Institutional reform and technological practice: the case of electricity', *Industrial and Corporate Change*, **17** (2): 233–65.

Littlechild, S. (2006), 'The market versus regulation', in F.P. Sioshansi and W. Pfaffenberger (eds), *Electricity Market Reform: An International Perspective*, Amsterdam: Elsevier, pp. xvii–xxiv.

Majone, G. (1990), *Deregulation or Re-regulation?* New York: St. Martin's Press.

Majone, G. (ed.) (1996), *Regulating Europe*, London: Routledge.

Murmann, J.P. (2003), *Knowledge and Competitive Advantage: The Coevolution of Firms, Technology, and National Institutions*, Cambridge: Cambridge University Press.

Nelson, R.R. and B.N. Sampat (2001), 'Making sense of institutions as a factor shaping economic performance', *Journal of Economic Behavior and Organization*, **44** (1): 31–54.

North, D.C. (1990), *Institutions, Institutional Change, and Economic Performance*, Cambridge, MA: Cambridge University Press.

Perez, C. (2002), *Technological Revolutions and Financial Capital: The Dynamics of Bubbles and Golden Ages*, Cheltenham, UK and Northampton, MA, USA: Edward Elgar.

Raineri, R. (2006), 'Chile: where it all started', in F. Sioshansi and W. Pfaffenberger (eds), *Electricity Market Reform: An International Perspective*, Amsterdam: Elsevier, pp. 77–108.

Saviotti, P.P. (1996), *Technological Evolution, Variety, and the Economy*, Cheltenham, UK and Northampton, MA, USA: Edward Elgar.

Soete, L. (1985), 'International diffusion of technology, industrial development and technical leapfrogging', *World Development*, **13** (3): 402–22.

Von Tunzelmann, N. (2003), 'Historical coevolution of governance and technology in the industrial revolutions', *Structural Change and Economic Dynamics*, **14** (4): 365–84.

Williamson, O.E. (1993), 'The logic of economic organization', in O.E. Williamson and S.G. Winter (eds), *The Nature of the Firm: Origins, Evolutions and Development*, Oxford: University Press, pp. 90–116.

Williamson, O.E. (1998), 'Transaction cost economics: how it works, where it is headed', *De Economist*, **146**: 23–58.

PART I

Institutions

2. Why reform infrastructures and with what institutional arrangements? The case of public–private partnerships in water supply

Claude Ménard

INTRODUCTION

Reforming public utilities has been high on the agenda of policy-makers. The 1980s were dominated by the major slogan of privatization. The late 1990s shifted to another one, public–private participation. In both cases, the underlying logic was that involving the private sector in the provision of public utilities meant the introduction of powerful market forces that would push toward higher investments and lower prices. It would thus benefit consumers and improve the general welfare.

There is a lot to question about this pseudo logical sequence (see Yarrow 1986). The goal of this chapter is different, however. After a brief overview of why reforms became considered a necessity, I will focus on why reforms based on contracts became so fashionable, and on some lessons we have learned about performance obtained through contracting. By reform I mean a substantial change in decision rights that modifies the governance and eventually the allocation of property rights of existing operator. In other terms, reform is viewed here as a structural change in the mode of governance.

Reforms of public utilities (PUs) vary widely across sectors because of substantial differences in the nature of networks, which depends on differences in their technologies (and the pace of their technological changes), on differences in market structures and transactions at stake, and on differences in their institutional environment. Broadly speaking, the range of reforms goes from full privatization with regulators monitoring the sector under consideration (such as telecommunications) to full control by public authorities over strategic components of the sector (for instance, the defense industry). In between different forms of public–private participation (PPP) develop, which can be interpreted as forms of franchising. The related modes of governance depend largely on sector characteristics and institutional possibilities and constraints. However, notwithstanding their differences, reforms increasingly tend to rely on contracts.

In what follows I examine the role of contractual arrangements as a tool for reforming public utilities through one category of networks, the drinkable water sector. My interest in this sector is motivated by the centrality of water to human beings and the low coverage and poor quality of water services in so many countries, which makes particularly surprising and worrying the slow pace of water reform. The chapter focuses on some questions raised by several attempts at reforming water systems. What forces are pushing toward using contractual arrangements as a tool for reforming the sector? What determines the choice of specific forms of franchising for reforming, as opposed to maintaining a public entity or to fully privatizing? And what difficulties may explain the slow pace of changes in this sector? In investigating these questions, the emphasis is on their institutional dimension, with the analytical apparatus mainly inspired by new institutional economics.

The empirical background of the chapter comes from three sets of studies. The first concerns reform of urban water supply in developing countries. It relies heavily on an extensive study for the World Bank of six cases selected among 53 major reforms (Shirley 2002). The second is based on an ongoing study of contracting practices in the provision of water in France. It involves over 2000 units and several thousand observations (Ménard and Saussier 2002; Huet et al. 2004). The third set of information comes from publicly available detailed case studies.

My arguments are developed in three steps. In the next section I briefly review factors that could explain the need for reform and the choice of contractual arrangements as a way for doing so. The third section examines the variety of contractual arrangements at hand, the diversity of forms actually implemented and some problems involved. In the fourth section I summarize lessons learned from different attempts to reform through contracts. Moreover, I identify strategic questions still to be explored.

WHY REFORM?

Reforms of public utilities, and particularly of water systems, do not depend on a single factor. The impulse usually comes from a complex set of forces that converge at some point, making the existing equilibrium unsustainable. The central proposition I promote in this section is that the combination of endogenous factors (such as sector crisis or tensions) and exogenous forces (that is, financial and political crisis) leads to reforms and to the key role attributed to contracts in that process.

Economic Factors Leading to Reform

In the case of water, sector tensions show up through a set of well-known indicators. First, the rate of connection may be low, signaling a crucial problem of accessibility. This remains a central issue in developing countries and may also exist, although to a much lower degree, in some areas of developed countries. Secondly, continuity in the provision of water for those connected signals whether appropriate investments have been made or not. (Geological conditions must also be taken into account in some cases.) Thirdly, the level of unaccounted for water (UFW) provides an important indicator of the deterioration of the system, because of under-investment, bad maintenance or a combination of both. Fourthly, prices most of the time emerge as a major issue. When one refers to prices in the context of reforms of PUs, the spontaneous vision that comes to mind is that they are too high. Actually the reverse might be the most common situation in water systems. Because of their political sensitivity, water systems tend to be heavily subsidized so that water is delivered at very low prices, which discourages investments and stimulates overconsumption. Fifthly, the collection rate also provides an important indicator of the organizational efficiency of the system.

All these factors tend to be aggravated by the very high level of sunk costs—up to 80 percent of the total costs according to data collected in the United States. This element is specific to the water sector compared to other utilities. It significantly increases the risk of opportunistic behavior by public authorities, by the operator or by both sides when contractual arrangements are introduced. Indeed, as is well known in the economics of networks, once irreversible investments are already made there is a strong incentive to keep the system going even if marginal revenues do not cover total costs.

When the factors above develop simultaneously, they result in a financial dead-end in the sector. Regulated prices, which are almost the universal rule in water networks, prevent self-sustainable investments. The seriousness of such internal disequilibrium can be hidden as long as public authorities can feed the system with subsidies. However, the disequilibrium becomes increasingly unmanageable when public finances face significant tensions or collapse: subsidies cannot be sustained anymore. Moreover most of the time a crisis in public finances combines with significant rates of inflation. In this configuration, operators become squeezed, whether they are private or public. Confronted by the gap between their revenues and their costs, they usually continue to operate, which is possible because of the importance of the initial sunk costs, but with low or even no investment and with much reduced maintenance. In the long run, the system rapidly deteriorates.

To summarize, from an economic viewpoint, reforms of water systems become high on the agenda when excess demand, signalled by low rates of connection, disruptions in the provision of the service, UFW and prices below their equilibrium level meet financial constraints either at the micro level of the operator, or most of the time at the macro level of public finances. There is one other factor that should be mentioned here, although it does not play, so far, a significant role in changes of governance of the water sector: it is the potential role of radical technological changes, that may either combine with the other factors or generate disequilibria that spread over these factors, as happened in other sectors such as the telecommunications industry.

Economic Forces Rarely Deliver Sufficient Conditions

Economic tensions in a specific sector, even spread over different sectors, rarely provide sufficient conditions for reforms in that sector. In order for equilibrium to change, even when it is a low equilibrium, political shifts are almost always needed. This introduces the important dimension of the political economy of reforms in the water sector.

Reforms involve winners and losers. Identifying these forces and their respective weight is a key element in understanding reform processes and their outcomes. For example, in many cases subsidies translating to low prices are particularly favorable to high-income households that consume more water. So there might be a convergence of interest between the wealthiest segment of the population and unions representing employees with vested interests in the existing system, which makes them opponents to reforms. Again there is a specificity of the water sector in that respect because of the political sensitivity of issues regarding water. This sensitivity results from three important components that make the sector highly politicized. First, there is absolutely no substitute for water, so that everybody is affected when there is rationing, through quantity as well as through prices. Secondly, consumers and voters (or constituencies of a dictatorship in that respect) form two sets that totally overlap, so that substantial changes in the system have a powerful impact. Thirdly, ideological factors tend to interfere, water being viewed as a gift of Mother Nature, a perspective that can even be formalized in religious dictums.

A major consequence is that reforms of the water sector depend significantly on swing voters. They determine changes in the equilibrium between winners and losers that can open a space for changes; and their attitude toward change conditions the stability of the ruling coalition, amplifying or reducing the range of contractual hazards. They also largely influence the timing of reforms, which is usually highly constrained. In most cases, the window of opportunity is very short because the support of swing voters is quite precarious, particularly for such a sensitive issue as water. This difficulty becomes even more significant in developing countries, with weak or quasi-absent democratic traditions.

There are two important consequences of this combination when it comes to the introduction of contracts as a tool for supporting reforms. The first consequence is an information problem. The window of opportunity for deep changes being short, particularly because of the role of swing voters, contracts have to be designed with largely incomplete knowledge of the exact characteristics of the network. This involves important problems not only for the design of the new arrangement, but also for its implementation, a difficulty confirmed by the very high rate of renegotiation of water contracts (Guasch 2004). The second consequence, the introduction of contracts, most of the time with a private operator, involves substantial changes in the allocation of decision rights as well as property rights, with the underlying assumption that contracts can help by relaxing the grip of public authorities on the water system.[1] This raises the issue of the credibility of commitments of public authorities, particularly when the political coalition initiating reforms is relatively unstable, making the enforcement of contracts a key factor.

In order to make reforms credible, several questions need to be answered first. What guarantees can be provided that commitments will be honored by the parties involved, particularly by public authorities? Do adequate institutions exist that make the reforms under consideration plausible? For example, if privatization is considered, does a credible financial market exist that makes it feasible? What role should guarantees provided by third parties such as donors play? This issue is often critical for developing countries, but also potentially sensitive in developed countries. For example, is there a financial guarantee provided by a central government to local authorities. Are political factors a source of credibility or elements that may hamper future initiatives, for example by imposing too many constraints on the operator?

In sum, the very nature of tensions pushing toward reforms in the water sector (see Figure 2.1) may explain why contracts are often viewed as a key tool for a successful approach and, simultaneously, why the institutional dimension is inescapable.

However, the forces at the origin of reforms also identify the difficulties to be expected. The financial dimension of the tensions, that is, the combination of lack of resources in the sector and of highly constrained public finance, is a major force pushing toward reform while the political sensitivity of water issues makes full privatization difficult. In that context, public–private partnership through contracts is often viewed as the ideal

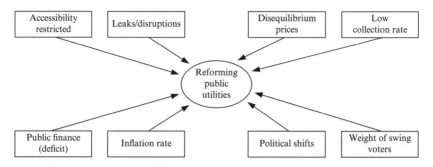

Figure 2.1   Forces pushing toward reform in the water sector

solution. In addition, this perception is reinforced by the possibility of a contractual approach to transfer a significant part of the risks and of consumers' anger to private operators. However, for reasons summarized above, changes of that nature involve political risks, particularly the risk of a backlash from swing voters: this may explain the very slow pace of reforms in this sector compared to other public utilities and the highly regulated nature of contracts implemented.

WHAT CONTRACT?

Once forces pushing toward changes have condensed into political will to reform, the main question becomes what type of reform. In transaction cost parlance, this translates into the question: should public authorities do it themselves, implementing internal changes in the governance of the public utility, or should they contract with an autonomous (usually private) operator in order to introduce market forces at the core of reforms? Our data-set on France as well as a relatively large set of case studies on reforms of water systems in developing countries converge in exhibiting the importance of financial pressures in the decision to look for contractual solutions involving private operators.[2] This trend has clearly been reinforced by the predominant economic approach of the 1980s.

A Dominant Perspective, with Serious Problems Involved

For reasons that by far exceed the scope of this chapter, most countries in the late 1970s witnessed a combination of the tensions identified above, so that pressures to reform became increasingly powerful. Progressively, a conventional wisdom emerged that a large set of transactions could be organized more efficiently either through full privatization or through outsourcing (in the water sector, typically through PPP). According to this perspective, the advantages of introducing private interests in the governance of public utilities would be threefold.

First, transferring initiative and responsibilities to private operators would considerably relax financial constraints on public authorities. However, this requires deciding the extension of rights to be conceded to operators. Should it be only decision rights, as in management contracts? Should it go as far as including total control over property rights, as in full privatization? If it should fall somewhere in between, what would be the optimal combination of rights? Secondly, there is the idea that the more involved are private interests, making operators the residual claimants, the more incentive they will have to perform efficiently and to innovate. However, since water systems remain regulated everywhere, incentives are conditional to the adequate design of the contract, particularly with respect to price formulas. Thirdly, involving private operators should help reducing significantly production costs since it would allow taking advantage of scale and scope economies that would result from putting the system in the hands of specialized operators benefiting from accumulated and cumulative know-how. However, potential benefits of different parties depend on the sharing rule and/or the transfer mechanisms to be implemented, so that operators in a monopolistic position will not absorb all gains.

Not surprisingly, as the conditionality of the three positive sources of advantages related to the introduction of private interests suggests, the efficiency of outsourcing public utilities through contracts, up to full privatization, raises problems that may be quite severe.

At the theoretical level, several recent studies have raised important questions in that respect. Transaction cost theory, as developed by Oliver Williamson (1976, 1999) has shown that the efficiency of any specific mode of organization, including contracting out, depends on the adequacy of the mode selected to the characteristics of the transactions to be organized: there are conditions under which an integrated entity, even a public entity, may perform better. An empirical study of the French water system largely substantiates this proposition (Ménard and Saussier 2002). From a different point of view, the incomplete contract theory has also exhibited potential distortions when contracts with private operators are incomplete, which is usually the case, for example in introducing difficult trade-offs between quality and costs (Hart et al. 1997; Hart 2003; Bennett and Iossa 2005). Last but not least, theoreticians of the agency approach have shown the possible counterproductive effects of high incentives (Tirole 1999).

At the empirical level, numerous studies confirm these difficulties. Let me illustrate with three examples that are particularly relevant. Early on

George Yarrow (1986) exhibited the ambiguous results of some leading privatizations in the United Kingdom. If we put aside the case of the telecommunications sector, in which technological changes played such an important role, benefits to different stakeholders were not that obvious. More recent contributions have shown mixed results of private participation from the reform of public utilities in Latin America, particularly because of the significant problem of repeated renegotiations and their impact on investments, which have been much less significant than expected (Guasch et al. 2003; Guasch 2004). Lastly, detailed case studies published by William Savendoff and Pablo Spiller (1999) as well as Mary Shirley (2002) revealed that very similar contracts may generate substantially different outcomes, depending on the institutional environment in which they are implemented. To summarize, we still need a detailed and objective assessment of the exact impact of contracting and of involving private operators in the reform of public utilities, particularly water.

Differentiated Contracts, with Distinct Problems

One reason that may explain the difficulty of this task is that there are many different types of contracts that raise different problems. Since there is so much emphasis on incentives that would come from public–private partnership and on the importance of who is supporting risks in order to determine who should be the residual claimant, a good way to illustrate this diversity is to differentiate contracts according to the allocation of property rights, with the implicit assumption that the allocation of decision rights perfectly overlaps that of property rights.[3] The types of contracts can be distributed on a spectrum (see Figure 2.2). At one end there is the full control by public authorities over both property rights and decision rights, for instance, the management of water by the Department of Public Works. At the other end there is the entire control of the same rights by a private operator, for instance, the case of full privatization. In between there are many possible variations within each broad category.

Note that this diversity of arrangement can exist even within the same institutional environment. Let me illustrate with the case of France, which

Figure 2.2   Forms of arrangements according to the allocation of property rights

has a long tradition of various arrangements in the water sector. In a recent study (Huet et al. 2004), the authors had access to detailed data about the modes of organization implemented for over 2000 units providing water to over 75 percent of the total French population. In 2002 the distribution of arrangements was the following: 42 percent of water units were managed by (local) public authorities, either directly (39 percent) or through relatively autonomous boards (3 percent), while 58 percent were under contracts, with a massive dominance of lease contracts (51 percent) followed by management contracts (4 percent) and concessions (3 percent).

An interesting aspect that these static data do not reflect is the evolution toward an increasing role of lease contracts, which is particularly significant since it points out the growing reluctance of private operators to assume financial risks. Not surprisingly, this evolution is even more significant in developing countries. Another very significant aspect that the detailed study of these contracts exhibits is the diversity of their clauses, even for the same type of contracts. A good illustration is provided by clauses regarding price formulas. In a preliminary study, researchers have been able to identify 11 substantially different ways of determining prices, from firm-fixed price with no possible renegotiation at one end of the spectrum, through to systematic renegotiations anticipated in the contract at the other end (Athias and Saussier 2006).

How are Choices Made?

If public authorities turn toward contracting for implementing a much needed reform, what contract should be selected? Why endorse one contractual form rather than another? Without getting into details, transaction cost economics provides a very useful approach to this problem in the context of PPP. Basically the theory emphasizes the key role of the specificity of investments paired with potential opportunism of parties to an arrangement in explaining why one form could perform better than another. This also means that, from a normative point of view, there would be advantages in choosing it. The central proposition from this theory is that the more specific investments are, the higher are contractual hazards associated with the potentially opportunistic behavior of parties, and therefore the more powerful are incentives to integrate. When it comes to public utilities, integration can take the form of a public entity, for instance, a bureau or a public corporation, or of a tightly regulated private monopoly.

Fundamental characteristics of the water sector fit well within this theoretical approach. Fixed physical investments are very high in the sector, up to 80 percent of total investments, and represent sunk costs that are much more significant than with other public utilities, making the sector particularly close to the standard definition of a natural monopoly. Part of the explanation for these highly specific investments comes from the significance of site constraints. Moreover, and contrary to some received ideas, transactions in the water sector are not that simple. Producing safe drinkable water may involve complex operations, particularly when the quality of the source of water is quite low. In addition, delivering water to consumers also involves complex transactions, with factors that mix geology, demography and network effects.

The combination of these factors may help to explain some observable properties of reforms in the water sector. First, the high level of sunk costs combined with site specificity may account for the very limited cases of unbundling: in most cases, reforms maintain integrated firms, however radical these reforms claim to be. Secondly, the significance of contractual hazards resulting from the risks associated to this specificity of investments suggests that contracts with private operators will be tightly coordinated or regulated so that the type and forms of contracts are highly constrained. Thirdly, it also suggests that under some conditions, for example, if the geology or the quality of water available imposes very specific investments, a public bureau may be a valuable alternative. A detailed econometric study of the French system provides some evidence in that direction (Ménard and Saussier 2002).

The other dimension that particularly matters in a transaction cost perspective is the risk of opportunistic behavior from one or both parties. Note that this risk becomes particularly significant when there are specific investments, so that the effects of the two variables combine: without the mutual dependence created by these investments, competitive markets could discipline parties. Reforming water systems and doing so through contractual arrangements is usually viewed as a way to reduce hazards due to specific assets as well as to the discretionary power of public authorities. However, there are important limitations that create obstacles to that process and may feed opportunism. First, it is often difficult to specify services delivered over a long period of time, and would require the presence of the important sunk costs already noted, for example, because urban planning is lacking or deficient, or because of unexpected demographic changes. Secondly, there is very often a small number of bidders, or even no competition at all notwithstanding a public call for bidders. This is because either the risks resulting from the importance of sunk costs are so high that few parties are interested, or the high concentration ratio of private operators in the water sector mean that the potential number of bidders is small anyway.[4] Thirdly, the general difficulty of organizing competition for the market that has been observed in all reforms of public utilities is amplified in the water sector by its closeness to natural monopoly. Lastly, price and quality are major issues in the provision of water, and almost inevitably involve a political dimension. There is no substitute for a good that is absolutely essential for the survival of all human beings. Award criteria in the sector have direct well-being consequences that particularly put the arrangements at risk of opportunism, on the part of public authorities as well as on the part of private operators.

Of course there are alternative explanations. Laffont and Tirole (1993), further developed by Tirole (1999), adopted an agency perspective, with an emphasis on the asymmetry of information between the government and the operator as the key factor in the provision of public utilities. Choosing the best information-revealing scheme *ex ante* is therefore at the core of the trade-off among alternative modes of governance. For example, if asymmetries are such that the franchisor, in this case the government, cannot obtain the relevant information, it may be better for him to provide the service directly, which is a form of integration. There are at least two difficulties with this approach. It does not allow differentiating clearly the different types of contractual arrangements and the rationale behind the choice of a specific form, which transaction cost does through the modes of allocation of rights. In addition it overemphasizes the *ex ante* design of incentive mechanisms, which are usually much simpler than this theory would predict, and it neglects *ex post* adaptation that requires devices built into the mode of governance. Another approach, the incomplete contract theory, focuses on the allocation of residual property rights in the decision to outsource a service versus providing it in house (Hart et al. 1997). The emphasis here is on the trade-off between quality and cost in providing a collective service with the assumption that there exists an adverse effect between quality and cost. That is, it is not possible systematically to increase quality and decrease costs at the same time. The choice of the mode of governance must be made according to given priorities, with public bureaus emphasizing quality factors, since their lack of control over residual rights provides them little incentive to reduce costs, while private operators react the other way around. This analysis raises important issues, the trade-off between quality and cost being so central in the provision of water; but it ignores the variety of potential contracts between the polar cases of private versus public operators. Therefore, besides its difficulties in shaping testable propositions (Whinston 2003), it does not provide an explanation for the diversity of contractual arrangements and for the rationale behind the selection of a specific form.

One last interpretation emphasizes the role of political forces in choosing an organizational arrangement (World Bank 1995; Savendoff and Spiller 1999). Because of their nature, public utilities would be at high risk of capture by public authorities, so that the choice of governance would be highly politicized. This is particularly so in the water sector. I would not deny that political forces play a role in decisions regarding the provision of water. I will come back to this aspect in the next section. However, the explanatory power of the politicization perspective remains too vague. For example, if politics is at the command of decisions regarding the choice of the mode of governance, we would expect a sharp distinction in the type of arrangement selected by leftist parties as opposed to conservative parties. Our extensive study of the French system does not show a significant correlation supporting this view (a point already made by Derycke 1990).

In sum we find strong support for the transaction cost approach and its emphasis on institutional arrangements in which transactions are embedded for explaining the diversity of modes of governance and the logic of choice among these modes. However, recent reforms have been inspired largely by alternative theories, particularly the agency approach. As such they have focused on *ex ante* conditions, particularly the choice of the right operator, with the right incentives. The emphasis has been on the type of auctions that should be implemented; on pre-qualification criteria; on determining rules shaping the stream of future revenues; on the allocation of risks among parties; and on clauses regarding the characteristics of services to be delivered. This perspective does not seem to work that well. Several empirical studies show that most problems develop *ex post*, at the time of implementation of contracts, so that there is a wide margin for renegotiations (Shirley 2002; Guasch 2004). Contracts provide a framework. However, the nature of the mode of organization selected and the characteristics of the institutional environment become the leading factors when it comes to *ex post* adaptation. The neglect of these dimensions may explain why so many international organizations and donors have been taken aback by results of reforms they have contributed to, designed and implemented!

WHAT RESULTS?

Notwithstanding the diversity of methods adopted, a large set of recent empirical studies concur in exhibiting mixed results, to say the least, in reforms in the provision of water, particularly but not exclusively in developing countries.[5] There have been mitigated improvements in the water sector, particularly if one considers the significant investments made and the trumpeted expectations accompanying reforms. In this section I briefly review this discrepancy between expectations and results before turning to a possible explanation.

What is Expected and What Outcomes can be Observed?

Expectations are high when contracting out is considered for reforming the water sector. Priorities vary, of course, according to parties involved. Consumers are essentially hoping for improved accessibility and increased reliability; that is, a higher rate of coverage with continuous availability, a particularly significant issue in developing countries. Reformers always promise consumers that this will be attained at lower prices and improved quality, at least in the long run. Operators expect sustainability, which requires prices to be determined through formulae that guarantee costs coverage, including a normal rate of return on capital. The underlying rationale is that this would provide adequate incentives to invest in order to make productivity gains while simultaneously improving quality and reducing unaccounted for water. Public authorities expect mainly to alleviate their financial burden while guaranteeing minimum advantages to their constituencies. And in total, welfare gains are expected for the entire society, with a positive balance of costs and benefits for consumers, normal capital gains for private operators and reduced deficits or even positive returns through taxes for public authorities (Ménard et al. 2002).

This optimistic view is rarely confirmed by facts. Notwithstanding situations in which significant gains were obtained, contracting out generates also severe *ex post* problems that must be faced. There are constant delays in construction and in the provision of services. Renegotiations tend to be the rule, despite the clauses that pretend to regulate the relationships between parties. There is often a lower level of quality than was committed to in the agreement with respect to health criteria, rate of connection and UFW, particularly in developing countries. Absence of responsiveness from operators in relation to maintenance and delays in repair are also a recurrent complaint. And last but not least, significant increases in prices are observed almost everywhere. This is particularly troubling since the rationale behind price increases is that this would provide resources for investing and improving the system. However, there is a clear trend to switching from concession contracts to lease contracts in recent reforms, which means that risks associated with the heavy sunk investments of the water sector are no longer on the side of the operator and that public authorities can no longer rely on PPP to escape the financial burden of required investments.

A more detailed analysis of the recent evolution of contractual arrangements shows significant efforts to find contractual solutions to these problems. Let me mention four of them and point out some difficulties they encounter. First, numerous contracts have introduced tougher dissuasive penalty clauses, particularly with respect to delays and quality.

However, one major difficulty has to do with the implementation of these clauses without bringing the system to the verge of collapse. This is particularly acute in developing countries; but it is also becoming increasingly a concern in developed countries with decaying infrastructures that would require major long run investments from private operators. Secondly, efforts have been made to define enforceable sanctions paired with finer monitoring procedures in order to develop accountability. However, this raises serious problems of expertise and competencies, even in developed countries. Water systems are almost universally decentralized: how can small communities invest in human capabilities specific enough to monitor properly their relationships with private operators who are highly concentrated and backed by a large pool of experts? Thirdly, there has been a lot of emphasis on developing open-book policies and information transparency. This is particularly obvious in the role attributed to regulators. Besides the problem already mentioned of the availability of human assets next to public authorities, there is some ideological blindness in the claim for transparency since it neglects or ignores that contractors have good reasons for keeping a substantial part of their information private when they operate in a competitive environment. There is some naivety in the ideal of transparency of information that brings us back to illusions of the 1960s regarding the regulation of natural monopolies. Lastly, yardstick competition that worked relatively well in other sectors in which substantial reforms were introduced (for instance, the telecommunications industry) has also been considered as a way to improve PPP in the water sector. However the variety of sources of drinkable water, the diversity of demographic evolution, and the differences in urban development and population density, make yardstick competition difficult to implement in a sector as decentralized as water.

An Institutional Perspective on these Difficulties

All concerns and solutions mentioned above are relevant. What is missing is an integrated perspective that would embed these difficulties and these solutions into their institutional environment, thus making sense of dispersed elements and taking into account what may be the determining factors in the last resort.

Indeed approaches underlying the solutions considered above are mostly inspired by a perspective focusing on asymmetric information and related agency problems, with an unambiguous emphasis on factors located at the micro level of specific contracts, or at the sector level, so that the main issue would lie in the appropriate design of contracts. A transaction cost approach intends to go further in pointing out the maladaptation of contracts to specific characteristics of transactions at stake and its consequences on *ex post* implementation and adaptation. As emphasized by Oliver Williamson (2002): 'The common error to be avoided is to pronounce that governance structures are efficient or inefficient without reference to the transaction . . . [T]here are transactions for which the firm is superior to the market, its bureaucratic disabilities notwithstanding.' For example, the lack of consideration for the adequacy or inadequacy of specific arrangements with conditions such as the degree of uncertainty that varies according to population density, geology, hydrologic conditions, and so on, may command types of investments for which one mode of organization is better suited than another. Incentive issues, particularly tariff policies over time, need to be reassessed from that perspective: the choice of a specific contractual arrangement and the design of the related contract cannot be disconnected from the properties of the mode of governance in charge of implementing that contract *ex post*. Adequacy to transactions at stake is central here.

There is also another question that may require getting deeper in the explanation of the difficulties reforms are facing: can the problems raised above be overcome at the micro or sector level? Elements of solution exist at that level and cannot be ignored, particularly if we combine *ex ante* conditions with more attention to *ex post* conditions. *Ex ante*, conditions implemented for selecting the operator obviously play an important role, although several fashionable solutions over the last period have also exhibited serious flaws. For example, the development of a menu of auctions tends to neglect the basic idea that all contractual arrangements have flaws, and that selection must therefore operate comparatively. Pre-qualification criteria tend to ignore that there are often very few bidders. Bids formulated in terms of constant revenue stream tend to be complex and costly to implement, with a risk of shifting back to the old cost-plus system (Engel et al. 1997). Allocation of risk among parties has tended in recent years to increasingly transfer risks to public authorities, which signals a relative failure of what was expected from public–private participation. *Ex post*, efforts have been made to define conditions for a better execution of contracts, although much less energy has been spent by theoreticians on this aspect than on *ex ante* conditions. Examples have been provided above. There are now discussions about what should be dissuasive and realistic penalty clauses (otherwise there are repeated renegotiations and challenges). Sanctions must also be enforceable, which requires adequate monitoring and accounting procedures as well as available human competences. Yardstick competition has been proposed as a way to improve information transparency. However it is astonishing how little progress has been made toward benchmarking, a situation that may reflect the fact that comparative analysis at the micro level remains so underdeveloped in economics.

These solutions are plagued with severe flaws because they neglect a major dimension, the key role of the institutional environment in which contractual agreements are embedded. Taking into account the role of institutions is at the core of any satisfactory explanation of successes and failures of reforms, including the adoption of contractual solutions. However, this requires going further than long talks about how institutions matter, a ritual statement nowadays among international organizations and donors.

The Role of Micro-institutions

I would like to emphasize the particular significance of micro-institutions, beyond the very broad perspective of the general institutional environment such as the legal system or the political system, now quite fashionable among economists. This is not to say that the global institutional framework does not matter. However, exclusive focus on that general level misses the conditions that make these institutions operational. Three dimensions deserve specific attention.

First, there is the key role of local and regional institutions. For example, it is necessary to go beyond the standard approach which focuses on central regulations and the ideal properties of a central regulator. This is particularly important for decentralized networks such as water systems, with so many differences in local conditions and, most of the time, with different levels of public authorities involved. In this sector, local authorities everywhere play a key role in designing and monitoring the mode of organization that provides drinkable water. It is often necessary to understand local institutions, for instance, municipal councils, in a broader setting since organization of the network and potential trade-offs among alternative usages of water depend also on a higher level of decision-making. French basin agencies provide an interesting example of regional coordination and regulation. There are two other advantages to paying more attention to this interaction between levels of institutions and, from a normative point of view, in developing the role of micro-institutions: they help in understanding the requirements for more adequate supportive capabilities, particularly administrative competences at the local level; and they may provide indications on how to compensate inadequate human assets at that level. Recent studies on regional regulators in the telecommunications industry, with regions defined at a higher level than national borders, also provide interesting elements in that perspective (Barendse 2006; Baudrier 2006).

Secondly whatever the mode of organization chosen, but even more so when it is a contractual arrangement, developing adequate conflict resolution mechanisms is essential. Indeed, most contracts are incomplete, which means that there is always room for diverging interpretation, without clear rules for arbitrating between them. On the other hand, going to court presents serious disadvantages: it sends very negative signals to the other party as well as to potential partners; it transfers problem-solving authority to an institution that may not have the necessary competence or may not be able to observe or verify what parties are claiming; and it may involve high transaction costs. Hence the important role of autonomous arbitrators filling the blanks of contracts or helping to overcome their ambiguities without going as far as the formal settlement offered by courts. And beyond formal arbitrators jointly appointed by parties, there may even be a less formal institution, let us call it 'mediation', in which insiders are appointed by parties to a contract for solving problems with a potential for conflicts. Actually this is a lesson to be learned from private contracts: there are at least three levels of institutional arrangements that play a role in conflict resolution, from the relatively informal status of internal mediators to the formal role of courts, with the intermediary step of arbitration.[6]

Finally, the political dimension must be assessed in a less negative perspective than it is usually done nowadays. When it comes to the water sector, there is an almost inescapable role of politics. As already emphasized, water networks involve very significant sunk costs, much higher than in other networks. Moreover there is no substitute for water: this is an almost unique case in which needs are universal, which means that it concerns all citizens without exception. As a result, users and voters systematically overlap. Techno-economic factors reinforce this: water networks are particularly close to the traditional concept of natural monopoly. Technological innovations have allowed the introduction of competition in the telecommunications industry, even without access to fixed networks. In railways and electricity, the distinction between competitive and noncompetitive segments has opened the door to market forces in the competitive segment, paired with tight regulation of the monopoly segment focusing on conditions of access to the network. In the water sector, there is no example of such unbundling, notwithstanding some propositions in that direction that have been viewed as rather exotic by almost all practitioners. The consequence of all of the above is that there is some legitimacy to public interference in this sector. The problem then becomes the appropriate framing of these interferences. Thanks to the extensive literature on regulation during the past 20 years, risks associated with political activism are now well known. Beside the risks of capture and/or corruption, there are risks associated with the dispersion of decisions among different bureaus, and the risk of micro-management by public authorities. One hypothesis that has been explored recently is that multiple competing layers of government might favor more transparency and better accountability (Weingast 2005). Empirical evidence on this issue remains mixed. We need more in-depth analyses of the impact of multiple layers of government, and of their associated costs, particularly when it comes to the organization of transactions involving numerous parties, which is the case in the water sector.

In sum we have to explore institutional designs that would restrict the discretionary power of the principal, namely, public authorities, as well as the opportunistic possibilities of agents, namely, the operators, without sacrificing the legitimacy of public control, which remains the core of a democratic society.

CONCLUSION

Other aspects, partially related to this political dimension, would deserve careful examination: the existence or not of adequate administrative capabilities; the credibility of commitments of the different levels of public authorities; the adequacy of the definition and implementation of property rights; and the specific role of checks and balances. These items should be high on our research agenda. Nevertheless there are several lessons we can already draw from reforms of public utilities, and particularly from water system reform relying on contracts.

First, there are economic forces at work behind the choice of contractual arrangements. Politics does not explain it all; it may not even be the leading force. Secondly, we can observe significant changes in the approach to partnership between public authorities and private operators, due to substantial changes in institutional rules of the game coming from endogenous forces that push toward reforms or from pressures from international organizations and donors. These changes signal an increasing consciousness among economists and policy-makers that institutions matter. Thirdly, there is an increasing concern about credibility issues in public–private partnership. For example, penalties based on observable and verifiable clauses, such as quality standards of water delivered, may be much more efficient than less credible threats, such as the breach of contract. Fourthly, our French data set and several case studies developed for the World Bank show a recent movement toward transferring most or all sunk investments to public authorities. This is very similar to integration in the private sector, and suggests that private operators are increasingly reluctant to share major contractual hazards. And it is noticeable that this trend is not limited to developing countries. Fifthly, if we keep in mind the considerable efforts of the last two decades to build a more competitive environment in public utilities, there is, surprisingly, almost no benchmarking in the contractual agreements we have examined, which suggests that a comparative approach remains largely ignored. Sixthly, there are almost no contracts with positive incentives, such as rewards to private operators if targets are surpassed. The explanation likely relates to the very high political sensitivity of the governance of water systems. The significance of renegotiations in the water sector comforts this point. Seventhly, this brings into the picture the key role of institutions, which goes far beyond the general level of the political or judiciary system, all the way down to how local or regional authorities are organized and interfere, and how local or regional institutions are shaped and embedded in more global institutions.

The central message of this chapter is, therefore, that contractual arrangements remain a limited tool for reforms because they depend so much on the institutions in which they are embedded, and that in order to understand this dimension, the analysis cannot remain at the level of general statements on global institutions. In order to understand the reform of water systems and, more generally, the provision of critical infrastructures, we need to go deeper in the examination of the micro-institutions that shape our modern economies.

NOTES

1. The creation of a public corporation is a case in which contracting does not involve a private operator.
2. Main published references are Ménard and Saussier (2002) and Huet et al. (2004) for France, Savendoff and Spiller (1999), Shirley (2002) and Guasch (2004) for developing countries. Numerous case studies, particularly from the World Bank, are also available.
3. This assumption is disputable. Very often decision rights and property rights do not coincide or overlap only partially, as illustrated by an abundant literature from Berle and Means (1932) to the analysis of franchising, joint ventures, and so on (Ménard, 2004).
4. This statement actually needs to be nuanced. What we basically have is either local operators, often public operators with no competitors, or bids open to international competition that confront the very high concentration rate in the water sector, with five major operators dominating the market.
5. Many of them, particularly case studies, are available only as working papers, either with specialized research centers, such as ATOM and CIRANO, or with international organizations, particularly the World Bank. However probing material is provided in Shirley (2002), Ménard and Saussier (2002), Ménard et al. (2002), Guasch (2004) and Savendoff and Spiller (1999).
6. I am grateful to Aad Correlje and Peter Spaans, from Delft University of Technology, for having pointed out this aspect. To my knowledge, there is very little in the literature

on this issue, but there are already very interesting indications in Palay (1985) and more recently in Rubin (2005).

REFERENCES

Athias, L. and S. Saussier (2006), 'Contractual design of toll adjustments processes in infrastructure concession contracts', working paper, Centre ATOM, University of Paris–Panthéon-Sorbonne.

Barendse, A. (2006), 'Regional regulation as a new form of telecom sector governance: the interaction with technological socio-economic systems and market performances', doctoral dissertation, Delft University of Technology.

Baudrier, A. (2006), 'Coûts de transaction, coordination réglementaire et environnement institutionnel: une analyse de la structure de gouvernance de la régulation du marché européen des communications électroniques', doctoral dissertation, Centre ATOM, University of Paris–Panthéon-Sorbonne.

Bennett, J. and E. Iossa (2005), 'Contracting out public service provision to not-for-profit firms, working paper 05/124, CMPO, Bristol University.

Berle, A.E. and G.C. Means (1932), *The Modern Corporation and Private Property*, New Brunswick, NJ: Transaction, rev edn 1991.

Derycke, P.-H. (1990), 'Typologie des services publics locaux et choix d'un mode de gestion', in *Performances des services publics locaux: analyse comparée des modes de gestion*, Paris: Litec.

Engel, E., R. Fischer and A. Galetovic (1997), 'Highway franchising: pitfalls and opportunities', *American Economic Review*, **87** (2): 68–72.

Guasch, J.L. (2004), *Granting and Renegotiating Infrastructures Concessions: Doing it Right*, Washington, DC: World Bank.

Guasch, J. L., J.-J. Laffont and S. Straub (2003), 'Renegotiations of Concession Contracts in Latin America', working paper, 3011, World Bank.

Hart, O. (2003), 'Incomplete contacts and public ownership: remarks and an application to public–private partnerships', *Economic Journal*, **113** (486): 69–76.

Hart, O., A. Shleifer and R.W. Vishny (1997), 'The proper scope of government: theory and application to prisons', *Quarterly Journal of Economics*, **112** (4): 1127–61.

Huet, F., C. Ménard, S. Saussier and C. Staropoli (2004), *Mode de gestion et efficacité de la distribution d'eau en France: une analyse néo-institutionnelle*, Paris: Report to the Ministry of Environnent.

Laffont, J.-J. and J. Tirole (1993), *A Theory of Incentives in Procurement and Regulation*, Cambridge, MA: MIT Press.

Ménard, C. (2004), 'The economics of hybrid organizations', *Journal of Institutional and Theoretical Economics*, **160** (3): 345–76.

Ménard, C. and S. Saussier (2002), 'Contractual choice and performance', in E. Brousseau and J.-M. Glachant (eds), *The Economics of Contracts: Theory and Applications*, Cambridge: Cambridge University Press, pp. 440–62.

Ménard, C., G. Clarke and A.M. Zuluaga (2002), 'Measuring the welfare effects of reform: urban water supply in Guinea', *World Development*, **30** (9): 1517–37.

Palay, T.M. (1985), 'Avoiding regulatory constraints: contracting safeguards and the role of informal agreements', *Journal of Law, Economics and Organization*, **1** (1): 155–75.

Rubin, P. (2005), 'Legal systems as frameworks for market exchanges', in C. Ménard and M. Shirley (eds), *Handbook of New Institutional Economics*, Berlin: Springer, pp. 205–24.

Savendoff, W. and P. Spiller (1999), *Spilled Water*, Washington, DC: Inter-American Development Bank.

Shirley, M. (ed.) (2002), *Thirsting for Efficiency: The Economics and Politics of Urban Water Reforms*, Amsterdam: Elsevier-Pergamon.

Tirole, J. (1999), 'Concessions, concurrence et incitations', *Revue d'économie financière*, **51** (1): 79–92.

Weingast, B. (2005), 'The performance and stability of federalism: an institutional perspective', in C. Ménard and M. Shirley, *Handbook of New Institutional Economics*, Berlin: Springer, pp. 149–73.

Whinston, M. (2003), 'On the transaction costs determinants of vertical integration', *Journal of Law, Economics and Organization*, **19** (1): 1–23.

Williamson, O.E. (1976), 'Franchise bidding for natural monopolies: in general and with respect to CATV', *Bell Journal of Economics*, **7** (1): 73–104.

Williamson, O.E. (1999), 'Public and private bureaucracies: a transaction cost economics perspective', *Journal of Law, Economics and Organization*, **15** (1): 306–42.

Williamson, O.E. (2002), 'Transaction cost economics', in C. Ménard and M. Shirley (eds), *Handbook of New Institutional Economics*, Berlin: Springer, pp. 41–65.

World Bank (1995), *Bureaucrats in Business: The Economics and Politics of Government Ownership*, New York: Oxford University Press.

Yarrow, G. (1986), 'Privatization in theory and practice', *Economic Policy*, **1** (2): 324–77.

3. Creating institutional arrangements that make markets work: the case of retail markets in the electricity sector

Jean-Michel Glachant

INTRODUCTION

Over the course of the past 15 years, the electricity industry has experienced a series of remarkable innovations—in particular, the creation of open markets. Wholesale markets come first, then retail. These markets replaced the vertically integrated and quasi-integrated structures that had prevailed mostly during the second half of the twentieth century. Few economists truly anticipated or forecast this revolution in electricity markets. The notable exception was Paul L. Joskow and Richard Schmalensee. Their book *Markets for Power* (1983) anticipated the opening of the English wholesale market in 1990 by a full seven years. The notion of a retail market for electricity had even less currency than that of a wholesale market. Stephen C. Littlechild, another economist, and British regulator from 1989 to 1998, merits being designated as the inventor of the retail electricity market. Previously this concept was so novel, so unfamiliar, that it is nowhere to be found in the White Paper (United Kingdom, Secretary of State for Energy 1988), with which the British government prepared the way for the electricity reform, nor does it occur anywhere in the Electricity Act 1989 (United Kingdom, Ministry of Justice 1989). At that time only a wholesale market for generators, distributors and large industrial users was envisaged.

However, the most salient feature of this innovation was not simply the introduction of markets into the industry, but rather that their creation required so much institutional activism. The competitive reforms of the electricity industry literally consisted of elaborating gigantic and complex architectures for trading on markets—comparable in some ways to architects designing skyscrapers or engineers erecting suspension bridges

(Glachant and Finon 2003). In no place were market forces harnessed to build their markets themselves. Consequently, electricity reforms are better characterized as market design than as competitive opening. 'The market cannot solve the problem of market design,' as captured in a nutshell by W. Hogan (2000).

Thus we are confronted with a question that is representative of applied neo-institutional economics. What is meant by creating a retail market? Since the wholesale market already serves as a market for the commodity electricity, what specific role does the retail market play? Are the operations conducted on this retail market identical to or different from those on the wholesale market? Do the differences pertain to the object being transacted, because not exactly the same thing is traded? Or are the differences procedural, for trades do not occur in exactly the same way?

Wholesale and retail operations would indeed differ if the transactions conducted on these markets were not on the same commodities. This notion is already present in business organization practices and in wholesale and retail operators' commercial strategies. As a rule, wholesalers add a few complementary services that are important to their clients to the output of the production process (that is, the producer's good). Thus they provide an incentive for customers to buy from wholesalers rather than directly from producers. Retailers in turn add yet more services, which may be complementary or supplementary, and in so doing create another source of value added for their specific category of customers (Coughlan et al. 2001). The upshot is that neither sells the same good, the same set of characteristics, as producers.

Conversely, another take is that these two markets, wholesale and retail, essentially transact the same commodity, but do so in a different fashion. It is mainly the transactional procedures that differ. Here wholesalers and retailers are viewed as market intermediaries. It is, in fact, intermediation services that they sell to their customers. These are typical of transactional services provided by third parties who interject themselves between producers and consumers when the latter find this arrangement preferable to engaging in a direct transaction (Spulber 1999).

The goal of this chapter is to identify how retail electricity markets are created, to define the essence of these market designs, and therewith to find a logical explanation for the space created for entrepreneur-retailers. To accomplish this, we first explore retailers' involvement in the adaptation of the product between generation and consumption, and then how the wholesale and retail markets manage transactions within the framework of their market design. At the end of the chapter, we illustrate a typology of retail market design using three examples of the creation of retail markets in Europe.

RETAILERS' INVOLVEMENT BETWEEN THE GENERATION AND CONSUMPTION STAGES

When a product exits from the production facility, it may not necessarily possess all the characteristics that are of use to all consumers. It can subsequently be more precisely tailored to the needs of consumers by adding assorted complementary services. Specifically, these services may be transportation and storage, classification and sorting, disassembly and reassembly, pairing with other products and exhibiting to consumers.

The electricity industry does indeed make use of several of these adaptation services. Transmission substitutes, at least partially, for storage—which is economically not feasible—by tightly interlinking all generating plants within a zone, so as to make all power generated at any point within the zone permanently available throughout it. Since electricity is a highly normalized industrial product, and remains very homogeneous at the plant exit and on the transmission grid, it is not necessary to sort or categorize it. On the other hand, the disassembly and reassembly functions are very important and systematic. To render transmission economical, the tension of the electrical current is raised to levels much higher than are useful to consumers, at the point of exit from the generating plant. Thus, at the downstream end of the transmission grid, the tension must be reduced to its consumption level. Furthermore the transmission grid serves a very specific purpose—it is not designed to connect to all points of consumption. The link that carries the electricity to consumers' homes is the distribution network. Finally, by virtue of this funneling into households by an exclusive distribution grid, the product becomes permanently available to consumers; but it is now impossible to pair it with other goods.

We here see that the functions of adapting the product to consumers, after it leaves the generating plants, are highly industrialized and automated, and that they are dispersed between the activities of the transmission and the distribution grids. However none of these adaptation functions are actually performed by retailers. Thus, in the competitive electricity industry, the retailer does not directly play a role in adapting these characteristics of the gross industrial product to the uses of consumers. So in this sense the retailer adds no value to the product (Joskow 2000; Littlechild 2002).

WHOLESALE MARKETS, THE EXCHANGE OF RIGHTS AND THE IMPLEMENTATION OF TRANSACTIONS

The concept underlying wholesale electricity markets is that several sellers will simultaneously face several buyers to offer them supply contracts. However, all these rights, having been individually traded between sellers and buyers, will ultimately be executed on the same shared grids and will take the form of a single, collective form of power on the electrical current. This is why procedures for managing transactions are of considerable interest for understanding the creation of electricity markets (Glachant and Lévêque 2005).

When exchanging contracts for electrical energy, buyers and sellers find themselves in typical inter-individual relationships. However, at the time they seek to implement their contracts, they enter into collective interactions. The electrical current that flows from generating plants to consumers cannot be stored or divided into exclusive and transferable units. All injections and withdrawals are pooled in the shared flow of electricity that circulates through the grid. Thus what we refer to as the wholesale electricity market in fact consists of several complementary modules that trigger a sequence of operations as required for satisfying the claims on the commodity. This chain, by which transactions are implemented, includes at least three distinct modules. The first module handles the individual contracts between sellers and buyers. This is simply the exchange of rights, which does not provide for the effective delivery of the corresponding product. The following two modules manage the actual, though collective, application of these rights. The transfer of products corresponding to the rights and duties of individual contracts can only occur in a collective framework that manages all transfers at the same time.

Managing the Individual Exchange of Rights

The most well-known module of the wholesale electricity market is the individual exchanges compartment, in which rights are negotiated between sellers and buyers—either bilaterally such as over-the-counter markets (OTC) or multilaterally such as organized markets of the power exchange (PX) type. However, after the conclusion of individual agreements, the corresponding actions on the commodity cannot be directly taken by the buyer–seller pair. It is not possible to undertake direct inter-individual delivery on electricity transmission grids, for they are not point to point like communications networks. Since electrical energy is not storable, the right ceded by the seller is at most a certificate providing the right to withdraw, on demand, from the shared energy resources of the grid and covering a specified period, or at least a commitment to compensate the difference between the price contracted *ex ante* and the real cost of the power.

Managing the Collective Feasibility of Individual Exchanges

Since the commodity is neither storable nor separable into exclusive and transferable units, the execution of all individual exchanges occurs over the intermediary of the shared flow of power on the grid. Collective management of this process makes use of a third party, the manager of the transmission grid, known as the system operator (SO). This third party plays no role in the negotiation of the individual programs; but it has authority over the collective management of the corresponding shared energy flows.

The first order of business for this collective implementation is to ensure that the aggregation of the individual programs is feasible, given the grid's capacity and security constraints. If forecasts indicate that some of these constraints may be violated, the SO announces that the grid is congested. Consequently, some individual exchange programs will be designated unrealizable, and these must be modified under the SO's aegis.

Examining the interplay of the management of collective congestion and the operation of inter-individual transactions reveals at least four architectures for executing individual programs. First, collective constraints can be managed with hardly any impact on the individual transactions negotiated *ex ante* between buyers and sellers, who were powerless to anticipate these constraints. To accomplish this, the SO assumes certain generators' commitments not being feasible given the state of the grid and obtains an equivalent output, from the perspective of the buyers, from other generators on a less congested part of the grid. The cost of this maneuver is subsequently spread over all participants in the wholesale market, curbing their unit cost. This class of collective management operations may be called 'redispatching' or 'countertrading', depending on the exact details of the procedure. We observe that this process assigns greater weight to supply contracts that are negotiated individually *ex ante* than to the constraints and collective costs of implementing them *ex post*.

Secondly, we can oblige contracts that are negotiated individually *ex ante* to account up front for the constraints and collective costs of their future execution. If this *ex ante* internalization of collective constraints occurs on an organized market (PX), it takes the form of direct incorporation into the prices and volumes of inter-individual exchanges on the market. As a result only operable individual contracts are exchanged *ex ante*. This internalization of collective constraints into individual exchanges can be exhaustive if the SO and the PX collaborate closely to identify the contribution to the congestion from each elementary unit of the grid (that is, each of its hundreds of nodes). Thus the term 'nodal pricing' is used to describe this way of managing collective constraints.

Thirdly, the internalization may also occur at a much higher level of aggregation, so that only a few broad zones are differentiated and becoming autonomous submarkets of the same PX. The threshold for the volume of exchanges between zones at which the PX is splintered into submarkets is set by SOs. They behave as if the impact of each zone on the collective constraints was homogeneous, and all traded contracts are thus realizable. This maintains sufficient liquidity on each submarket of the PX to ensure that there is a single energy price throughout the zone. Consequently, this way of managing collective constraints is called 'zonal pricing'.

Fourthly, there exists another means of *ex ante* internalization of grid constraints on either bilateral (OTC) markets or organized (PX) markets that does not require an *ex ante* coordination of markets with the SO. In this fourth category of collective constraint management strategies, the SO makes his own *ex ante* commitment to guarantee that a firm capacity will be available on a given segment of the grid and sells it off at auction. Thus the grid is de facto divided into zones; but these zones are only delineated by virtual entry and exit points or gates. Here SOs are acting like traditional road, railway and air transporters. They are not directly involved in the collective adaptation of individual energy supply contracts on either side of the gates. It is rather incumbent on sellers and buyers to separately and independently arrange their contracts on the basis of what they can foresee in terms of common consequences solely from the signals yielded by the capacity auctions.

The diversity of market designs corresponds to different architectures for negotiating and implementing energy transactions (Glachant and Lévêque 2005; Glachant 2006). These designs differ in how individual programs of exchange are negotiated (that is, bilateral against organized markets) in the first instance, and, in the second instance, in the provisions for rendering these individual programs compatible with collective constraints during their execution (for instance *ex post* redispatching arrangements, *ex ante* nodal, zonal or capacity auction arrangements). All these designs also define the role of a third party, the SO, the central agent for the collective implementation of the claims acquired during the individual exchanges.

Managing Collectively Uncertainty in Individual Programs

The execution of individual programs is not only subject to uncertainty attributable to collective constraints on the grid. A further category of uncertainty arises from the individual conduct of buyers and sellers. Will they strictly adhere to the exchange program they agreed on? Or will they digress from it, for any reason whatsoever? In principle, in most other industries, any divergence of buyers and sellers from a contractual agreement is a matter strictly between themselves. This cannot apply to the electricity sector, owing to the fact that this commodity is neither storable nor divisible into exclusive and transferable units, so the shared flow of power is immediately influenced by any individual deviation from the programs.

To ensure the overall feasibility of the individual programs, SOs' responsibilities also extend to managing the continuity and quality of the shared flow of power. To accomplish this they administer an ongoing service of adjusting the flow of electricity on the grid, reacting every 10 or 15 minutes to continual fluctuations in injections and withdrawals. This is possible because they have access to generating capacity that is held in reserve and ready to kick in, as well as rapid upward and downward sources of power. This arrangement can be called 'balancing'. Though this service was originally conceived as a network reliability feature during the era of vertical integration, it clearly functions during the era of open markets as an energy market. It is in fact the only real trading place for physical energy, since all inter-individual negotiations that precede the opening of the balancing only actually deal with promises for future delivery, and not with the direct exchange of a product that is available immediately.

In an open-market context, the SO cannot manage a physical energy market without billing the users directly for this supply. For obvious reasons of incentives, it is necessary that the costs of individual deviations from the exchange programs be assumed by those who cause them. This cost cannot be socialized, as in some of the formulae for managing congestion. However, to be able to charge this balancing to those who are liable for it, it is necessary to be able to record all individual deviations from the injection and withdrawal programs. Thus all private programs need to be collected— in principle one day ahead. It is also necessary to have a complete series of physical measurements of individual injections and withdrawals operated on the grid over the day. Since the price of electrical power is determined on wholesale markets every hour or half-hour, individual physical metering must be performed by special meters with the same degree of precision. This is true for both generators and buyers. Consequently the SO must conduct a full physical accounting of the compensating operations of the grid users' programs and the suppliers of balancing services. This physical clearing of wholesale market transactions allows the collective implementation of individual transactions to be concluded. Thanks to physical clearing, the SO can initiate financial settlement of individual deviations. This completes the collective framework for individual transactions.

Being responsible for the provision of balancing power, the SO is in charge of both a clearing service and a settlement service. These two services, founded on accounting and measuring individual exchange programs, constitute the core of this second and last module of collective implementation of the wholesale transactions.

A Shared Measurement System

The interface that links the three modules required for implementing the wholesale transactions is known as the architecture of wholesale electricity markets. In principle, buyers and sellers cannot anticipate *ex ante* the *ex post* feasibility of their individual transactions without the intervention of a third party, the SO, who functions as the architect of the markets. Similarly, sellers and buyers are in no position to manage the uncertainties associated with their individual injections and withdrawals in an exclusively bilateral fashion. Therefore, the SO's collective management activities are indispensable for implementing individual transactions—not merely supplementary services that add some product value with the exception of reliability, which is really valuable but not necessarily priced. While several market designs are possible, and hence several operating modes for SOs, all of these market designs are mainly institutional infrastructures for executing individual transactions on the wholesale electricity market. We here have a striking illustration of what Ronald Coase (1992) was talking about: the institutional structure of production.

Nonetheless the fact that a designated third party, the SO, manages this collective infrastructure, this governance structure of the market (Williamson 1985, 1996), does not invalidate all wholesalers' economic functions on wholesale markets. They still play a role in the elaboration and administration of purchase and sales contracts.

During the establishment of contracts on PXs, traders can intervene between generators and buyers and play the traditional role of price-makers by exploiting the existence of a purchase/sales price spread with their ability to understand or anticipate market movements, or to arbitrate differentials within the market. Outside of PXs, brokers can offer traders similar opportunities on the bilateral market (OTC). All these electricity trading activities can include transactions that internalize the collective constraints on the grid *ex ante*.

Similarly aggregators of individual power exchange programs may intervene between buyers and sellers to aggregate the individual programs before submitting them, at time minus one unit, to feasibility control by the SO. This position of intermediary also allows aggregators to conduct an initial, private clearing of their clients' imbalances prior to addressing aggregate physical clearing and financial settlement with the SO.

The two typical functions of wholesalers, namely, trading and the aggregation of programs, can also be accomplished by generators (upstream integration) or large consumers (downstream integration such as Norway's Norsk Hydro in continental Europe). Upstream or downstream integration of these wholesale activities by producers or consumers does not affect the function of the transaction. Trading and program integration are typical activities of market intermediaries who capitalize on their knowledge of the market, on economies of scale, or on the frequency with which they repeat transactions to reduce transaction costs.

The functions of the SO and of the wholesaler are thus complementary. Wholesalers manage private units of transactional services; the SO, the collective infrastructure for all transactions. The two roles, however, are not symmetric. The creation of the SO and market architecture is an absolute prerequisite for the existence of a wholesale market, while independent wholesalers can be dispensed with. Nonetheless, despite the absence of symmetry, there still exists a pronounced mutual interdependence around a shared measurement system.

On the one hand, SOs would be utterly incapable of carrying out their collective duties if most of the bilateral or organized transactions on wholesale markets (PXs) were not already semi-aggregated by several dozen wholesalers—vertically independent or integrated—who bring their credibility to the table as intermediaries by assuming responsibility from a business and financial perspective. On the other hand, SOs would be unable to accomplish their clearing and financial settlement tasks without access to private data preformatted for these calculations. Even assuming that all generators are directly hooked into the transmission grid (which is not always the case), and that their injections are thus directly measured by the SO, it would remain necessary to have access to hourly or half-hourly meter readings of individual consumption and to group them aggregator by aggregator. To allocate these individual readings to the aggregators, a pre-configured registry identifying the affiliation of each consumer with an energy seller would be needed. In practice, the performance of collective tasks by SOs thus presupposes that they can make use of large amounts of private data from metering systems. Consequently there is a great deal of interdependence between the two systems for monitoring transactions information, private and collective.

RETAIL MARKETS, THE EXCHAGE OF RIGHTS AND THE IMPLEMENTATION OF TRANSACTIONS

What else is required for the exchange of rights between sellers and buyers on the retail electricity market, and for implementation of these transactions that cannot already be found in the architecture of whole-sale markets? It is not some requirement to adapt the commodity gross electricity to the needs of individual consumers, since we know that this is automatically done by transmission and distribution grids. Nor is it any inability of wholesale markets to handle individual consumption data, since we know that the functions of the SO and the wholesalers are articu-lated around a shared metering system. However, from the perspective of the wholesale market, the structural particularity of the retail market—and its Achilles heel—is this measurement system.

Of course, orders of magnitude separate the measurement system that manages several hundred or thousand large corporate consumers from one that manages millions and tens of millions of consumers in the mass market. This distinction does not necessarily imply a structural difference between wholesale and mass markets. The structural constraint on the wholesale market is that the data communicated to it must be formatted according to its own rules of operation. It assumes in particular that meter readings of individual consumption are taken hourly or half-hourly, and that all these individual volumes are assigned to the various aggregator accounts to ultimately yield physical clearing and financial settlement.

Then the essence of market design for the retail market is the organization of its measurement system, since this constitutes its interface with the two modules of collective governance of the wholesale market. Consequently, what we find are four potential architectures for retail markets, which are also variants on their market design. In the first variant, the retail market is not really distinct from the wholesale market, since they both share the same hourly metering system for individual consumption. Things are very different for the three other variants. None of them feature the hourly metering system of the wholesale market, but rather consumption approxi-mations computed from profiles of demand proxies, simply known as profiles. These measurement proxies are applied to consumption volumes that have been accurately metered, from the perspective of the wholesale market but that apply to a very large number of consumers who are the customers of different sellers. It is with the border effect, resulting from the design of the zones for which these measurement proxies are computed, that these three variants of profiling within the retail market design differ.

Nodal Retail Design

The first variant of the retail market is a simple internal compartment of the wholesale market, since their measurement systems are identical. Each consumer is equipped with a smart meter. This counter transmits hourly or semi-hourly consumption data to a database that allocates it using a registry matching consumers' affiliation with sellers. With this type of system, no equalization between consumers, sellers and aggregators is required for the SO. In an analogy with the terminology of wholesale market design, this could be called a 'nodal measurement system', where each consumption node is metered individually and can be handled independently of the others. This specific type of retail market appeared subsequent to the introduction of competitive electricity reforms. It was, in fact, not distinguished from the wholesale market as such, until questions arose concerning the barriers to entry for small-scale consumers raised by the cost of metering equipment.

System Operator Retail Design

In the following three variants, the retail market is distinct from the wholesale market, because its measurement system is different. Rather than proceed with hourly metering of individual consumption, volume approximations are computed from demand curve types or profiles. These profiles serve as keys for allocating hourly volumes of global consumption that are not based on individualized data. These global volumes are computed from the perspective of the wholesale market; but they sum over very many consumers who are clients of different sellers. Underlying this system of profile-based metering is a systematic equalization between consumers having the same profile. It may also involve transfers between profiles. Thus several types of cross-subsidies are affected between consumers, sellers or aggregators when treated by the SO.

In the first of the three profiling variants, the allocation keys or the profiles are computed on the same scale as the clearing and financial wholesale balancing operations. They are performed by the SO or an equivalent agent. While distinct from the wholesale market, this type of retail market still functions as an approximation to it, since the proxies sent to wholesale clearing and financial settlement are computed on the same scale, sometimes even by the same services. The logic underlying this design is that the retail market is treated like a single zone of measurement proxies for the wholesale, rather than as an accumulation of local markets.

This retail market design closely corresponds to the case of England and Wales. While the defunct compulsory wholesale market, the Electricity Pool, was not responsible for the overall architecture of the retail metering system, it profoundly affected the clearing and settlements system. In addition, the profiling standard, based on eight domestic consumption profiles, was designed by the British Electricity Association. Each year the forecasts of electricity consumption are updated for each profile on the basis of real data dated from two years back (Maclaine 2003).

Zonal Retail Design

Conducting profiling on the same scale as the wholesale market—as in SO retail design—is in fact a very particular choice. In practice all elementary data necessary for computing the profiles are collected on a more disaggregated scale, the local level. Locally, that is on the level of the distribution grid or the supplier at the point of consumption, one can maintain a registry of consumer–supplier affiliations, updated when a consumer changes supplier; one can conduct precise hourly metering of the global consumption of a population of profiles; and one can perform periodic metering of actual individual consumers within the population of profiles. Finally, by combining these various data, one can refine or rapidly adjust the profile definitions or conduct various operations to reconcile the data.

However, when that much emphasis is placed on the local scale, where the data are directly accessible, the market becomes highly splintered in terms of calculating profiles and settlements. These profiles may be closer to the consumers or the places of consumption, but they also become zonal profiles for purposes of zonal settlements. The national consumption-profiles market dissolves into a collection of proxies embedded in various zonal profiles with a non-negligible potential for border effects between the zones.

One can nevertheless mitigate these potential border effects between local profiling zones by adopting common calculation methods as well as a shared interface for querying and exchanging data. Consequently, in an analogy with the terminology of wholesale market design, this could be called a 'zonal metering system'. Each consumption profile is metered and handled within a single distribution zone; but since all zones apply open and equivalent procedures, it is no gross exaggeration to state that they tend to function as a common infrastructure for the interface between the retail and the wholesale market.

This type of retail market design corresponds to the case of Norway, where each distribution grid computes a single consumption profile for its zone and then directly derives the settlement owing from each supplier. While this profiling standard, with a single consumer type in each zone, appears very simplistic, the fact that it is updated weekly goes some way toward mitigating its inherent lack of precision. Finally, on the national level, this methodology is framed by the regulator (NVE 1999), while a common national system for querying and transmitting data (EDIEL) facilitates exchanges between all suppliers and all distribution grids.

Borders Retail Design

When local distributors are collecting data, computing profiles or determining the corresponding settlements, they may have no obligation, incentive or inclination to adopt common procedures or to converge toward a shared data query and exchange protocol. Thus it is possible for border effects between retail zones to be of the same order of magnitude as those between noncoordinated wholesale zones. Moreover it would be inappropriate to designate these local entities as zones of a retail market, since each is in fact a self-contained retail market. It is the extent of border effects between profiling zones that motivates the division into local retail markets. Thus we can define this retail design as a measurement system with borders. Consumption profiles are measured and handled differently within each zone. There are no open and equivalent procedures that might constitute a common articulating infrastructure between these various retail markets and the wholesale.

This type of retail market design corresponds to the case of Germany, where each distribution grid has its own approach to computing consumption profiles for its zone and then dictates the settlement due from each supplier. In the absence of national regulation and a national regulator until 2005, only voluntary participants, including the four largest generator-transmitters, subscribed to a shared protocol for computing and exchanging data. By comparison approximately 80 percent of local suppliers and distributors retain retail practices that are essentially local (Müller 2005).

CONCLUSION

The goal of this chapter has been to identify how retail electricity markets are created, to define the nature of their market designs, and therewith to find a logical explanation for the space created for entrepreneur-retailers. We can ask what is meant by creating a retail market, since the wholesale market is already a market for the commodity electricity. Of course the assumption is that the retail market will conduct operations that differ from those on the wholesale market. However these differences can bear on the object of the transaction such as exchanging differentiated goods or on procedures such as differentiated market mechanisms.

We have observed that retailers do not play any significant role in adapting the electrical commodity between the stage of generation and that of final consumption, and that adaptation of the commodity is automatically performed by the transmission and distribution networks. We have established that the core of market designs consists of the layout of a chain of transactional modules necessary for implementing the rights exchanged. First, there is a module of inter-individual transfers of rights between sellers and buyers, with trade places that are bilateral (OTC) or organized (PX). Secondly, there is a module for the collective management of the feasibility of individual exchange programs (congestion management). Thirdly, there is a module for the collective management of uncertainties involving individual conduct for imbalances management, clearing and settlement. Within this institutional architecture, it is a common third party, the SO, who manages the collective part of the transactions governance structure. All the while market intermediaries (wholesalers) sell private services to facilitate transactions, notably trading and program aggregation. Between the common third party and the private intermediaries there exists an extensive interface over a measurement system that allows monitoring and executing individual transactions within the externalities-rich context of the grid.

Retail market design is one particular derivation of this interface which coordinates private intermediaries and a common third party around a measurement system. It specifically deals with market situations in which the consumption of individual consumers is not metered, though they maintain direct access to the shared resource—the electrical current. Thus new types of market design appear with retailing. They are characterized by the introduction of proxies into the measurement system to support the collective implementation of individual transactions.

On this new type of market, retail market intermediaries sell private services to assist their customers' transactions. Like wholesalers, they also sell trading and program aggregation; but they add services that are typical of electricity retailing, demand aggregation which opens access to trades on OTC and PX wholesale markets, and data-processing logistics, which notably begins by registering customers within a proxy measurement system and ends with sending them the bill.

Empirical evidence shows that to open new doors for competition several layers of hard institutional foundations have had to be built. These institutional foundations first covered the definition of rights and duties of generators, transmitters, distributors, traders, suppliers and consumers having to result in a feasible set of exchangeable rights. It then needed a chain that controls the consistency of individual rights and of registering and clearing of the uses of these rights. It assumed that commercial and financial consequences of these uses can be identified, measured or proxied and assigned to any user according to defined circumstances of individual use.

REFERENCES

Coase, R.H. (1992), 'The institutional structure of production', *American Economic Review*, **82**: 713–19.

Coughlan, A.T., E. Anderson and L.W. Stern (2001), *Marketing Channels*, 6th edn, Upper Saddle River, NJ: Prentice Hall.

Glachant, J.-M. (2006), 'Retail markets in the electricity industry: an overview', working paper, Florence, Florence School of Regulation, European University Institute.

Glachant, J.-M. and D. Finon (eds) (2003), *Competition in European Electricity Markets: A Cross Country Comparison*, Cheltenham, UK and Northampton, MA, USA: Edward Elgar.

Glachant, J.-M. and F. Lévêque, (2005), 'Electricity single market in the European Union: what to do next?', discussion paper of the European Regulation Forum on Electricity Reforms.

Hogan, W.W. (2000), 'Regional transmission organisations: millennium order on designing institutions for electric network system', working paper, Harvard J. Kennedy School, Cambridge, MA.

Joskow, P.L. (2000), 'Deregulation and regulatory reform in the US electric power sector', in S. Peltzman and Clifford Winston (eds), *Deregulation of Network Industries: The Next Steps*, Washington, DC: Brookings Press, pp. 113–88.

Joskow, P.L., and R. Schmalensee (1983), *Markets for Power: An Analysis of Electric Power Deregulation*, Cambridge, MA: MIT Press.

Littlechild, S.C., (2002), 'Competition in retail electricity supply', working papers in economics, University of Cambridge, Faculty of Economics.

Maclaine, D. (2003), 'Determining the limits of competition: a critical evaluation of the process to introduce electricity supply competition', doctoral dissertation, University of Sussex.

Müller, C. (2005), 'Responding to regulation: operating in Germany within a (non) regulated market', paper presented at the Electricity Markets Conference, Toulouse, June.

Norway, Ministry of Petroleum and Energy (NVE) (1999), *Regulations Concerning Metering, Settlement and Co-ordinated Action in connection with Electricity Trading and Invoicing of Network Services*, reg. no. 301, 11 March.

Spulber, D.F. (1999), *Market Microstructure: Intermediaries and the Theory of the Firm*, Cambridge: Cambridge University Press.

United Kingdom, Secretary of State for Energy (1988), *Privatising Electricity: The Government's Proposals for the Privatization of the Electricity Supply Industry in England and Wales*, White Paper, London: HSMO.

United Kingdom, Ministry of Justice, *Electricity Act 1989*, London: HMSO, ch. 29.

Williamson, O.E. (1985), *The Economic Institutions of Capitalism*, New York: Free Press.

Williamson, O.E. (1996), *The Mechanisms of Governance*, New York: Oxford University Press.

4. Liberalization and privatization of road management in Finland and Spain

Mónica Altamirano and Martin de Jong

INTRODUCTION

Roads are technologically and institutionally less complex than other infrastructure types. Rolling stock consists of buses, lorries, taxis and private cars—all of which are owned by others than the infrastructure manager. Neither is the underlying technology for producing asphalt, maintaining it properly, eliminating ice, snow and other disturbing elements from the road surface exceedingly complicated. And yet road reform is in the context of growing car use and congestion, budgetary restrictions, environmental considerations and lacking technological innovation in the past decades, a subject to be reckoned with.

Several organizations have a large role to play in the debate on the why and how of road reform. Examples of these organizations are the World Bank, the Organisation for Economic Co-operation and Development (OECD), the European Union (EU) and the World Road Association (PIARC). More often than not, individual countries take the sketches of models to be emulated as reference frames for how to restructure the institutions for their own road management system. One could say that among experts and policy-makers in the international arena and transfer agents carrying ideas from international organizations to the national scene and vice versa, a worldwide pool of ideas on road reform exists from which national governments can borrow. For instance, the World Bank emphasizes that public policy in roads requires a thorough restructuring of the existing organizations involved. This implies entering a new paradigm, in which public agencies are transformed into client organizations responsible for tendering all phases of road construction and maintenance activities (PIARC 1995; Talvitie 1996, 1999; Parkman 1998).

This process of moving from an in-house organization to a client organization is often referred to as the privatization process of a governmental

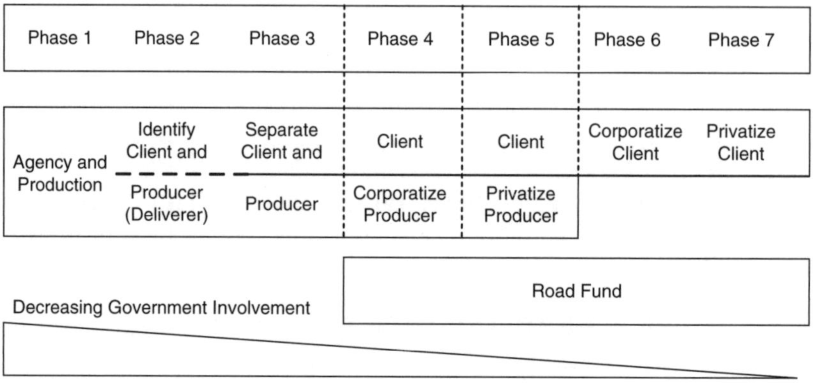

Phase 1	Phase 2	Phase 3	Phase 4	Phase 5	Phase 6	Phase 7
Agency and Production	Identify Client and	Separate Client and	Client	Client	Corporatize Client	Privatize Client
	Producer (Deliverer)	Producer	Corporatize Producer	Privatize Producer		

Decreasing Government Involvement	Road Fund

Sources: Talvitie (1996, p. 100), adapted by Pakkala (2002, p. 17).

Figure 4.1   The seven phases in road reform

agency (Madelin and Parkman 1999; Pakkala 2002). The process is described as comprising seven phases that increasingly separate the client-related aspects of road management from its service-providing parts (see Figure 4.1). In this terminology, the client represents the principal, for instance, the public agency ordering the services, while the provider is the agent, the company that delivers the requested services. This is accompanied by a gradual opening of the market (liberalization), the selling out of the public provider (privatization), the creation of a road fund from which investments exclusively to roads can be made and, eventually, even the privatization of the public agency acting as a client. However these last two phases of the model have not yet been implemented anywhere

Not only do the proposed phases in the reform seem fairly standardized, so do the objectives and drivers to engage in such a reform (Talvitie 1996; Dunlop 1999; Heggie 1999a). According to the World Bank:

> the objective is nearly always the same. To introduce a more commercial approach to management of roads, by creating: (i) more autonomous and accountable management; (ii) a more market-based approach to setting priorities; (iii) better staff incentives; (iv) a more flexible staffing structure; and (v) better accounting systems combined with tighter financial discipline (World Bank 2002).

Four trends seem dominant in road contracting (Altamirano and Haraldsson 2005; Altamirano and Herder 2006). First, projects are contracted for the whole life cycle of the road. Secondly, contractors are given increasingly more freedom of design, as the indicators used for monitoring their work become less operational and more performance based (Cervera and Minchin 2003). Thirdly, more projects are financed by private investors (Miller 2000). Fourthly, contracts tend to be granted for the longer term (Altamirano et al. 2007). Britain, New Zealand and Australia are presented as leading, because they materialized most of these trends. Other countries are seen as lagging behind them, but still following largely the same developmental path, albeit slower and later. This would suggest that road reform occurs more or less uniformly around the world, with countries following the same steps.

In this chapter, we show that the institutional starting positions of various countries can differ so markedly that they are bound neither to follow the same developmental paths nor to produce similar institutional outcomes after the reform. Put differently, multiple institutional equilibria exist, which result from differential starting positions leading through different histories of interaction between players to differential institutional equilibria (Aoki 2000, 2001, 2007; Groenewegen and de Jong 2008). While Finland, Norway, Sweden and the Netherlands have no or little experience with funding road infrastructure through toll-levying or transferring the financial or managerial responsibility of entire projects to private parties, in Spain, Portugal, France and Italy road users are accustomed to paying for the use of infrastructure because these countries have a long-standing tradition in private or mixed entrepreneurship and finance in road construction and maintenance. As a consequence, the reform process of liberalization, privatization, private finance and growing design freedom for contractors puts very different types of strains on these countries. The steps taken to push through the reform as the policy-makers in each of the countries defined it, also diverged. Although each of the above mentioned countries have their individual features, we believe it is justified to make a broad-brush distinction between the North and South European models of road reform, apart from the Anglo-Saxon model (Esping-Andersen 1990).

In order to demonstrate the different starting positions, developmental paths and eventual institutional outcomes after the reform process, we have taken two countries, Finland and Spain, widely seen as daring reform pioneers within their general group. For both countries, the institutional situation before and after the reform will be presented, after which the specificities of both developmental paths are laid out, as well as what ideas were borrowed from the worldwide pool of ideas for reform. Finally, general conclusions are drawn in light of the main research question on differential developmental institutional paths. Our findings are based on case study research. Documents were consulted and interviews were held with the main stakeholders and experts in the field in both countries.

The Road Sector and its Reform Agenda

The public obligation of providing a transportation network can be divided in four different kinds of tasks: capital projects, the construction of green-field projects or new roads; routine maintenance, which includes daily activities that ensure the continuous availability of the road, like roadway and shoulder maintenance, drainage and winter maintenance; periodic maintenance, the management of pavements and the planning of activities required to return the state of the road to its original condition by repairing road damage and thereby substantially altering the asset condition; and, finally, operation of roads, which mainly includes incidental traffic and safety services.

In general the agenda for reforming the road sector can be described as follows. First, there are two overarching goals, to introduce a more commercial approach to road management and to ensure an adequate and stable supply of funds to the road sector. These goals can be achieved by applying different policy measures (see Figure 4.2), such as introducing a 'more flexible staffing structure' (Heggie 1999b, p. 41) or the introduction of the user pays principle (Estache et al. 2000; Heggie and Vickers 1998). In some cases, normally when the road authority counts with a large operational division, carrying out construction or maintenance work directly, the implementation of these principles requires restructuring the existing

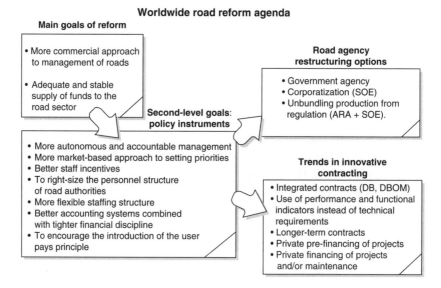

Figure 4.2   Agenda for road management reform

road agency. This can be achieved by creating a vertically integrated government agency under the supervision of the Ministry of Transport (corporatization); by transforming the entire road agency or road administration into a user-financed service-producing state-owned enterprise (SOE) with a contract-based relationship with the government; and by unbundling production from regulation. The last option involves the creation of an administrative road authority (ARA) taking care of regulation, and a separate service-providing SOE, carrying out construction and maintenance tasks. The seven phases model depicts the implementation path for this last reform option. Apart from an internal reorganization, the application of these measures normally also requires a reorganization of the work packages or services to be outsourced. This is how different countries have come to experiment with innovative contractual arrangements for the procurement of road construction and maintenance.

New Governance Modes

These innovative practices have caused a shift in governance from a public bureau to a market-like arrangement. In the old situation the public road authority did outsource, but did so by tendering work orders. Contracts were signed directly with each contractor. The road authority had its own staff looking after the management and coordination of all project activities. Private parties only acted as a hired hand in the public sector (Salminen and Viinamäki 2001). In the new situation, the road agency signs a single contract for an entire project or a service agreement for a particular network for a particular time-span. Subcontracting of specialized works or particular work orders still occurs, but now under the responsibility and supervision of the main contractor. The new role of the private contractors is that of a service provider (see Figure 4.3).

The first column shows a traditional design–bid–build (DBB), whereas the second represents the common structure for a design–build (DB) project. In a DB contract, design and construction aspects are contracted for with a single entity, known as the main contractor, usually the general contractor; but in some cases it is also the design consultant. Where the design–builder is the main contractor, the design consultants are typically hired directly by the contractor. By making both phases overlap the road agency or infrastructure owner aims at minimizing project risks and delivery times; by allowing the construction contractor to bring his construction expertise into the design process; cutting the extra tendering process for the design phase and realizing payments upon completion. Besides functional requirements, instead of technical requirements, are used in combination with lump-sum payments—a total price for the whole project

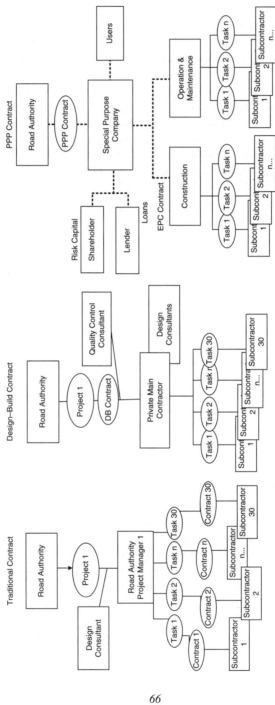

Figure 4.3 Old versus new organization of contracting entities

negotiated upfront, instead of unit prices—ensuring the owner against cost variations. Integration of different life-cycle phases and use of functional requirements in contracts entail larger design space for contractors, freedom to choose different technical solutions.

The third column is illustrative of a public–private partnership (PPP) or concession contract. All life-cycle phases of the infrastructure are tendered in a single package. The main contractor, often a special purpose company, finances the project and takes care of design, construction, operation and maintenance of the infrastructure for a certain period of time, between 15 and 30 years. Payment is subject to completion and linked to performance, during the operation period. Practically all technical risks are shifted to the main contractor. The main contractor subsequently manages his risk efficiently by closing an engineering–procurement–construction (EPC) and an operation and maintain contract (OM) with experienced suppliers, often daughter companies. The EPC contract is similar to a DB, but here both parties are private. Upon completion of the project a functional completion certificate is issued and the infrastructure is transferred from the supplier to the main contractor. From that moment on the OM contract starts.

THE INSTITUTIONAL SETTINGS BEFORE THE REFORM

In the road sector in Spain and Finland, what institutional structures existed in 1996 before they were reformed? To answer this question, we will present the main actors, the positions they had in the system, their preferences vis-à-vis the reform and the institutional rules and practices in existence then. Since road reform hinges strongly on government action and party-political preferences, we pay extra attention to this aspect.

Actors and their Positions in Finland

In Finland the main political parties are the Social Democrats (SDP), the Center Party and the National Coalition. In 1996 and in 2001, when the three laws needed for separating road administration and road enterprise were finally approved, each of these three parties had approximately 25 percent of the votes. The SDP predictably was closest to the labor unions. The National Coalition, a center-right party, represents private enterprises and the business community. Meanwhile the Center Party especially defends the interests of small and rural municipalities, it supports decentralization, free will, free and fair trade, and small enterprise.

Three actors were actively promoting the reform of road management in Finland: the Ministry of Finance, the Ministry of Transport and the Finnish Road Administration (Finnra). The reform being proposed required the unbundling of the road authority into a road agency and a road enterprise. Therefore it initially met with criticism and opposition from nearly all actors. Drivers for change were basically to cut public spending and reduce staff. In addition Finnra aimed to promote innovation in the sector. In the political arena, the SDP and Communist Party (Left Wing Alliance) represented the majority in Parliament. They supported the labor unions and therefore opposed reform. Nevertheless, later in 2001, they came to approve the laws required, because Finnra had succeeded in convincing the labor unions of the benefits of the creation of a public enterprise and the benefits that will accrue to them.

Finnra also faced internal criticism. Staff at the operational level were hesitant to transfer so much design freedom to private contractors. It was difficult for them to go from being project managers telling contractors what and how to do things, to contract managers only having a say in the acceptance of the final quality delivered. Labor unions came out in defense of their affiliates. The creation of a separate public enterprise that would compete as any private company threatened the jobs of many workers within Finnra. They were externally backed by the left-wing political parties. Consultancy firms were moderately opposed: they had their doubts as to the speed with which the reform would be pushed through. They also feared losing their role as privileged advisors and becoming only subcontractors of construction companies. Road contractors in general were against the reform. Large contractors feared more competition, especially from foreign companies and the new public enterprise. Medium and small contractors feared becoming subcontractors, losing their direct contracting relationship with Finnra. Meanwhile other contractors active in construction but not yet in roads feared unfair competition from the large enterprise to be created. Foreign contractors were the only private players interested in the reform. Swedish and other foreign players wanted access to the Finnish market. The position of the banks seemed neutral.

All these parties had a stake in the problem and key resources to either block the reform or ensure successful implementation. Examples of the former were labor unions, political parties represented in Parliament and the Ministries of Transport and Finance. Among the latter we count the contractors, consultants and the staff at Finnra. Contractors not yet active in the road sector are an interesting case; not being directly involved, they could not stop the reform but were key for the creation of a new market for maintenance activities. If they had confidence in the reform, they would deploy their expertise and resources in order to become active in this market.

Actors and their Positions in Spain

In Spain the two main political parties are the conservative Partido Popular (PP) and the social-democratic Partido Socialista Obrero Español (PSOE). Together they represent over 80 percent of the votes. In addition there are two parties representing regional interests, the Partido Nacional Vasco (PNV) for the Basque Country and Convergencia i Unio (CiU) for Catalonia. The PP was the main opposition party until 1996, while the PSOE was in power. The roles were reversed between 1996 and 2004. The PSOE won the elections again and regained power in 2004. The two other regional parties support one national party or the other, depending on their support for greater regional autonomy.

The initiator of the reform was the recently chosen PP government. This government, supported by the Ministries of Transport and of Finance, declared privatization as one of its main objectives. It proposed, for public roads, to go back to the concession model; an alternative quite in line with its drive for privatization. An ally in this particular issue was the PNV, which was aware that neither the national state nor their region could control roads under concession.

The political arena was far from agreement on the issue. As in Finland, strong opposition was shown by the left-wing parties, PSOE and the CiU, who had a majority in Parliament at that time. The reason was different, however. In Spain they represented the interests of the smaller contractors instead of the labor unions, which believed the new practices would favor large vertically integrated companies, increase their profits, lead to higher market concentration and leave small contractors subject to abusive contract terms. Furthermore, they were against a longer duration of project concessions, the extension of existing concessions and pre-financing and/or toll-financing of roads. They feared public control over expenditure would be lost. For the CiU an additional concern was that national players would gain control over regional roads.

Compared to Finland, private players, large contractors and concessionaires (having the expertise and financing capacity to compete in the proposed model), banks and consultants seemed more favorably inclined. However the position of road users was mixed. They were unhappy to see the numbers of toll roads increase, while acknowledging the need to augment investments in the road network.

The Institutional Framework in Finland and Spain

Before the reform was initiated by both countries in the late 1990s, they followed the traditional procurement model. Operation and maintenance tasks were realized mainly by road agency in-house personnel and infrastructure projects were financed directly, with public funds. Outsourcing took place on an ad hoc basis. Projects were normally divided into small tasks or work packages for which private companies were hired. The road authority was then acting as the main contractor. Given the limited scale of the tasks assigned to contractors, contracts were prescriptive. *Ex post* monitoring was done with a focus on the contractors' effort and by checking technical requirements. Price was the overruling selection criterion. Contractual relationships were valid for a relatively short period of time, normally the time needed to complete the particular task. And payments were made on the basis of unit costs. This system was designed under the principle that all operational risks and the entire responsibility toward users were to be fully and directly borne by the public authority.

There were also important differences between Finland and Spain before the reform. In 1996 the Finnish Road Authority still fully operated the routine and winter maintenance tasks in-house. It had no recent experience with private financing methods. Meanwhile, in Spain, at least 40 percent of the maintenance tasks were outsourced; and, in exceptional cases, the road authority could even make use of the traditional concession model developed in the late 1960s.

THE INSTITUTIONAL SETTING AFTER THE REFORM

Here we will describe the institutional structures in Finland and Spain which prevailed after the reform. The main actors in both countries are roughly the same as before the reform, except for the newly created state-owned Finnish Road Enterprise (FRE).

Actors and their Positions in Finland

Actors and their positions have been shown to be decisive for the final choices made. The opposition of most of the stakeholders made it last 10 years before the required legislative changes were approved. The reform succeeded mostly due to agile negotiation with stakeholders by Finnra. Before the reform, support from the Minister of Finance was key to place the issue on the political agenda. Later on that same actor became the main obstacle for a wider-scale implementation of private financing.

In Finland, once the reform had been implemented and the different stakeholders experienced the new system, they came to adopt different positions. In general they were satisfied with the process, especially public bodies such as Finnra and the Ministries of Transport and Finance. These had realized their goals, including downsizing of the road agency and the creation of a competitive market for routine maintenance. They even intend to copy and implement the same model to other infrastructure sectors, such as the railway sector. Most of the actors have adjusted to their new role. Finnra has become a professional client. The workers represented by the labor unions are pleased with their status as staff of a successful autonomous company. The FRE is the largest contractor with a competitive advantage over its competitors, because of its experience and familiarity with the client. However recently it has lost some market share in routine maintenance activities to other companies such as YIT, a construction company especially active in the area of water and environmental services that joined the newly created market of routine maintenance in 2001.

Contractors have learned to compete in the new maintenance market and have become service providers. Foreign contractors have been more successful in obtaining capital projects than in gaining maintenance projects. Skanska, a large Swedish contractor, has been the leader of the winning consortium for the only two PPP projects until now realized in Finland, the E-75 and the E-18 motorways. Medium-sized contractors appear to be the biggest losers after the introduction of the large innovative contracts. They do not have the financial strength needed to act as main contractors, and are often less specialized than smaller contractors, which makes becoming a subcontractor hard. Meanwhile, most consultants have become partners rather than subcontractors. Some of them are even developing long-term alliances with contractors. Others have specialized as quality auditors of contractors' work.

However, when specific future developments are discussed, disagreements pop up again. While Finnra would like to transfer more responsibilities to the private sector by promoting private financing and the use of large integrated PPP schemes, the Ministry of Finance and Parliament are halting this development. They either fear loss of control over future spending or simply do not believe that total life-cycle costing saves money. Large contractors instead lobby for further implementation of these innovative practices, because comprehensive long-term contracts grant them more design space. Their complaint about the implementation of private financing, thus far, is the uncertainty about the number of future projects using this scheme. They believe a larger pool of projects, announced long in advance, is crucial to ensure the participation of more contractors, since tendering costs are much larger and companies need to invest in a set of completely new skills.

Actors and their Positions in Spain

The position of the actors in Spain is not only influenced by the results of the reform but also by the change in government in 2004, with the Socialist Party gaining office again. The main opponents in 1996, PSOE and CiU, came to realize that even though they are now a parliamentary majority, it is practically impossible to revert to the traditional model and shift back to budgetary financing of infrastructures. They now opt for supporting a shadow-toll model instead of direct toll-levies. Shadow tolls are payments made from the public budget to contractors, based on estimates of numbers of road users, a price for each of them. The new government is defending this position by pointing to the right of citizens to universal and free access to public infrastructure.

As in Finland, the results of the road management reform are generally appreciated in Spain. At the national level, authorities like the Ministry of Transport are satisfied with the expansion of the network and its relatively good condition. After 2004 they have begun to make use of shadow toll schemes, where a levy is not paid directly by users but by the government. They are currently replicating the concession model, either direct or through shadow toll, to already existing roads, to finance maintenance expenses. At the regional level, the positions of road agencies depend on the political situation. Most are satisfied with new practices and are extending the concession model to maintenance. Many also have created public corporations that fulfill the role of concessionaires and hire competitive subcontractors for the various life-cycle phases, to keep some control over their income from tolls. Large contractors and concessionaries, as expected, are satisfied with the new model. However, they are not totally convinced of the shadow toll model, for they miss control over market risks and tariffs and they do not like being used to only finance projects. These new shadow-toll concessions are used in combination with performance-based payment determined by government, which reduces their degrees of freedom and poses new risks.

It is interesting to note that even smaller local contractors have benefited since they can participate in temporary alliances or consortia with large national companies for various local projects. The change has also served the interests of consultants. In fact they were more used to collaboration with contractors than their Finnish counterparts. Concessionaires in Spain are normally vertically integrated and have large engineering departments, from which some consultancy companies evolved. Only some smaller consultancy companies are upset, because of what they consider arbitrary tendering practices by public concessionaires. The financial actors seem pleased: three national banks have been very active in this area of private infrastructure finance and have therefore developed expertise, making them competitive in the entire European arena. Finally, users directly affected by the new model are generally used to the user pays principle, even though they find it sometimes hard to swallow toll charges for already existing roads and for maintenance. A number of pressure groups have shown resistance against the growing number of shadow toll projects, which are believed to lead to much higher expenses in the long run.

Changes in the Institutional Framework in Finland and Spain

Finnra has become a government agency operating under the jurisdiction of the Ministry of Transport and Communications, but relatively independent from it. In Spain roads have remained under the jurisdiction of the Spanish Directorate General of Roads, which is part of the Ministry of Transport, and of the autonomous communities. Both countries are comparatively advanced in using innovative contracting and in the implementation of their own reform agendas. While Finland is already implementing its third procurement strategy after the reform of 2001, Spain has refined its contract law to support the further development of the concession model, not only for use in green-field capital projects, but also for the rehabilitation and maintenance of existing roads.

From the four main trends in procurement, the Spanish model can be characterized by its experience in private financing, first with direct tolls and recently with shadow tolls, and very long-term contracts. Spain could already build on experience developed since the 1970s. The use of contracts that integrate design with construction do not seem to be a priority. This is probably due to the bad experience they had in the 1990s when a DB scheme, with payment in unitary prices and not as a lump sum had been implemented.

Nevertheless, the Spanish seem pioneers in integrating safety related tasks into their integrated maintenance contracts. The Finnish procurement model is, in turn, specific in its great advance in the use of integrated contracts—with 60 percent of projects tendered as DB—and their experience in the use of performance based contracts for routine maintenance.

The use of quality-related criteria for the selection of contractors is more advanced in Spain than in Finland. This is partly due to certain informal institutions to be discussed in the subsection below. Both countries implemented integrated maintenance contracts at around the same period, in 1998. The difference is that while Finland first had to realize a restructuring of the road agency and create a completely new market, Spain was already outsourcing a greater part of it and only had to reorganize the tendering of these tasks.

Periodic maintenance has remained rather traditional in both countries. In Finland contractor selection remains totally based on price and in both countries contracts are prescriptive, detailed and very short term. Consequently, there are plans to make important reforms in this sector, either by combining periodic with routine maintenance in one contract or by developing long-term rehabilitation contracts for a whole road network.

As explained previously, in both countries these new contracting practices have caused a shift in governance from a public bureau to a market-like arrangement. These practices have also resulted in innovative arrangements for *ex post* management of contracts. A common method used is the so called 'own responsibility principle'. Contractors have to submit, alongside their offers, a quality control plan and regularly prepare reports for Finnra; and, consultants are hired to check if contractors are following plans and procedures as promised. If not, penalties will follow.

In Finland one of the main concerns expressed was the lack of trust between the various players, preventing the creation of long-term alliances. This is surprising in light of the substantial attention paid by Finnra to transparency, open competition and efficiency. There is no guarantee that a contractor will win a maintenance contract in the next term just because it won the previous one. Its offer has to be objectively better to win the new round, so the time horizon is rather short. Finnra actively promotes the participation of international companies in Finnish projects, which objective was successful when in 2006 two routine contracts were won by an Estonian company.

The situation in Spain is characterized by more frequent informal contracts between road authorities and contractors. They seem less cautious about a regular information exchange, even during tenders. This is partly because transparency is not as highly valued as in Finland. Contractors in Spain accept more easily than in Finland that the selection of the winner is not completely objective. Many other selection criteria than price are used, without use of detailed guidelines as to how quality points are assigned. Moreover the success of Spanish companies in the national and international markets is deemed very important in Spain, more so than efficiency or the existence of a solid competitive market. This attitude reinforces the already existing principle of nonintervention among contractors, for instance in a quota system for distribution of the sales of raw materials.

The *ex post* management and monitoring of contracts in Spain is also very different than in Finland. The relationship between road agency and contractor is much richer than merely a written contract. The contract is not the last word, but rather the beginning of a continuous process of negotiation. As a result, there can be a great gap between the contract signed and actual practice. An example is provided in an interview with the Operations Director of Maintenance Concessionaire in Spain (20 June 2007):

> In the contract between the Public Concessionaire (Bidegi) and the special purpose company (Bidelán) signed in 2003, there were certain levels of service and values for performance indicators agreed. These however have not been monitored the first four years. This is the result of a later agreement between the contracting parties, where it was recognized that the condition in which the existing roads were delivered was also different than provided in the contract, and, therefore those levels of service required were impossible to be achieved.

THE NATIONAL PATHS AND REFORM PROCESSES

Not all the measures presented in the worldwide reform agenda can be applied at the same time, at least not with equal focus. Some of them could even be contradictory. In the two national models described above, it appears that countries pick different objectives and measures from this global pool, depending on the priorities their national actors have. Once such a selection is made and the reform process set in motion, it proves that some ideas are hard to combine or even exclude each other, making the course chosen hard to change. In this subsection, we review how the Finnish and Spanish paths developed. We look at the main elements of their national agendas, the consequent objectives that were chosen and the path-dependent process that evolved.

The Finnish Path

Traditionally Finland was not an open market economy. In the 1960s the government had a firm grasp on many economic sectors, including the financial sector. For instance, all banks were government owned. A series of events in the early 1990s caused a change in the public management of infrastructures, from the welfare state toward a market-orientation state (Salminen and Viinamäki 2001). The main events were the economic recession of 1992, the collapse of the banking system and the collapse of the Soviet Union, Finland's largest trade partner. These events demanded a radical and urgent response from the Finnish government and created a window of opportunity for the new public management paradigm.

From the beginning of the 1990s Finnra's top management promoted reform, and, in 1996, a proposal was presented to Parliament. Parliament rejected it but this setback did not stop the initiators of the reform. They kept discussing possible reform with several stakeholders (Ojala and

Sirvio 1998). The years 1998–2001 were a period of intensive preparation to safeguard a smooth transition, after the new legislation was approved. When Parliament did approve it in 2001, the FRE was officially born.

Although various options were considered by the Finnish government, 'full privatization' was not among them (Ojala and Sirvio 1998, p. 3). The government preferred an SOE, allowing for substantial state control. Finnra's top management was also more concerned about achieving formal unbundling of agency and enterprise.

Once new legislation was in place and the FRE officially born, it was time to liberalize the sector and open the market to new players. Working groups were created in which a transition plan was discussed with which most stakeholders could concur. This transition process leading to an open market lasted two years for design and construction and four years for periodic and routine maintenance. This gradual opening meant the gradual phasing out of negotiated contracts between Finnra and FRE, and an increase in the number of contracts decided by competitive tendering. Full competition has been in place in the sector since 2004.

The path followed by Finland coincides with the seven phase-model proposed by the World Bank, with the only difference that a road fund has not been created. The situation in 1996 can be compared with phase 1. Then, between 1998 and 2001, promoted by strong leadership within Finnra, phases 2 and 3 were carried out. The necessary steps to move on to phase 4 were taken by gradually opening the market and FRE now operates in a fully competitive market. There are plans to open the enterprise to private investors; but no decision on this matter has been taken yet. There are no discussions about taking the reform further than phase 5.

The Spanish Path

Compared to other European countries, Spain has had a democratic regime only since 1975 and has been a member of the European Union since 1986. Ever since, Spain's governments have made serious attempts to stabilize and strengthen their economy. And yet, when the Partido Popular (PP) gained office in 1996, they inherited an economy with serious problems that, along with plans to join the European Monetary Union, set the stage for a reform of the public sector.

The dominant road procurement model Spain had used until 1996 was traditional. Infrastructure construction and maintenance were completely financed with public funds. Only in exceptional cases did legislation allow government roads to be given in concession to private entities. It should be mentioned that the old system of toll highways, which had been introduced in 1965, was stopped in 1982 by the then socialist government.

The situation in 1996 made a revision of their infrastructure delivery model urgent. Key factors responsible for this sense of urgency were a serious infrastructure deficit in comparison with the most advanced members of the European Union and tough requirements to control public spending. The new government focused on the liberalization of the economy and the privatization of many national companies. The road reform being proposed basically consisted in going from the traditional direct financing of infrastructures to private financing. It consists of returning to the old concession model, where infrastructure projects are financed by direct contributions from users through tolls. And since the projects planned concerned roads with probably much less traffic than those given in concessions in the 1960s, it was proposed to lengthen the maximum concession period to 75 years, for existing concessions and for new projects. Other project delivery methods being considered were DB or *llave en mano* (turn-key) that would defer the payment of the infrastructure to the delivery moment.

The government, aiming at involving the private sector in the delivery of infrastructures, implemented a series of fiscal, administrative and social measures that set the legal basis of the new infrastructure delivery model. These were adopted throughout the Aznar administration from 1996 to 2000. They implied important changes in the legal framework and particularly in the Highway Concessions Law, which had been left outdated since the concession regime was stopped in 1982. Even though the new infrastructure delivery model had the old concession model as a basis, its wider reimplementation required a new legal framework and, equally importantly, a pool of projects, mature enough to be given in concession. Some of the measures adopted were the incorporation of lump sum contracts within the General Contract Law for Public Works (art. 147, L13/96) and the creation of the legal figure 'contracting for integrated maintenance services' (art. 60, L55/99); the modification of the Law on Highway Concessions making it possible to use the concessionaire figure for complementary activities, to extend the concession period to a maximum of 75 years and to extend the concession to neighbouring road sections (art.157, L13/96), all with the goal of making projects more profitable and attractive to private investors; the extension of the concessionaire as a legal figure to also cover maintenance and exploitation of already existing road sections (art.59, L55/99); and making possible the creation of a state company or public concessionaire able to acquire debts (art.158, L13/96) (Izquierdo and Vasallo 2004).

In 1996 the size of the public sector in general and road authority in particular was already moderate. This was partly due to the 1982 Autonomy Statute that already transferred many tasks and staff to the autonomous communities, and partly to the first stream of privatizations carried out by the socialist government from 1982 to 1996. Levels of outsourcing were also comparable to Finland and even higher for routine maintenance. As mentioned before, there had been an old tradition of toll roads and concessions since the 1960s when the first highways, like the Barcelona–La Junquera and Bilbao–Behobia, were given in concession. There was a pool of contractors, therefore, experienced in this model. The different stakeholders unanimously agreed that the main drivers for the reform and implementation of many innovative contracting practices was the need to reduce the public debt and the need for further expansion of the network.

THE TWO MODELS IN A NUTSHELL

The reform process has followed different paths in the two countries. Though in both countries the goal was to move toward what, according to new public management, is a more efficient way of organizing procurement of public infrastructures; the specific drivers as well as the specific practices that have been implemented are different.

In Finland the main goal of the road reform is the selection of a more commercial approach to road management (see Figure 4.4). This results from a combination of external factors (mainly the process integration with the EU and the fiscal discipline it required), initial conditions (an oversized road authority) and historical and cultural circumstances generating particular preferences among different actors (like the lack of experience in private financing). This first selection conveys a particular focus on efficiency and reducing the size of the road agency. Consequently, from the list of second level goals, Finland has chosen primarily to right-size the personnel structure of road authorities and better staff incentives in the second place. Both goals predictably lead to a radical restructuring of the road agency through unbundling production from regulation.

Spain chose the road reform to ensure adequate and stable supply of funds to the road sector (see Figure 4.5). It has a different national agenda marked by the need to reduce the public deficit from 5.7 percent to 2.7 percent in less than a year, an evident backlog in infrastructure and recent experience in the use of private financing. The most logical policy instrument to achieve this goal was to encourage the introduction of the user pays principle, which in Spanish terms meant a return to the old concession model. Since Spain did not have a significant production portion in-house or problems of an oversized road authority, efficiency was not a key

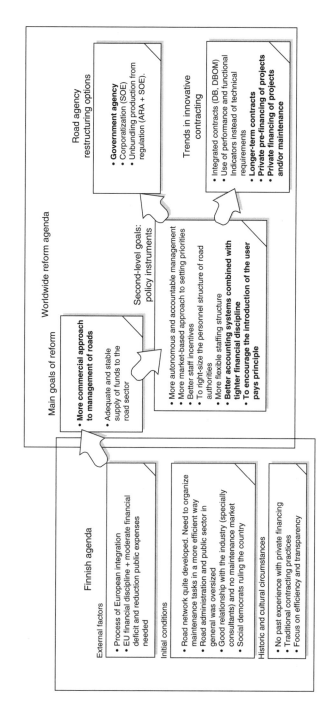

Figure 4.4   The Finnish reform path

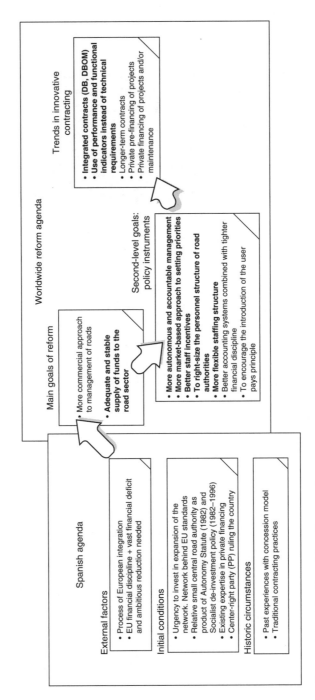

Figure 4.5 The Spanish reform path

driver, and restructuring the existing road authority was not considered necessary.

The choices of these two countries have also had an important impact on the contracting practices they have developed. Spain has become a pioneer in private financing schemes and longer-term contracts, allowing them to expand their transport network without increasing the financial deficit. Finland has become a pioneer in integrated and performance-based contracts reducing the agency staff needed to keep contractors under control. In financing delivery methods, Finland has experience only with pre-financing methods, as they do not require the introduction of the user pays principle. Broadly speaking, one could say that Spain mainly went through a privatization process, while Finland focused on the liberalization aspects of road reform.

Spain's most recent changes in procurement practices reflect an interesting example of path dependency. In 2004 the socialists gained power again and, as could be expected in the light of their position before the reform in 1996, they have tried to turn back the clock. However, it was not possible for them to go back to the model of direct financing of infrastructure projects prevalent before the reform. At the national level, they have introduced a system of shadow toll concessions instead of direct toll. This essentially implies a shift from total private financing to private pre-financing. Probably this change was made possible, because the public deficit in 2004 was smaller than in 1996.

With the shadow-toll model, the socialist government gained more control over the infrastructure investments, something they argue makes the decision-making process more transparent and democratic. Some other actors think this model is actually less transparent, as it can result in uncertain and large payments in the future, which are not readily visible in the budget.

CONCLUSIONS

In this chapter, we have seen how the particular institutional starting positions of Finland and Spain made a significant difference, not only to the path of the reform process, but also to the eventual institutional equilibrium that evolved. By comparing the initial and final institutional structures, reviewing the preferences of the actors in these two countries before and after the reform, and the particular reform paths they followed, it became evident that Finnish and Spanish actors have selectively taken ideas from the worldwide pool of ideas on road reform. Their initial circumstances kept them from adopting all ideas from the worldwide agenda, at least with the same emphasis. Instead, these countries have chosen the reform ideas most suitable to them. This selection process has resulted in a new institutional equilibrium in which a particular subset of ideas, for each of the countries, has been absorbed. One could claim that Finland typically represents a successful example of liberalization in which direction a number of countries in Northern Europe are headed, whereas Spain can be seen as a forward-looking representative of the Latin model, in which the aspect of privatization comes more to the fore. The way the reform was implemented, as well as the relative advance each of them has shown in the use of innovative contracting, made evident that even though both countries have taken up the challenge of road reform, they have done so in very different ways. Surprisingly enough, both countries have become world examples and pioneers in their own right. Both can be pleased with the extent to which they realized their objectives, within the context of their own national system.

Finland has succeeded in downsizing the road agency and in creating a brand new market for routine maintenance, and has achieved savings of up to 40 percent. Spain has succeeded in expanding the national transport network and updating it to meet European standards, all within the financial strictures of the European Union. The question is whether their current equilibria are sustainable. Challenges are not over yet.

In Finland the strong focus on efficiency and competition is causing cutthroat competition that threatens to affect negatively the development of the sector. If profit levels are too low, Finnish companies will not be able to invest in research and development, nor deliver the innovation hoped for in these innovative contracts. In the long run, they may become less competitive in the European and other international markets. Contractors may start to act in their defense and push toward a new wave of reforms. In Spain the recent developments in the use of shadow tolls for the financing of projects is expected to create serious financial problems in the future, which may necessitate a new wave of reforms. In both cases, the current institutional equilibria may still turn out to have been suboptimal and temporary ones.

ACKNOWLEDGMENTS

We would like to thank Juha Aijo (Ramboll) and Pekka Pakkala (Finnra) in Finland, and Jose Maria Sarriegi (University of Navarra), Luis de los Mozos (Diputacion Foral de Gipuzkoa) and Guillermo Albrecht (Typsa) in Spain, for their assistance, the valuable discussions we had with them and the many doors they opened for us.

REFERENCES

Altamirano, M.A. and H.V. Haraldsson (2005), 'Resolviendo juntos los problemas de las Infraestructuras de la Próxima Generación', paper presented at the III Congreso Latinoamericano de Dinámica de Sistemas, Cartagena, Colombia, 30 November.

Altamirano, M.A. and P.M. Herder (2006), 'Systems dynamics modeling for road contracting', paper presented at the Transport Research Arena Europe 2006, Gothenburg, 12–15 June.

Altamirano, M.A., W.M. de Jong and P. Herder (2007), 'Cross-national benchmark of innovative contracts in road infrastructure: the use of games for investigating future scenarios', paper presented at the 23rd World Road Association Congress, Paris.

Aoki, M. (2000), *Information, Corporate Governance and Institutional Diversity: Competitiveness in Japan, the USA and the Transitional Economies*, Oxford: Oxford University Press.

Aoki, M. (2001), *Toward a Comparative Institutional Analysis*, Cambridge, MA: MIT Press.

Aoki, M. (2007), 'Endogenizing institutions and institutional changes', *Journal of Institutional Economics*, **3** (1): 1–31.

Cervera, A. and R.E. Minchin (2003), 'The change to end-result specifications: where are we now?', *Proceedings of the Transport Research Board 2003 Annual Meeting*, Washington: Transportation Research Board.

Dunlop, R.J. (1999), 'The New Zealand experience in restructuring road administration New Zealand road reform', *Transportation*, **26** (1): 55–66.

Esping-Andersen, G. (1990), *The Three Worlds of Welfare Capitalism*, Cambridge: Polity Press.

Estache, A., M. Romero and J. Strong (2000), 'The long and winding path to private financing and regulation of toll roads', working paper 2387, World Bank, Washington.

Groenewegen, J. and W.M. de Jong (2008), 'Assessing the potential of new institutional economics to explain institutional change: the case of road management liberalisation in the Nordic countries', *Journal of Institutional Economics*, **4** (1): 51–71.

Heggie, I.G. (1999a), 'Commercially managed road funds: managing roads like a business, not like a bureaucracy', *Transportation*, **26** (1): 87–111.

Heggie, I.G. (1999b), 'Examples of legislation establishing an autonomous road authority', www.worldbank.org/transport/roads/ism_docs/annex5.pdf (accessed 23 November 2007).

Heggie, I.G. and P. Vickers (1998), 'Commercial management and financing of roads', *World Bank Technical Paper*, 409: 158.

Izquierdo, R. and J.M. Vasallo (2004), *Nuevos Sistemas de Gestión y Financiación de Infraestructuras de Transporte*, Madrid: Colegio de Ingenieros de Caminos, Canales y Puertos.

Madelin, K. and C.C. Parkman (1999), 'A review of contract maintenance for roads', http://www.worldbank.org/html/fpd/infrastructure/toolkits/Highways/Highways/pdf/48.pdf (accessed 20 November 2007).

Miller, J.B. (2000), *Principles of Public and Private Infrastructure Delivery*, London: Kluwer Academic.

Ojala, L. and E. Sirvio (1998), 'Restructuring highway agencies: the Finnra case: options for Africa?', *Africa Transport: Technical Note*, 15, Road Management Initiative, World Bank.

Pakkala, P. (2002), *Innovative Project Delivery Methods for Infrastructure: An International Perspective*, Helsinki: Finnish Road Enterprise.

Parkman, C.C. (1998), 'Transferring road maintenance to the private sector: preliminary literature review and proposed study area for the project', working paper, Transport Research Laboratory, Wokingham.

PIARC (1995), Road Management Committee Papers, World Road Congress, Montreal.

Salminen, A. and O.-P. Viinamäki (2001), *Market Orientation in the Finnish Public Sector: From Public Agency to Privatised Company*, Helsinki: Ministry of Finance and University of Vasa.

Talvitie, A. (1996), 'International experiences in restructuring the road sector', *Transportation Research Record*, 1558: 99–107.

Talvitie, A. (1999), 'Restructuring of road administrations: a paradigm shift', *Transportation*, **26** (1): 1–3.

World Bank (2002), 'Institutional and management structures for roads', www. worldbank.org/transport/roads/inst&sm.htm (accessed 20 November 2007).

PART II

Technology

5. Regulatory practices and the role of technology in network industries: the case of Europe

Matthias Finger and Frédéric Varone

The purpose of this chapter is to identify the key characteristics of the emerging modes of governing European network industries. With Giandomenico Majone (1990, 1996), we make the case that a European model of network industry regulation has developed since the liberalization of the telecommunications industry. Yet we go further than Majone by explicitly taking into account the technical systems underlying both liberalization and regulation of network industries. At present regulatory practices in Europe cover both the functions of regulation (that is, the different aspects that are being regulated: competition, market creation, and technical and political aspects) and the institutions of regulation, generally a more or less independent regulatory agency.

However these practices—and their underlying model—appear to be increasingly at odds with the technical and systemic evolution of the network industries. Thus we argue that the future European model of network industry regulation will have to evolve by taking better into account the technical nature of network industries, as this will better reflect the coevolution between the technical systems, on the one hand, and their institutional governance, on the other. As we have argued elsewhere (Finger and Varone 2006), 'bringing technical system back in' will pose substantial challenges to the current practices and underlying model of network industry regulation in Europe. Therefore, we suggest that at least three diverging policy options or scenarios are thinkable in the near future: the top-down creation of sector-specific regulators at the European level; the bottom-up emergence of differentiated regulations, either at a regional level or across customers' categories; or the devolution of new regulatory powers to major market players such as self-regulation by transnational multi-utilities. Our research question thus pertains to the likely evolution of network industry regulation in Europe, considering the growing acknowledgement of the importance of their technical and systemic nature.

In this chapter, we first begin by highlighting the key features of the present European regulatory model, as it is currently practiced across network industries. Secondly, we identify the coevolution between institutional governance and technical systems. Thirdly, we formulate three scenarios for the future European regulation of network industries, namely, European regulators, differentiated regulations and self-regulation by significant market operators. Finally, we conclude by reflecting on the likelihood and implications of each of these three models.

EUROPEAN REGULATION OF NETWORK INDUSTRIES

The underlying assumption of this chapter is that there is indeed a European model of network industry deregulation and reregulation. This assumption can be questioned, considering in particular the fact that the European Commission does not have much power to impose a mandatory institutional model and that European Union (EU) member states still have substantial leeway when it comes to organizing their infrastructures as well as the delivery of services of general interest. Nevertheless the original model of liberalization and reregulation in network industries is without doubt the telecommunications industry: this is the first, and so far only, industry that has been successfully liberalized by the European Commission. The Commission introduced competition, reduced regulatory intervention after initially regulating market opening, and ultimately generated benefits for the consumers. While this original model has inspired the deregulation and at times the reregulation of electricity, postal services, railways, and so on, these other industries have proven to be much more complicated and the model has become significantly complex as a result.

The European Union as a Regulatory State

On the theoretical level, Giandomenico Majone (1996) had already argued that there was a model of a 'regulatory Europe' emerging. National regulation, according to him, must still be considered to be relevant and indeed sovereign; but new forms of regulation that operate independently of the individual member states are indeed appearing. In addition, he declared the EU to be a new 'regulatory state'. In the same vein, other scholars also stressed the rise and diffusion of a new order of 'regulatory capitalism' (Levi-Faur 2004).

Traditional forms of regulation included public ownership, regulatory functions assumed by government departments under political control and self-regulatory arrangements. However, the liberalization and sometimes privatization of network industries in Europe today creates the need to find new institutional venues for regulating competition, market imperfections and private operators, and to protect consumers. The central feature of such institutional reform in Europe at both national and supranational levels is indeed the delegation of regulatory action to independent bodies. Consequently, the so-called independent regulatory agencies (IRAs)[1] are emerging as the most important and most characteristic mode of regulating Europe's network industries. These IRAs are indeed the key feature of the European model (Thatcher 2002; Gilardi 2005a). In other words, statutory regulation by independent bodies is gradually replacing other and older forms of state intervention. The regulatory state is considered to be less bureaucratic, more efficient and more independent of political influences. It is also supposed to be less prone to political bargaining, more geared to pragmatic problem-solving and better able to protect consumers' interests rather than defend operators' (Thatcher 2005).

In short Majone has a convincing argument for the development in Europe of a 'regulatory state', an expression that became his label. Majone's message is that market development does not lead to deregulation but rather to reregulation. According to him, the regulatory state is neither social nor interventionist. It pertains to the correction of market failures and tries to increase the welfare of consumers. It institutionalizes a branch of government which guards against possible regulatory failures through its insulation from majoritarian and political influence. The newly created IRAs are non-majoritarian institutions. They possess and exercise some grant of specialized public authority; but they are neither directly elected by people nor directly managed by elected officials. The nonmajoritarian IRAs managing European regulatory politics and the majoritarian institutions of the member states complement each other. Distributive policies are, in Majone's view, dependent upon majoritarian legitimization and must remain the domain of the member states (Joerges and Roedl 2004).

Characteristics of the European Regulatory Model

A few decades ago network industries were mostly vertically integrated. This was particularly the case of telecommunications, postal services, public transport, electricity, gas, water distribution and the audiovisual sector. The air transport sector also functioned de facto in such an integrated manner. Furthermore, network industries were organized at the national level in general and at the regional level in federal states. If they were not totally integrated within the same enterprise, the professional nature of these industries ensured that all concerned actors collaborated at national and international levels. Economically these industries operated under what is called a 'cost-plus regime', thus paying primarily attention to the technical aspects and only secondarily to financial and/or customer considerations. Finally, these industries generally had more or less important public service obligations. However, corresponding public service objectives were not ensured by means of regulation, but by means of public ownership. The reasons for this regulatory approach stem from the technical and systemic nature of the infrastructures, market failure and public service objectives. This vertical integration is being put into question, however, by the process of liberalization that started in the 1980s. The European Commission is a very significant actor in this process.

On the basis of neoclassical economic theory, such liberalization in Europe takes the form of simultaneous unbundling—a primarily technical endeavor—and competition, whereby unbundling is a prerequisite for competition. As a consequence, the formerly integrated industries are becoming fragmented; and the different actors within the industry, which were previously cooperating, are now increasingly competing or otherwise behaving strategically.

It appears that the liberalization of network industries cannot entirely be assimilated to the liberalization of other industries and sectors, given in particular their specific technological nature. More precisely, in most network industries only some segments can be liberalized, while others remain monopolistic for both technical and economic reasons (for instance, railway and air traffic control infrastructures). By definition imperfect, this liberalization of the network industries requires the creation of functions previously assumed by the vertically integrated firm and/or by the industry or sector itself through cooperation, but lost after liberalization. These functions pertain to the technical integrity and systemic nature of the network industries, namely, in terms of interoperability, interconnection, capacity management and system management (Finger et al. 2005).

Consequently, in the age of competition, these systemic technical functions need to be assumed by a third-party actor that can be either the regulator him/herself or an actor supervised by the regulator. This is to ensure that technical regulation is distorting the market as little as possible. Finally, one must also mention the fact that, in the age of liberalization, public service objectives are no longer automatically guaranteed and must therefore be defined and enforced by some external entity. All this leads to the fact that network industries must be reregulated after liberalization (and ideally in parallel to it) in order to ensure their proper functioning for the benefit of both citizens and customers. The above considerations constitute the technical argument, which underpins Majone's observation of reregulation.

Although the European Commission did have very logical and coherent arguments for the liberalization of network industries, it quickly become clear that reregulation was not only needed, but was also going to be a pragmatic, messy, complicated and incremental process. Not only did liberalization lead to reregulation, but reregulation also led to more reregulation. Overall one can detect in the EU's reregulation four different types of arguments, which justify four corresponding types of regulatory intervention.

First, economic arguments are being used for reregulation. Liberalization often does not seem to proceed as planned. Further regulatory intervention is therefore required to (further) create the market. The privileged means to create competition here is so-called third-party access (TPA), that is, the granting of rights to use the infrastructure of the incumbent. Third-party access was initially developed in the telecommunications sector and subsequently spread to all network industries. Today it is even used where there are no physical networks, for instance, in postal distribution. Access problems are now found everywhere and access regulation becomes the generic solution for market creation.

Political arguments also become necessary. Competition leads to the fact that nonlucrative services, which previously had been cross-subsidized within a public enterprise, have to be specifically identified and financed. Incumbents and especially new entrants have no incentives to provide nonlucrative public services. Therefore, public service regulation must be developed to force an operator to do the job or to pay for other operators to do it.

Increasingly technical arguments for reregulation can be observed in Europe. Such technical arguments pertain to interoperability, interconnection, capacity management and system management—all regulatory functions which become problematic once technical systems are unbundled and fragmented (Finger et al. 2005). The successful regulation of such technical functions will ultimately decide whether the infrastructure will function at all and be sustainable in the long run (see below).

As a result of competition, and economic growth more generally, network industries grow and the usage of the networks increases. This poses challenges to the usage of the scarce resources upon which some network industries rely, such as water, airspace and telecommunication spectrum, the usage of which subsequently also needs to be regulated.

The institutionalization of such reregulation is again a pragmatic and stepwise process. Indeed, regulatory institutions, especially the sector-specific IRAs favored by the EU, constitute an institutional novelty within the European continental political-administrative system. Thus the new

IRAs somewhat overlap with—in several member states—pre-existing competition authorities, which are also concerned with the functioning of the markets in network industries or the lack thereof. In general, these four functions are attributed to the IRA, even though competition authorities sometimes get involved. Furthermore attributing these four regulatory functions to IRAs, leads to compromises between the IRAs' public policy objectives, market creation and sustenance, and technical functions.

In our view, the creation of the IRA in general and the fact that the IRA simultaneously must fulfill the above mentioned regulatory functions triggers five issues. The first is the tension between sector-specific regulatory authorities and competition authorities, and sometimes even the judiciary. Sector-specific regulators are in charge of technical, political and at times resource attribution functions, as well as the market creation function. However, when it comes to competition regulation, there is generally an inbuilt conflict between the sector regulator and the already existing competition regulator; even more so because technical and public service regulatory functions all do have implications on competition. So far there is no coherent and satisfactory institutional arrangement to reduce this tension (see, for example, the diversity of solutions adopted in the United Kingdom, the Netherlands, France or Germany), other than having these two regulatory functions and corresponding institutions reporting to two different ministries, thus balancing the power and raising conflicts among these two to the level of a political debate. In some countries there are other organizations involved in sector regulation. Such is the case, for example, in Germany, where the judiciary plays a significant role in *ex post* regulation or in Switzerland where price surveillance is a function fulfilled by a specific regulatory authority. While the judiciary should only play a role once all other regulatory interventions fail, price surveillance should, in our opinion, be integrated into sector-specific regulation, as it constitutes simply a subelement of public service regulation.

The second issue concerns the ownership of the incumbent operator. Indeed, in many network industries, one or several publicly owned operators will remain. This situation generally creates a tension between the sector regulator (as well as the competition regulator), on the one hand, and the administrative authorities historically in charge of steering and supervising the historical operator, on the other. At first these two functions generally remain within the same ministry, even though they represent two totally different interests, that is, ownership interests versus consumers' interests. However, over time, the political authorities must clarify and separate these two interests. European Community law generally requires some separation by attribution to two different ministries. Ideally, the interest of protecting the consumers and of making the industrial sector function properly should prevail over the interest of protecting the incumbent by means of ownership measures. But even if ownership objectives are reduced to purely financial objectives—comparable to a shareholder' s interests in a listed company—a tension will necessarily always remain between the regulators (sector-specific and competition), on the one hand, and the owner(s), on the other. The only institutional solution to this tension is to attach these objectives and functions to different ministries or levels in order to balance power relations or to privatize. For example, the shareholding objective should be attached to the finance ministry or to the political authorities of other, especially lower, levels such as regional or local political authorities.

The independence of the regulator is a third very sensitive issue. By definition sector (and even more so competition) regulators are independent from the operators they are supposed to regulate. The term 'independence' is used for the institutional separation between the regulator and the political authorities. European Community law only requires some separation when the state is also present on the market as an owner of one of the players. Indeed, the general philosophy is that regulators should also be at arm's length from government (Coen and Thatcher 2005). However, the only intellectually solid argument for this is public ownership, the fact that one of the operators being regulated remains owned by the state. In other words, the regulator' s independence is thus yet another institutional means to prevent the confusion of the various functions political authorities inevitably assume: the ownership function, the sector-specific regulatory function and the competition regulation function. This issue of independence has a bearing in particular on questions pertaining to the nomination of regulatory bodies' members (Who nominates? And for what period of time are regulators nominated?), reporting structures (To whom does the regulator report, to the government, the parliament or a special commission?), oversight mechanisms (Who oversees the regulator, the parliament, the judiciary or still another body?) and power (see next point) (Gilardi 2005b).

Indeed independence is only one of two key elements to be considered, the other being the power of the regulator. This is the fourth issue. A regulator can be very independent yet have little power. It is therefore important to consider the regulator's power attributes, such as legal attributes (Can the regulator decide on its own or simply recommend? Can it investigate on its own or only act upon complaints? Can it intervene *ex ante* or *ex post*? Does it have to consult with other bodies, such as, for example, the price surveillance authority before acting?), the financial resources (What is its budget?), the human resources (What are its competencies?), as well as the financial autonomy (By whom is the regulator paid, the government, the consumers, the operators or a combination thereof?). These attributes, together with the institutional independence, ultimately determine the pressure the regulator can exert and the results it can achieve. While the European model goes so far as to urge the creation of a sector-specific IRA, it leaves significant leeway when it comes to the real power of the regulator. Yet the entire model of sector-specific regulators can only function if these regulators have power.

Finally, there is the issue of the level of regulation. The original idea was that regulation occurs at the national level and that regulatory bodies should be set up nationally. Over time one can observe a process of gradually moving up this sector-specific regulatory function to the European level, thus Majone's argument for a regulatory Europe. This is already the case of air safety regulation assumed by the European Air Safety Authority, as well as of some rail regulation functions which falls under the responsibility of the European Rail Authority. It will certainly extend to other sectors and functions in the future.

BRINGING TECHNICAL SYSTEMS BACK IN

A preliminary analysis of the European model of regulating network industries clearly supports Majone's assertion of an emerging regulatory Europe, which is structured around sector-specific regulation and regulators. We also notice that such sector-specific regulators combine market regulation with other noneconomic regulatory functions such as technical and political functions. Thus they are creating new institutional arrangements which go far beyond network industries and touch other public policy areas such as the environment. An assessment of the above evolution and subsequent institutional framework leads us to three critical observations

First, the liberalization of network industries was done from a nontechnical perspective, more precisely from a neoliberal perspective aiming at introducing markets to create competition and increase efficiency, quality and customer satisfaction more generally. The overall objective was to dismantle the monopolist, and this was done monopolist by monopolist, sector by sector. Moreover, dismantling the monopolist was achieved by introducing competition into one of the monopolist' elements (activities), assuming that all the other (infrastructure) would remain unchanged, thus rather neglecting the systemic nature of network industries.[2] It was also assumed that the technical characteristics of networks would remain unaffected by these changes or that technology would change automatically according to the new economic incentive structure. This assumption may well prove to be wrong in the medium term and especially in the short run (Finger et al. 2005; Künneke 2008).

Secondly, subsequent regulation according to the new European model, which became more and more necessary as liberalization progressed, was conceptualized in a quite static manner: further markets were to be created mainly by means of granting ever more TPAs; technical problems as they arose were to be solved; traditional public service objectives were to be guaranteed; and so on. Furthermore, such static or at times even backward-oriented regulation was being institutionalized in the sector-specific IRAs, which, precisely because of their relative independence, started to develop a life of their own, namely, by seeking to increase their discretionary power.

Thirdly, the dynamics thereby introduced into formerly vertically integrated industries has, not astonishingly, triggered some technical and often systemic innovations, which in turn led to the evolution of the technical system, the sector and the industry. The most telling example here is mobile telephony; but analogous examples can be found in all the other network industries. The question that now arises is whether the institutional arrangements set up and institutionalized along this new European model are not going to be, or are already, at odds with, the state of the technical system, and this to the point where institutional arrangements no longer foster but hinder the evolution of the technical system.

In other words, the emergence of the European model of regulating network industries seems to be—and increasingly so—at odds with the technical and systemic evolution of the network industries (which, however, has been triggered by this very deregulation and reregulation). This situation must be conceptualized as a problem of coevolution between technology and institutions in general, but more precisely between technical systems (infrastructures), on the one hand, and the institutional arrangements governing these technical systems (in particular regulation), on the other (Finger et al. 2005). Figure 5.1 summarizes this coevolution.

Based on the above observation of an emerging new European model of regulation and against the background of this framework a series of research questions can thus be formulated. What are the consequences of deregulation and reregulation on the technical systems? To what degree does it trigger technical innovations in systems? What are the core technical functions of systemic nature that must be assumed even after liberalization and reregulation? Preliminary research shows that the four core functions are interoperability, interconnection, capacity management and systems management (Finger et al. 2005). To what degree and how are these core technical functions of systemic nature reflected in institutional arrangements? And what happens if they are not? How does the performance of network industries reflect this dialectics between technical and institutional systems? Answering these questions goes far beyond the scope of this chapter.

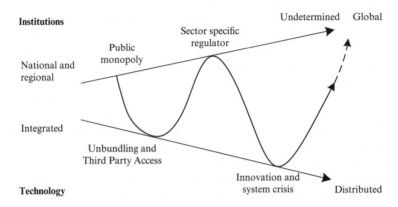

Figure 5.1   Coevolution between institutions and technology in network industries

We limit the demonstration to three potential but alternative developments of the European regulation of network industries, which lead to three corresponding ways network industries are likely to evolve.

We argue that such regulatory developments are plausible as several crisis situations in the infrastructures (for instance, electricity blackouts, shortages of supply of energy, accidents involving trains and airplanes) lead the European Commission to interpret these systems failures as a failure of national regulation and try to increase its intervention and decision-making power. Many examples can be found here, notably in the electricity and the air transport sectors, where the European Commission has used crises to further its power and to develop an updated regulatory framework. Furthermore the EU is also actively supporting, by means of subsidies, the construction or rehabilitation of trans-European networks in energy, transport and communications. Subsidizing such networks automatically leads to a more integrated and systemic approach, which inevitably leads to regulating the access to technical management and security of such transnational networks.

EUROPEAN REGULATORS, SELF-REGULATION BY MARKET OPERATORS AND DIFFERENTIATED REGULATIONS SCENARIOS

The main challenge to be addressed by the future European model of regulating the network industries—if intended to integrate the above technical considerations into the overall regulatory framework—is how to design an institutional framework for regulating the liberalized network industries. A particular aspect of this challenge pertains to how and to whom the new regulation powers are to be delegated? For Majone (2001), there are in fact two basic modes of delegation, agency and trust relationships.

On the one hand, power relationships can be characterized as principal–agent relationships. This is a social interaction in which the agent makes decisions and carries out actions that are intended to fulfill the principal's interests. Thus the principal (in our case political authorities) delegates some of its authority to the agent (the sector-specific IRA). Agency theorists usually discuss two main types of agency loss. Because of hidden information, principals may select agents who have preferences that are bound to conflict with theirs. This is the problem of adverse selection. Because the agent's action may be hidden while in office, the agent may not even be sanctioned for acting detrimentally to the principal's welfare. This is the moral hazard problem. Thus the asymmetry of information between the principal and the agent allows the latter to engage in opportunistic behavior that is costly and detrimental to the principal and, at the same time, difficult to detect. However, a key assumption of the principal–agent approach is that specific institutional rules and arrangements can be designed in such a way that they guide delegation and accountability in response to these agency problems. These rules and arrangements include both *ex ante* contract design, screening and selection, as well as *ex post* monitoring, reporting and institutional checks (Lane 2007).

On the other hand, the idea of trust relationship is derived from the trusteeship relation in Anglo-American law. According to Majone (2001: 113):

> [A] trust is a situation where the owner of some property, the 'settlor', transfers it to a trustee with the stipulation that the trustee should not treat it as her own but manage it for the benefit of the 'beneficiary', who could be the settler himself. Since agency may possess the element of trust and confidence of a fiduciary relation, both agents and trustees can be classed together as fiduciaries for many purposes, but the two concepts are distinct . . . A trustee is an agent and something more. The trustee's fiduciary duty is not simply a personal obligation but is attached to a piece of property—the trust assets.

As regards European governance, Majone states that political property rights, that is, some elements of national sovereignty, are transferred from national governments to the European institutions for the benefit of these governments. This is the case, for example, with the European Central Bank, whose role consists of preserving the property rights of the member states in the area of monetary policy. In the same vein, some provisions of the Treaty give the Commission real property rights in order to safeguard the *acquis communautaire*, to begin with the right of initiative.

The main difference between the situation of the agent and of the trustee is the level of independence with regard to the principal. Contrary to the agency relationship where the agent's preferences must be in line with those of the principal in order to avoid or minimize agency losses, in the case of a trustee relationship, these preferences can be to a certain extent different from those of the principal in order to safeguard the credibility of the policy proposals put forward by the trustee.

Because regulation is by its very nature independent from the political authorities, we consider that such a trust relationship is at work when delegating powers to regulate markets, public service obligations and technical systems integrity of the network industries. The governments and legislatures of the member states have delegated regulatory powers to IRAs and to the EU to enhance credible commitments, for instance, fair competition between historic operator and newcomers and long-term investments in networks capacities. Of course, it is even more the case if regulation is delegated by national governments to a supra-national level, such as in the case of European regulators or networks of national regulatory agencies (Coen and Thatcher 2008). Who, therefore, will be designated as trustee of the European Union for managing the technical systems? Three scenarios are thinkable, which all go beyond the actual sector-specific IRA at the national level and the competition regulation at European and national levels.

European Regulators

The first scenario consists of applying the actual regulatory design of the air (European Air Safety Authority) and rail (European Rail Authority) safety sectors and to the other network industries. Thus, a sector-specific European regulator is institutionalized in order to regulate access to and pricing of the infrastructure, to monitor and sustain technical integrity and innovations, and to guarantee its overall security. This solution seems to have strong advantages from both a technical and an economic point of view. In such a case trans-European networks are merely understood as a natural monopoly within the European market. However such a scenario, which corresponds to the model envisioned by Majone, will face strong resistance from the member states, as well as from the actual owners of the infrastructures. In the air and railway sectors delegating regulatory authority to a supra-national European body was made possible because of strong public policy concerns, mainly in the area of safety. But one can also imagine similarly strong public policy concerns in other areas such as the environment.

Self-regulation by Market Operators

The second scenario assumes that European institutions will never gain sufficient knowledge and expertise to regulate complex technical systems. Thus they will delegate the regulation of network industries to major market operators, and basically intervene only on competition (antitrust) issues. This scenario will end up with some kind of self-regulation by market operators, who act either as trustee of the European authorities or on a voluntary basis. It is quite obvious that already the big market operators are cartelized and have reached at times oligopolistic positions in several of the network industries (mainly in transnational multi-utilities), and as such cannot be avoided by the European Commission when it comes to regulatory matters. Clearly the question of political control and accountability of these trans-European operators—should self-regulation prove to be ineffective and inefficient—will remain a crucial issue. Examples, here, abound in matters of technical standards, where the major market players are indeed the drivers of standard-setting in particular and regulation in general.

Differentiated Regulations

The third scenario does not emerge as a conscious institutional design by the European institutions. On the contrary, it results from a gradual bottom-up process. This evolution leads de facto to a physical and technical integration of networks as infrastructures and to a harmonization of the sector-specific regulations implemented by neighboring countries with similar socioeconomic standards and shared values regarding the services of general interest to be provided. In such a case, both market operators and national IRAs work hand in hand, even across borders, to secure their own integrated market. This scenario seems to be very attractive as the national attitudes toward the quality of services of general interest, the privatization of public enterprises, and so on, still vary significantly across Europe (Hall and Soskice 2001, Thatcher 2004). The recent enlargement of the EU will certainly reinforce this tendency. Thus, every member state will pay for the services and the security he wants. But the development of this *service à la carte* also means the death of a really integrated European market. Finally, one could imagine that the scenario of differentiated regulations will not only spread across member states but also across various types of consumers such as industry and households. In this respect, the cream-skimming strategies pursued by the market operators could increase inequities among social groups, as well as between countries. In short, the risk of this last scenario is that the network industries no longer contribute to social, economic and territorial cohesion, at least not at the European level.

CONCLUSIONS ABOUT THE SCENARIOS' LIKELIHOOD AND IMPLICATIONS

We have seen so far that the currently emerging European model of regulating network industries is not yet systematic, let alone coherent. We have in particular highlighted the technical aspects that will have to be regulated in order for these network industries to function properly. Indeed, if these technical aspects are not properly regulated, failures of systemic proportions will result in blackouts for instance. As these systemic failures— be it in the areas of safety, security, security of supply or environmental degradation—will have strong political repercussions, they will accelerate the evolution from the current situation toward one of the three above outlined institutional scenarios.

However the concrete institutional arrangements of such reregulation, resulting from the above dynamics, are far from obvious. We have outlined three possible scenarios of such institutional arrangements: European regulators, self-regulation and differentiated regulation. In terms of likelihood, one would have to better understand which scenario is supported by which institution, at both the EU and member state levels, and by which private actor, such as operators and consumers. In doing so, one should give more consideration to particular types of pressures, for example, systems' breakdowns, safety and security problems, environmental pressures and others. One could also envision that the three scenarios are not independent from one another: the first scenario can be combined with the second, and the second with the third.

In terms of implications, one should asses the viability and efficiency of each of these three scenarios on the different network industries as technological systems (for example, security aspects and technological innovations), as well as on the delivery of services of general interest (that is, quality of services, affordability and accessibility). Last but not least, one could evaluate the impacts of the three scenarios on the institutional balance of power between the EU institutions themselves (for instance, the Directors-General of the Commission, European Parliament and the Council), between various levels of governance (from the EU, to member states, to local authorities) and between the various bodies engaged in a specific regulatory framework (in this case, competition authorities, sector-specific regulators and ministries). All these constitute as many further research activities and projects, which should contribute to a better assessment of both the likelihood and implications of each of the above three scenarios.

NOTES

1. Some authors also use the term 'national regulatory authority', given that the independence of the IRAs is the most contested feature of the model.
2. The aim of the reform in the telecommunications and postal sectors, at least, is to fully liberalize.

REFERENCES

Coen, D. and M. Thatcher (2005), 'The new governance of markets and non-majoritarian regulators', *Governance*, **18** (3): 329–46.

Coen, D. and M. Thatcher (2008), 'Network governance and multilevel delegation: European networks of regulatory agencies', *Journal of Public Policy*, **28** (1): 49–71.

Finger, M. and F. Varone (2006), 'Bringing technical systems back in: towards a new European model of regulating the network industries', *Competition and Regulation in Network Industries*, **1** (1): 87–106.

Finger, M., J. Groenewegen and R. Künneke (2005), 'The quest for coherence between institutions and technologies in infrastructures', *Journal of Network Industries*, **6** (4): 227–60.

Gilardi, F. (2005a), 'The institutional foundations of regulatory capitalism: the diffusion of independent regulatory agencies in Western Europe', *Annals of the American Academy of Political and Social Science*, **598**: 84–101.

Gilardi, F. (2005b), 'The formal independence of regulators: a comparison of 17 countries and 7 sectors', *Swiss Political Science Review*, **11** (4): 139–67.

Hall, P.A. and D. Soskice (eds) (2001), *Varieties of Capitalism: The Institutional Foundations of Comparative Advantage*, Oxford: Oxford University Press.

Joerges, C. and F. Roedl (2004), *The 'Social Market Economy' as Europe's Social Model?*, Florence: European University Institute.

Künneke, R.W. (2008), 'Institutional reform and technological practice: the case of electricity', *Industrial and Corporate Change*, **17** (2): 223-65.

Lane, J.-E. (2007), *Comparative Politics: The Principal–Agent Perspective*, London: Routledge.

Levi-Faur, D. (2004), 'The global diffusion of regulatory capitalism', *Annals of the American Academy of Political and Social Science*, **598**: 12–32.

Majone, G. (1990), *Deregulation or Re-regulation?* New York: St. Martin's Press.

Majone, G. (ed.) (1996), *Regulating Europe*, London: Routledge.

Majone, G. (2001), 'Two logics of delegation: agency and fiduciary relations in EU governance', *European Union Politics*, **2** (1): 103–22.

Thatcher, M. (2002), 'Regulation after delegation: independent regulatory agencies in Europe', *Journal of European Public Policy*, **9** (6): 954–72.

Thatcher, M. (2004), 'Varieties of capitalism in an internationalized world: domestic institutional change in European telecommunications', *Comparative Political Studies*, **37** (7): 751–80.

Thatcher, M. (2005), 'The third force? Independent regulatory agencies and elected politicians in Europe', *Governance*, **18** (3): 347–73.

6. Network modernization in the telecom sector: the case of Wi-Fi

Wolter Lemstra, Vic Hayes and Marianne van der Steen

INTRODUCTION

This chapter presents an account of the technological and economic development of Wi-Fi, from its genesis to the emergence of a global ecosystem. It provides detailed observations on the life cycle of Wi-Fi. What determined the emergence and success of Wi-Fi? What role does it play in the network modernization within the telecommunication sector? To answer these questions, we focus on three dynamic aspects: the evolution of Wi-Fi technology, the role of strategic management, and the coevolution of industry structure and the institutional environment. These aspects will shed light on several intriguing questions about Wi-Fi. Why did it start in a firm, NCR, operating outside the traditional telecom industry? How did the institutional changes in the United States (US) radio spectrum regulation support it in its early years? How did NCR, as a rule-breaker, forge the creation of an open standard? And how did supporting institutions of the global and regional economic system provide an incentive for further growth of Wi-Fi?

Based on evolutionary economic theory, we assume that new technology develops along a relatively standard track from the time it is born to its maturity, and that the firm structure evolves with the technology. We take into account that technology coevolves with the development of institutions in response to changing economic conditions, incentives and pressures. Following the methodology suggested by Wilber and Harrison (1978), we develop themes and typology based on the case study. Our approach is to discuss an analytical narrative in which we interpret the case study in terms of the evolutionary notions of knowledge interactions, coevolution of wireless technology, institutions and firms, and sector structure.

We discuss the evolution of Wi-Fi during three subsequent periods: the genesis of Wi-Fi, toward an open standard, and public domain networking. Further on we discuss stylized facts derived from the case study, linking the empirical facts to elements of evolutionary theory, such as notions of variety generation, selection and transmission, and retention to better understand the emergence and the success of Wi-Fi. This chapter concludes with the application of a typology of network modernization based on Wi-Fi technology.

WI-FI AND TELECOM NETWORK MODERNIZATION

For an appreciation of the role of Wi-Fi in the modernization of today's telecommunication networks, its developments should be placed in the proper context. The Wi-Fi related developments are thereby in stark contrast with the traditional developments in the telecommunication sector. Telecommunication network modernization has traditionally been the responsibility of network operators, either as government entities or as tightly regulated private companies. For decades the focus of modernization has been the core network, with the main objective to improve the network capacity and the operational efficiency. The network design principles were being derived from the characteristics of the primary service being supported, that is, voice telephony. Wi-Fi, however, has its roots in the field of local area networking in support of data communication between computers. This is the market segment of private networking for business users, that is, at the edge of the public network. This segment is characterized by private entrepreneurship in an unregulated market environment, whereby the end users invest in their own networking facilities.

The use of radio spectrum provides another contrast. As spectrum capacity is considered a scarce resource, the use of radio waves is highly regulated. Hence governments apply a tight licensing regime to regulate the use of frequency bands among a variety of users and applications. Tight regulation is also intended to prevent interference among different applications and users. These objectives and principles can be recognized in the governmental licensing policy in the area of cellular or mobile telecommunication, which regulated in the early 1980s the use of analogue systems, in the early 1990s narrowband digital systems and, more recently, the use of third generation wideband systems. On the other hand, Wi-Fi operates in unlicensed frequency bands. The original assignment was in the bands set aside for noncommunication use in relation to industrial, scientific and medical applications (ISM bands). The World Radio Conference (WRC) 2003, however, allocated 455 MHz of spectrum at coprimary level in the 5 GHz band to 'wireless access systems including Radio LANs'.

Wi-Fi competes in this band with many other radio services. In addition to devices of other coprimary services it shares the spectrum with other Wi-Fi systems, and hence the 'signal of one user is interference to the other'. A coprimary status means that proposed changes to regulation in the related bands have to be accompanied by proof that no harm is done to the incumbent primary services.

Wi-Fi originated in the field of the unregulated data communication environment, being targeted at the business user. With the advent of the Internet it has become the leading platform for home networking. Subsequently it has moved outdoor, providing Internet access at hotspots, thereby providing alternative access to the public telecom infrastructure. In the context of citizens' initiatives it has become a tool for neighbourhood area networking, partly in competition with the public telecom infrastructure. Through mesh-networking and in nomadic mode it provides other access and networking alternatives to the existing public telecommunication infrastructure. Through the application of voice-over-Internet protocol (VoIP) it also provides capabilities in the voice-telephony domain. Wi-Fi presents alternative ways of network modernization, whereby users take a much more active role. The network thereby reflects more the model of the traditional commons, than the for-profit model deployed by telecom operators.

THE GENESIS OF WI-FI

Traditionally peripheral equipment, for instance input–output devices, was connected to computers using a dedicated wired infrastructure. Also computers were being interconnected using a wired infrastructure, within an office building or factory complex often through a local area network (LAN). As a consequence, so-called 'moves and changes' were both costly and time-consuming. In traditional stores located on primary business streets of cities, the wish to preserve the architecture of fine wooden paneling and marble floors did not combine very well with the increasing need for wired infrastructure. Moreover it was lacking flexibility, for instance, required in connecting additional cash registers during summer sales and the Christmas season. This was a customer concern well known to suppliers, including NCR, the leading provider of cash registers in the 1980s.

Strict regulation of the radio spectrum did not allow alternative solutions based on wireless technology to be developed until 1985. That year the US National Regulatory Agency, the Federal Communications Commission (FCC), opened up the 915 MHz, and 2.4 and 5.8 GHz bands designated for ISM applications for use by radio systems. The condition was that spread spectrum techniques would be used to limit interference with other applications and users, on the one hand, and to be able to operate in a hostile environment, on the other hand.

The FCC's decision is a landmark change in one of the most important and formal institutional arrangements of the telecommunication sector, which is concerned with the regulation of the use of radio frequency spectrum as a shared communication medium. Radio spectrum is considered to be a scarce resource. This resource is managed worldwide as a publicly owned asset by the national administrations, typically assumed by a governmental department within the Ministry of Communications. They allocate and assign the usage through a system of licenses to specific services using a system of frequency management to prevent interference from one service to another. Examples of services are the broadcasting, aeronautical mobile and radio navigation, maritime mobile and radio navigation, mobile satellite and amateur services. The administrations typically have to satisfy more requests than they have spectrum available, hence they have to be creative in allocating the same part of the spectrum to multiple services in such a way that the probability of users being subject to interference by other users is minimized. The services allocated in the same band receive rights according to a certain hierarchy. The highest level services are allocated primary rights. If they experience interference from users of a lower service, they can request this user to be shut down. The service(s) in the next lower hierarchy are allocated secondary rights. They are not allowed to interfere with users of a primary service; but they can request a user of a lower service to be shut down. The lowest level services in the hierarchy are assigned in the band at a noninterference, nonprotected basis.

Throughout the radio spectrum, the regulators have set aside frequency bands designated for ISM applications. In these bands the industry is allowed to use radio waves for research and industrial processes, such as diagnostic purposes and heating. The bands, 12 in total, range from 6 765 KHz to 246 GHz. The radio regulations of the International Telecommunication Union (ITU) state the following regarding these ISM bands:

> Radio communication services operating within these bands must accept harmful interference which may be caused by these applications. Administrations shall take all practicable and necessary steps to ensure that radiation from equipment used for industrial, scientific and medical applications is minimal and that, outside the bands designated for use by this equipment, radiation from such equipment is at a level that does not cause harmful interference to a radio-communication service and in particular to a radio-navigation or any other safety service operating in accordance with the provisions of these. (ITU 1998, part 1, articles)

In the beginning of the 1980s, Dr Michael J. Marcus was contracted by the FCC to find yet other ways to deregulate the use of spectrum available for communications. His proposal was to use a spread spectrum system to maximize robustness of receivers and to minimize interference by the transmitter. So far spread spectrum was only considered for military applications. On 9 May 1985 the FCC adopted spread spectrum rules in bands designated for ISM applications intended for civil use.

Within the notion of spread spectrum two methods can be distinguished. One, called direct sequence spread spectrum (DSSS), requiring a transmitter to multiply the transmitted data by a pseudo random code or pseudo noise (PN) code. As a result the transmitted spectrum is widened by a factor equal to the length of the PN code; but, at the same time, the energy is spread over that wider range, thus lowering the power density. The larger the code, the lower the power density is. The military would use a code so wide that the transmitted signal would be buried in the background noise. At the receiver, the signal is divided by the same PN code to recover the original transmitted data, while reducing the narrow band interference by a factor equal to the length of the code.

The other spread spectrum method, frequency hopping, requires the transmitter to limit the duration of a transmission at a particular frequency, and to use a specified number of other frequencies in a pseudo random pattern before it is permitted to transmit again at that particular frequency. Receivers should receive the signal in the same pseudo random pattern. The devices using frequency hopping spread spectrum (FHSS) would therefore interfere with other, static, users in the band for just a very small portion of time. Other frequency hopping systems using other pseudo random patterns would also cause minimal interference among each other, assuming the number of hoppers is limited.

The interesting part of the new rules was that the end users of the devices were not required to have a license. However, the manufacturer had to obtain a type-approval license before being allowed to sell the devices. At the introduction of the new rules only a few members of the public were in support of the new rules, the large majority filed opposing comments at the FCC on the basis that the new rules were contrary to the rules so far imposed by the FCC, in that the devices were always required to minimize the use of the spectrum. The first commercial product using spread spectrum passed FCC approval in 1988. It was a LAN device. After this slow start, equipment authorizations have reflected an exponential growth curve.

THE DRIVE FOR AN OPEN STANDARD

Leading up to and following this landmark event in 1985 firms were starting to develop wireless local area network (WLAN) products for the US market; these included companies such as NCR, Proxim, Telesystem and Symbol Technologies. NCR would take the industry leadership role which ultimately led to the global success of Wi-Fi. NCR recognized the opportunity and value of being able to provide cash registers that could be connected wirelessly. The required LAN expertise within NCR resided with a small group of engineers located near Utrecht, in the Netherlands. This expertise had been obtained through the development of a new modem using signal processing techniques and through the development of a special low-cost extension to the Ethernet standard, which had become the leading platform for LAN since its introduction in 1985.[1] The necessary radio expertise was not available in-house and was acquired through the hiring of experts from Philips' Elcoma division and by providing radio frequency training to the engineers in residence.[2] These knowledge transfer efforts would lead in December 1990 to the release of the first product—a personal computer adaptor with external antenna—in the 915 MHz band, providing a single communication channel at 2 Mbit/s.[3] This release would be followed by products in the 2.4 GHz band.

For a provider of peripheral equipment, such as cash registers, the prevailing rule-of-the-game in the industry suggested that business success had to be pursued by being compliant with the interfacing protocols of the leading computer provider, at the time IBM, albeit this would at best result in a second place in the market. The alternative would be to align the interests of other players and build a coalition to create an open standard. This strategic option was chosen by NCR, moving them from a hitherto industry follower into an industry leadership role.[4]

The Institute for Electrical and Electronics Engineers (IEEE) was identified as the appropriate forum to pursue such an open standard.[5] In 1985 work started in a taskgroup already established as part of workgroup IEEE 802.4, which was responsible for the Token-Bus protocol. The representatives from the manufacturing industry in Workgroup 802.4 needed in their factories a wireless communication means to remotely control equipment, such as cranes and small vehicles. A year later the workgroup obtained approval for a project to extend the Token-Bus protocol with a wireless modem.

However, NCR found this task group to be inactive and decided it needed to take the lead to obtain results. After more than a year of study, the conclusion was that the Token-Bus protocol was optimally designed for use with a wired medium, but using the protocol for radio would imply a very inefficient use of the radio spectrum. An attempt to start a project for extending the IEEE 802.3 charter, which included the responsibility for the popular wired LAN standards based on the Ethernet protocol, with a wireless modem failed due to the lack of interest of the workgroup members.

This opened the way for the establishment of a new workgroup IEEE

802.11 in 1990. This workgroup was coestablished and being chaired by NCR.[6] By October 1991 the requirements for a WLAN standard were defined and agreed upon; the work on the specification of the physical layer (PHY) and the media access control (MAC) layer could be started.[7] The IEEE 802.x standards only affect the lower layers in the Open System Interconnection (OSI) reference model (see Figure 6.1).

In that same year AT&T acquired NCR. In November 1993 the foundations for the PHY and MAC were agreed upon.[8] One year later the design of the protocols had sufficiently progressed and was subjected to the workgroup ballot.[9] In a series of balloting and editing, the specification reached a level of maturity. A sufficient degree of consensus was reached to start the next higher level of approval, the sponsor ballot, in July 1996.

Also in 1996 NCR was spun-off through the AT&T Trivestiture, the split of the company into three new companies, and became an independent company again. However, the WLAN activities remained with the equipment division of AT&T, which was spun-off as Lucent Technologies. In June 1997 the IEEE 802.11 standard was ratified, and in November Lucent Technologies released its first IEEE 802.11 compliant WaveLAN product at 2 Mbit/s with an integrated antenna. In October 1998 an 8 Mbit/s version was released. In 1999 the International Standard Organization (ISO) endorsed the 802.11 standard through its ratification as ISO 8802 Part 11.[10]

Considering the commercial interests that were at stake, it should not come as a surprise that the process of standards-making was rife with rivalry among competing suppliers. Large and financially strong companies typically tried to influence the process through a high level of attendance at the workgroup meetings and by submitting many contributions.[11] See Figure 6.2 and for an illustration of the number of participants over time (Kamp, 2005).

As a WLAN chip-manufacturer, Intel recognized the potential of the market and had been very active in promoting its own variant, known as HomeRF, a wireless networking standard for the home, through the establishment of an industry workgroup. Supposedly the IEEE 802.11 standard was not suitable for voice applications, which was considered central in the scope of their targeted product. The task of the HomeRF workgroup was to exploit the frequency hopping variant of spread spectrum. In the meantime, workgroup IEEE 802.11 had started two projects for extending the standard with higher data transfer rates by making use of the direct sequence variant of spread spectrum techniques. In order to open the possibility for higher data rates using frequency hopping, the HomeRF Workgroup coerced the FCC to change the rules to permit 5 MHz wide channels instead of 1 MHz.

The HomeRF workgroup was disbanded before completing their task.

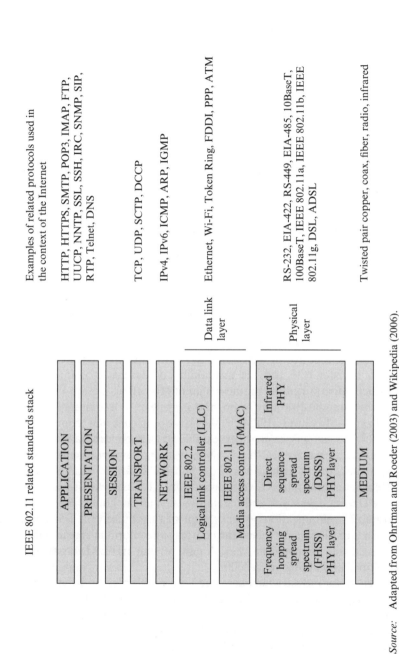

Source: Adapted from Ohrtman and Roeder (2003) and Wikipedia (2006).

Figure 6.1 IEEE 802.11 standards mapped to the OSI reference model

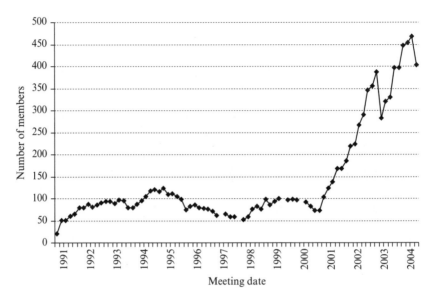

Source: Kamp (2005).

*Figure 6.2   Participation of members in IEEE 802.11 workgroups,
1990–2004*

This may be ascribed to the success of the IEEE 802.11 extension to 11 Mb/s data transfer rate and the availability of devices at competitive prices, which undermined the business plan of HomeRF.

   In another standardization forum, the European Telecommunication Standardization Institute (ETSI),[12] the European telecom equipment industry and telecom service providers established a European standard for WLANs under the name of HIPERLAN in 1991. Parties involved included WLAN manufacturers such as Motorola and NCR, future WLAN users Apple Computer and Sixtel (Olivetti), operators BT, Deutsche Bundespost and a few Danish operators, and regulators such as the United Kingdom (UK) Radio Communications Agency. Out of this initiative a Technical Committee ETSI RES 10 received the charter to develop such a standard. The standard was approved in 1996. A new version HIPERLAN type 2 was developed and approved in 2000.[13]

   Although major industry members had been developing prototypes, no product was brought to the market. The scope of the HIPERLAN standard was considered too wide and would lead to complex devices and high costs, which at the time of release would be too high to compete effectively with products based on the IEEE 802.11 standard.

Table 6.1   Overview of Wi-Fi related standards, 1997–2007

Standard	Released	Transmission speed	Frequency band	Range[1]	Functionality
802.11	1997	1 and 2 Mb/s	2.4 GHz	30–800 m	–
802.11b	1999	11 Mb/s	2.4 GHz	33–175 m	WEP-based encryption
802.11a	1999	54 Mb/s	5 GHz	2.5 m	Not compatible with b and g
802.11g	2003	54 Mb/s	2.4 GHz	7–18 m	WPA-based encryption
802.11i	2004				WAP2-based encryption
802.11n	2007	>100 Mb/s	2.4 GHz	12–27 m	Based on multiple inputs–multiple outputs (MiMo) and orthogonal frequency division multiplexing (OFDM)
802.16	2006	1–4 Mb/s	2–66 GHz	5000 m[2]	Wi-Max: long range, Not compatible with 11 a/b/g

Notes:
1. Theoretical distance for the highest data rate depicted between indoor area and free space circumstance based on 50 mW transmit power.
2. Range depends on frequency band and transmit power.

In Table 6.1 an overview is provided of the evolution of Wi-Fi related standards showing a constant push for higher bit rates and extension of the coverage.

THE QUEST FOR GLOBAL SPECTRUM USE

The standardization efforts in IEEE would only lead to truly globally applied products, and hence economies of scale, if the 802.11 standard could also be used outside the US. This required other nations to follow the 1985 initiative by the FCC and to assign unlicensed spectrum for the use of WLANs in the same frequency bands.

Soon after the establishment of workgroup IEEE 802.11, an ad hoc group was formed within the CEPT[14] consisting of representatives of the national regulatory agencies of the UK, the Netherlands and Sweden. This group prepared the recommendation that would provide radio spectrum for WLANs in Europe, to be approved in 1992. Because in Europe the 900 MHz band was already assigned to the use of the global system for mobile communications (GSM), CEPT only made available the 2.4 GHz band.

With the major industrial countries now having allowed WLAN devices, virtually all states on the globe followed their lead and allowed the use of WLANs in the 2.4 GHz band. Those countries having close relations with the US followed the rules as defined by the FCC, such as a maximum 1 W transmitted power with a maximum antenna gain of a factor of four and a minimum processing gain of 10 for direct sequence transmitters. Those countries having close relations with Europe followed the rules set by the CEPT Recommendation, such as a maximum of 200 mW output power, including antenna gain, and a power density requirement of maximum 10 mW/MHz, instead of a processing gain requirement.

The CEPT team did not stop with the assignment of the 2.4 GHz band, but identified another part of the frequency spectrum that could be used for WLANs. They assigned in July 1994, the 5150–5250 MHz band and the 17.1–17.3 GHz band, with a potential extension with the 5250–5300 MHz band in the future. This spectrum was reserved for devices operating according to the HIPERLAN standard being developed by ETSI. In 1999 the CEPT assigned the band 5470–5725 MHz for HIPERLANs and placed the allocation of the HIPERLAN bands on the agenda of the 2003 World Radio Conference (WRC).

The assignment of spectrum is in principle a matter of national governments. However radio waves do not stop at political or geographical borders. Hence the allocation of frequency bands has always been subject to close coordination among nation states. At the highest level, the WRC provides coordination under the auspices of the United Nations.[15] Because the use of 2.4 GHz for WLANs has been accepted worldwide, there was no need to involve the WRC. However the European Administrations (PTTs) were unhappy with the prospect that an incumbent user that received primary status at a WRC, on the promise that they could comply with the rules stated for HIPERLANs in the 5 GHz band, would subsequently be forced to reduce the permitted power for the HIPERLAN devices from 1000 mW without limits to 200 mW, and to indoor use. By requesting and obtaining an allocation at primary level for WLANs through the WRC, noninterference with existing WLANs would have to be assured for all new applications in that frequency band.

Lucent Technologies, through Vic Hayes, understood, on the one hand, the importance of this allocation for the future of Wi-Fi and, on the other hand, the significant effort it would take to coalesce the industry to make this allocation come true. In this respect, telecommunications companies have a long tradition of fighting for their rights and tend to allocate ample funding to defend their cases. Computer companies, however, operate with much lower margins and typically allocate lower budgets to standardization efforts. Moreover they lacked the experience to act successfully in this forum. At the beginning of 2001, Hayes successfully started a rally in the one-year old Wi-Fi Alliance to establish a committee with sufficient decision power to be able to act quickly in response to the events that would develop at the regulatory agencies, and with sufficient funding to engage a law firm to assist in the generation and implementation of all required actions.

The first order of business was to propose the establishment of new rules in the US for an allocation of spectrum in accordance with the proposal which was on the table of the 2003 WRC in order that the US representatives could support this proposal. Consequently the Wi-Fi Alliance made a petition to the FCC to start the rule-making process in line with the proposal. The next step for rule-making is a notice to the public to request comments on the petition. The response from the National Telecommunications and Information Administration (NTIA), the agency responsible for the spectrum assigned for governmental use, was strongly opposed to the allocation of spectrum between 5470 and 5725 MHz, because that frequency band was already allocated to US governmental use linked to the radio location service, which was applying radar technology. As a consequence the anticipated US position at the 2003 WRC would be negative.

Removing this obstacle was the beginning of a busy time for the regulatory committee of the Wi-Fi Alliance. They first contracted a radar expert to perform a sharing study for WLAN devices with a long list of radar devices. Based on the knowledge obtained, members of the committee worked the issue at national, regional and international level in close cooperation with the radar experts. This effort was concluded with a meeting between the NTIA, the FCC and the committee members, which resulted in an agreement on 31 January 2003 on how to share the band at coprimary level. This result was obtained just in time for the 2003 WRC meeting in June of that year (see NTIA 2003).

With the obstacle removed, the US position changed from violently against into absolutely in favor and the Wi-Fi Alliance received excellent support from the US delegation at the 2003 WRC. Thanks to the European initiative and the strong European support at the 2003 WRC, combined with the support from the US, the WRC ratified the allocation of nearly half of the 5 GHz band for use by Wireless Access Systems including RLANs at coprimary level.

THE ALLOCATION OF LICENSED SPECTRUM

The assignment of unlicensed spectrum for WLAN use presents a strong contrast with the allocation of licensed spectrum for the use of mobile telephony and the use of mobile data applications. In the 1980s the first licenses for analogue mobile telephony and the first licenses for digital mobile communication in the 1990s were typically assigned to the incumbent operator. The strong growth of digital cellular communication facilitated the introduction of competition in this segment of the market, and hence most countries in the Organisation for Economic Co-operation and Development area adopted a policy of gradual introduction of competition (OECD 2005).

The introduction of GSM in Europe implied, next to a modernization of the network from analogue to digital, a harmonization of the mobile communication standard being employed. In the analogue era, traveling and communicating across Europe would require the use of different mobile sets to work with a range of different standards (NMT450 and NMT900, TACS and E-TACS).[16]

Most of the second generation (2G) digital licenses were allocated on the basis of a tendering process in which commitments toward network roll-out played a more important role than the revenues that governments could obtain in the process. The position of governments changed dramatically with the introduction of the next generation of licenses (3G) for the deployment of broadband wireless.

This third generation of mobile systems enabled broadband data communication. It also implied a shift from the circuit-mode implementation of earlier generations, optimized for voice communication, toward packet-mode, optimized for data communication.[17] The tremendous growth of mobile communications, combined with the 'consensual vision' (Fransman 2002) that an all-encompassing e-world would emerge, led governments at the time to expect a high willingness-to-pay by the potential contenders for these new licenses 'to the future of telecommunications' (Lemstra 2006). For the assignment of these licenses, the use of auctions was considered to be the most appropriate mechanism for a competitive and transparent allocation of spectrum (Van Damme 2001). The first auction was held in the UK and generated the equivalent of US$600 per inhabitant. The total proceeds of the licenses awarded in the UK, Germany, the Netherlands and Italy amounted to approximately US$90 billion. The initial 3G auctions were held in 2000, at what appeared to be the peak of the Internet bubble. This financial drain and the collapse of the Internet–telecom bubble caused a major setback in the development of 3G technology and the roll-out of 3G networks, particularly in Europe.

CROSSING THE CHASM

The availability of an open and broadly supported standard in the telecommunication industry is a necessary condition for business success; but it is not sufficient. Following the release of an IEEE 802.11 compliant product in the fall of 1997, Lucent Technologies was selling its privately branded ORiNOCO products; and Micro-Electronics, Lucent's semiconductor and opto-electronic components division, was selling WaveLAN network cards to IBM, Dell, Toshiba and other computer manufacturers. The volumes, however, remained relatively small. The breakthrough would come in 1999 with the agreement to supply Apple with the WaveLAN chips for inclusion in the Apple Airport, a combination of wireless access point and an Airport card for the new Apple iBook. Lucent Technologies and Apple agreed to combine forces and to allow the package to be priced very attractively. With a speed of 11 Mb/s the WLAN could for the first time compete effectively with the available wired solutions.[18] This agreement became for Lucent Technologies the head pin in Geoffrey Moore's metaphor of the bowling alley describing the difficulty of moving the business from serving the early adopters to serving the mass market (Moore 1991).

In another strategic move the industry partners established in 1999, the Wireless Ethernet Compatibility Alliance (WECA) to promote 802.11 compliant products under the Wi-Fi label. The WECA started the certification process in 2000, and, six years later, the organization had certified more than 2500 products (Wi-Fi Alliance 2006). In 2002 the WECA changed its name into the Wi-Fi Alliance, recognizing the power of its Wi-Fi label.

Another boost came in October of 2001. Microsoft released its Windows XP operating system which includes support for IEEE 802.11 based communication, a result of close collaboration between experts of Lucent Technologies and Microsoft.

In 2003 Intel launched the Centrino chip with a US$300 million advertising campaign. This campaign transferred the success of the Intel Inside campaign to the mobile–wireless segment through Centrino Inside, which provides in-built Wi-Fi functionality. This step is a major landmark in the product life cycle of Wi-Fi. It implies that Wi-Fi is no longer a functionality that is added on afterwards, but that Wi-Fi has become a standard, built-in feature of modern laptop computers.

FROM PRIVATE TO PUBLIC DOMAIN NETWORKING

The idea of using Wi-Fi for public access to the Internet is attributed to Stewart, while working on the MAC protocol at AMD, following a

Table 6.2   Distribution of hotspot locations in the Netherlands and Belgium, 2006

The Netherlands			Belgium		
Location type	No.	%	Location type	No.	%
Restaurant	709	32	Restaurant	456	21
Hotel	633	29	Hotel	444	20
Café	260	12	Service routier	343	16
Conference centre	125	6	Petrol station	174	8
Petrol station	100	5	Other	173	8
Hotzone	91	4	Business area	125	5
Recreational centre	87	4	Café	88	4
Marina	74	3	Sports facilities	67	3
Business area	69	3	Recreational centre	64	3
Other	57	3			

Source: De Leeuw (2006).

licensing deal with Xircom (Bar and Galperin 2004). In 1993 he conceived Wayport, a company to provide high-speed wireless Internet access at hotspots frequented by business travelers, such as airports and hotel lounges. Public domain Wi-Fi became much more visible and popular after Starbucks made an agreement with MobileStar to equip all its outlets with Wi-Fi in 2001. (See Table 6.2 for an illustration of the distribution of hotspots in the Netherlands and Belgium.)

A plethora of providers helps to expand the availability of Wi-Fi. Although this extends the footprint of Wi-Fi, it does not necessarily increase the convenience for the user, as each provider has unique log-in procedures and billing arrangements. This has resulted in the emergence of so-called roaming providers who link a diversity of Wi-Fi network providers, while providing the user with a single interface.

NEIGHBORHOOD AREA NETWORKS

At home Wi-Fi access points (APs) are typically connected via ADSL or a cable modem to provide connectivity with the public network, and through the in-built router functionality an AP can support multiple computers. In this way, many users can share the access provided to the Internet. Depending on how the AP is configured, any Wi-Fi compatible computer within the coverage range of the AP may use it to access the Internet. This may be house guests, neighbors or passersby.[19] This is the infrastructure or managed mode of the IEEE 802.11 standard. Wi-Fi stations can also communicate directly with each other, that is, without an AP, in the peer-to-peer or ad hoc mode. The distance that can be covered is limited, typically 50 meters, depending on the propagation of the radio signals.[20] In this mode each personal computer equipped with Wi-Fi can be considered a Wi-Fi island, also called a Wi-Fi cell or pico-cell.[21] If more than two of these islands could be connected, a Wi-Fi based wide area network could be created. However the 802.11 standard does not provide an automatic means to communicate through intermediary stations. An alternative approach is using the repeater mode, whereby APs are connected using radio links rather than cables. This mode is used, for example, in the case of the neighborhood area network of Wireless Leiden, whereby network nodes are introduced with three APs, one using an Omnidirectional antenna to serve nearby Wi-Fi stations, and two APs with unidirectional antennas to provide a link to two neighboring nodes (Wireless Leiden 2006a).

In an alternative architecture, the Wi-Fi stations are considered to be nomadic and through additional software the stations are upgraded to provide routing functions. In this way, multi-hopping is being realized, and each station acts as a switching node for other stations, in a semi-stationary and semi-dynamic configuration. Some stations may thereby provide a link with the fixed public network (MeshNetworks 2002).[22]

Community initiatives to realize neighborhood area networks have sprung up in virtually every country. In spring 2006, the count in the Netherlands was 30 initiatives, of which the Wireless Leiden network was the largest with 100 nodes, covering most of the city and being linked to neighboring towns. The earliest start date of the initiatives is 2000, while the earliest in-service date is 2002.

A more recent development relates to metroWireless, whereby Wi-Fi technology is used to provide city-wide coverage. The region of Philadelphia is a typical example. Some 70 cities are claimed to have (partial) networks in operation and 130 cities with plans to follow. In Portland, Oregon, a network is under construction, whereby Microsoft is providing content and services with the objective to boost online traffic and advertising revenues. Portland is following the example of Google in San Francisco, by building a network in cooperation with Earthlink (Kharif 2006).

PERSPECTIVE ON FUTURE DEVELOPMENTS

Probing the future implies assessing the next steps in the evolution of Wi-Fi from a WLAN developed for corporate use, being widely deployed for home networking, and having crossed the border into the public

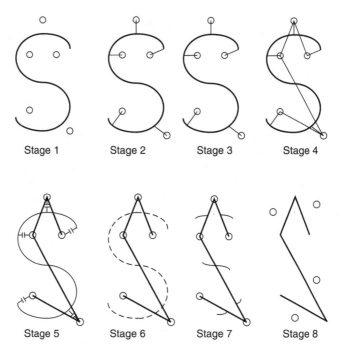

Stage 1   Stage 2   Stage 3   Stage 4

Stage 5   Stage 6   Stage 7   Stage 8

Source: Reprinted from H. Sawhney (1992), 'The public telephone network: stages in
infrastructure development', *Telecommunications Policy*, **16** (7): 538–52, with permission
from Elsevier.

Figure 6.3   Infrastructure development model according to Sawhney

domain in the form of hotspots and community networks. The work
agenda of the IEEE 802 workgroup already includes enhancements such
as radio resource management support, high throughput extension, fast
roaming and inter-working with other networks. Another way of assessing next possible steps is in comparing the Wi-Fi development to other
infrastructure developments. Sawhney has captured the development of
infrastructures, including telecommunications, in an infrastructure development model (IDM) (Sawhney 1992).[23] This model describing the development of infrastructures in eight stages can be summarized as follows (see
Figure 6.3):

Stage 1   Sprouting of infrastructure islands: 'The infrastructure tech-
           nologies first appear as technological islands. They are basically
           demonstration projects which test out revolutionary ideas. Their
           actual commercial potential is still uncertain.'

Stage 2   Development of a feeder: 'The new technology is found to be viable and its basic potential is seen in its role as a complement to the old system, reaching into areas which were inaccessible to the old technology. At this stage it is still a short-haul technology.'

Stage 3   Encouragement by the old system: 'The new technology in its role as a feeder generates additional traffic for the old system, by increasing the old system's catchment area. The old system encourages and aids the development of the new technology.'

Stage 4   Long-distance capabilities and system formation: 'The long-distance capabilities are developed. The islands become directly interconnected and start bypassing the old system; creating problems of coordination and standardization. Eventually the long-distance capability results in an integral system.'

Stage 5   Competition with the old system: 'The old system finds itself threatened and goes on an offensive, but soon assumes a defensive posture. Emerging competition is depicted as something wasteful. Finally an attempt is made to accommodate the new technology within the existing order.'

Stage 6   Subordination of the old system: 'The old system's rearguard action is unable to withstand the onslaught of new technological developments. Eventually the old system caves in or is pushed into a subservient role.'

Stage 7   Reversed feeder relationship: 'The old system disintegrates into fragments, serving niches. They either fill in a gap where it is not attractive to extend the new system, or they supplement it along routes where there is a specialized kind of traffic. These fragments now serve as feeders for the new system.'

Stage 8   Return of the cycle: 'The new system dominates until another technology appears. The newer technology then grows along the same cycle.'

Reflecting on this model, we may conclude that Wi-Fi has passed stages 1 and 2 and has arrived at stage 3. The old system is encouraging the new technological developments. We can observe long-distance capabilities being developed, for example, in the form of Wi-Max. However, true long-distance capability will most probably be provided through the (existing) fiber optic network. Albeit one could argue that the migration of internet protocol (IP) from the edge to the core of the telecommunications network is a development that is taking place in parallel. Once VoIP is fully deployed, the old telephony system will have been replaced by an all-IP system, with Wi-Fi as a part of this new all-IP system.

An alternative perspective could be based on the advancement of mesh-networking, whereby each and every Wi-Fi enabled computer becomes a hub in a nomadic network. The rapid growth of Wi-Fi enabled devices would support this perspective. However, up-scaling the system is not a trivial affair. This applies to the large-scale use of private devices for public use, the additional functionality required at the private device and the related consequences of resource and capacity utilization, as well as the availability of sufficient spectrum. This scenario also raises questions of an institutional nature in relation to sharing rights. The principle and the experience obtained with the commons may become applicable to the telecommunications world (see Ostrom 1990; Lehr et al. 2003 and Libecap 2005).

STYLIZED FACTS OF THE CASE STUDY

Based on the discussion of the development of Wi-Fi, we recognize theoretical notions of evolutionary theory, that is, novelty generation, transmission and selection, and retention. We observe that the type of process of change in Wi-Fi development connects to Nelson and Winter (1977, 1982). They argue that technical advance is an evolutionary process in which new technological alternatives compete with each other and with prevailing practice, whereby *ex post* selection is determining the winners and losers, usually with considerable *ex ante* uncertainty regarding the outcome. Thereby we recognize the Lamarckian metaphor of economic evolution which allows acquired characteristics based on learning to be passed on and which acknowledges purposeful intention with respect to changing behavior. This is in contrast to the Darwinian metaphor whereby change can only take place through mutations at birth and which is considered to be random (Van der Steen 1999).

First, selection in the early phase. The development of Wi-Fi was triggered by a major shift in the institutional arrangements, the assignment by the FCC of unlicensed radio spectrum for communication purposes. The technology to be applied had been developed in the military domain and was now prescribed for use in the private domain. This can be characterized as a change in the institutional selection environment.

Another interesting aspect related to the institutional environment is that Wi-Fi development was not confronted with the selection mechanism of the vested interest of incumbent telecommunication operators in exploiting their investments of licensed spectrum. Network modernization of the incumbent telecom operators took place along a certain technological path or trajectory, independent of the Wi-Fi related developments.

Based on the evolutionary economic literature, we have learnt that technological mutations are far from random. As in many other industries, technological progress in the telecom industry is mostly incremental; technological progress proceeds on the basis of yesterday's achievements. Trajectories are emerging as cumulative improvements are made along particular lines of progress, which reflect both what technologists understand they can achieve and what entrepreneurs believe customers will buy. These are referred to as technological regimes. Nelson and Winter defined them as:

> The sense of potential, of constraints, and of not yet exploited opportunities, implicit in a regime focuses the attention of engineers on certain directions in which progress is possible, and provides strong guidance as to the tactics likely to be fruitful for probing in that direction. In other words: a regime not only defines boundaries, but also trajectories to those boundaries. (Nelson and Winter 1977, p. 57)

Indeed, Wi-Fi was developed outside the traditional telecommunications trajectory. This may at least partly explain its success. Wi-Fi development took place within the private sector domain of enterprise data communications in a time when the Internet and mobile telephony industry were growing.

The start of its successful development can be ascribed to a major shift in the behavior of one important actor, NCR, by taking a leadership role in establishing a coalition. NCR's behavior can be connected to purposeful intention and to the role of the entrepreneur, as in the view of Casson: 'an entrepreneur is someone who specializes in taking judgmental decisions about the coordination of scarce resources' (cited by Ricketts 2002). A particular challenge for the entrepreneur is to move the business beyond the early adopter phase into the mass-market phase, from selling successfully to the technology enthusiast and visionaries to selling to the pragmatists. To reflect this difficulty, Moore (1991) uses the metaphor of crossing the chasm. He argues that it is important to target the right initial product segment to cross the chasm successfully. If properly selected and executed, the attack moves to adjacent segments. The success in the first market segment will work as the head pin at a bowling alley, ultimately leading to mass-market success (Moore 1995).

Although the FCC ruling prescribed a certain type of technology to be used, firms generated a broad variety of initial products using proprietary protocols. From a theoretical perspective, the FCC opened the possibility for novelty generation. The incompatibility resulted in a fragmented product market, increasing the risk for the users with respect to future developments.

Through NCR's initiative, novelty generation in the product market moved to the selection mechanism of the standardization process. The standardization process has been a process of retention and learning of the various firms involved in the development of Wi-Fi technologies.

A strong contribution to the development of the content of the standard, a high degree of participation, as well as skillful negotiation and maneuvering are the major ingredients that are determining the outcome of this process that has been facilitated through well-established formal procedures within the IEEE.[24] Wi-Fi emerged as the winner of the battle against HomeRF backed by Intel, and HIPERLAN developed by ETSI. As a result, the resources became directed to the winning technology platform, allowing it to be improved and expanded.

The product life cycle of Wi-Fi, to the extent it has been unfolded, reflects a long gestation period of almost 15 years, followed by a rapid take off in the last five or six years (see Figure 6.4).

The extensive period required for standardization illustrates the commitment, the tenacity and the resources required from an emerging industry leader involved in rule-breaking. In Moore's terms, the chasm was crossed in 1999 through a strategic cooperation of Lucent Technologies with Apple and subsequently Microsoft. This connects to the economic literature on how a dominant design emerges (Abernathy and Utterback 1978). Usually, after a period of time and competition, one or a few of the variants offered to the market come to dominate the others, and attention and resources become concentrated on these at the expense of the others. Once resources come to be largely focused on the leading technology further improvements may soon make it and its further developments the only economic way to proceed because competing design are left so far behind (Nelson and Winter 1977, 1982).

While Wi-Fi started as a technological innovation, its development became characterized by subsequent releases of the IEEE 802.11 standard. These standards were translated into chipsets that became incorporated in products, which in turn became part of communications systems. This connects to the economic literature. For instance, Nelson argues that, once a dominant design comes into existence, radical product innovation slows down and product design improvements become incremental. The attention shifts to the improvement of the related process technology. The growth in the number of people who own and use a particular technology variant plays an increasing role as skills develop that are particular to a certain variant, as are investments in complementary products designed to fit with a particular variant (Katz and Shapiro 1985, 1994; Arthur 1996). In our case study, we observe that first these WLAN systems were applied in the corporate domain, subsequently in the private domain, followed by the public domain. As a result the industry evolved from a component and product focus to a product and service focus. An expanding supply chain has been the result (see Figure 6.5).

Lucent Technologies, severely affected by the downturn in telecom-

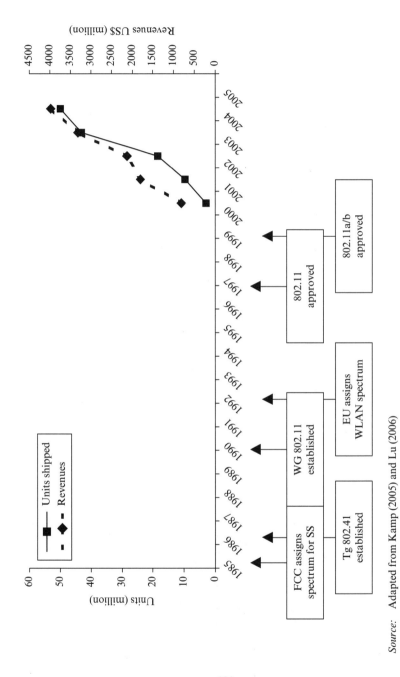

Source: Adapted from Kamp (2005) and Lu (2006)

Figure 6.4 Wi-Fi product life cycle by units shipped and revenues, 1985–2005

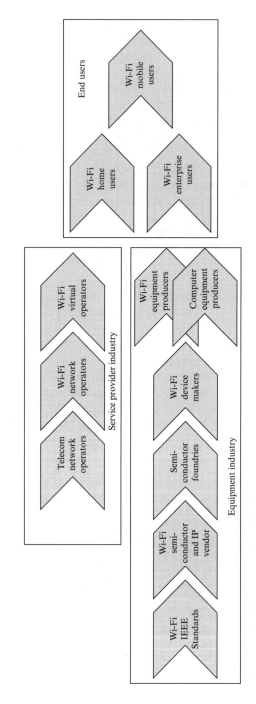

Figure 6.5 The expanding Wi-Fi supply chain

munication spending in the aftermath of the Internet bubble, divested its WLAN activities through the spin-off of Agere Systems in 2001. In 2004 Agere discontinued its WLAN development activities and the team in Utrecht–Nieuwegein was dissolved.

However, as the original radio expertise moved with the people from Philips to NCR, the success of Wi-Fi developments has triggered new start-ups by former staff of Lucent Technologies. For instance, Airgo was established in the Netherlands in 2001. Airgo continues to lead developments in the Wi-Fi space, in particular with MIMO (multiple inputs multiple outputs). Using multiple radio transmitters and receivers independent data streams are being transferred to increase the overall data rate of the connection. In NCR's footsteps, Airgo is contributing extensively to IEEE 802.11 Task Group 'n' (TGn), aimed at achieving high throughput extension (Van Nee 2006). Meanwhile Airgo designed chips which have resulted in the first ever MIMO consumer products being introduced to the market by a number of suppliers.

Next to knowledge diffusion through start-ups, former Agere staff have moved to other companies in the wireless industry, including Motorola, and they continue to push the limits in terms of innovation in wireless communications.[25]

The aspect of retention can best be illustrated by characterizing the Wi-Fi based ecosystem that has emerged and is evolving (Kamp 2005; De Leeuw 2006): In 2004–05 the Wi-Fi related product market was estimated at US$3.5 billion, the portfolio included chips and chipsets, personal computer–adapters, access points, bridges, gateways and routers, as well as Wi-Fi functionality in personal digital assistants, mobile phones, digital cameras, printers, video beamers and home audio-systems; being provided by more than 20 hardware manufacturers, supplying over 400 different products, The Wi-Fi service market included hotspots in excess of 26000. Major hotspot–roaming operators were iPass, T-Mobile, WeRoam, Trustive, Swisscom Eurospot, Boingo, BT Openzone, GoRemote (GRIC), GBIA, and NTT. Community initiatives have sprung up in both developed and developing countries.

NETWORK MODERIZATION REVISITED

We distinguish three types of network modernizations based on Wi-Fi technology, each with its own set of conditions for effectiveness. In addition a distinction should be made between wholesale replacement, through a new generation of technology, at one end of the spectrum of modernization and, on the other, localized upgrades. Another distinction can be made between modernization for the purpose of improving capacity and/or the efficiency of operations, and modernization for the purpose of increasing functionality provided to the customer or end user. In the case that wholesale modernization is to be based on substitute technologies, a close comparison in terms of functionality provided will be required to ensure continued operation toward the end user. In the case of telecommunication network modernization, a further distinction can be made between modernization of the public network infrastructure and modernization of the corporate network infrastructure, for which different organizations bear the responsibility.[26]

In the context of corporate networking, Wi-Fi is a clear case of network modernization based on new technology. Wireless connectivity provides flexibility and significantly reduces the costs of moves and changes. These are advantages that play into the corporate needs of flexible workspaces and hot-desking, related to an increasingly mobile workforce. What slowed down the adoption of Wi-Fi in the corporate environment are concerns about information security. Eavesdropping on radio waves is in principle more easily done than obtaining access to the wired infrastructure. Moreover, the initial version of WLAN did not provide for security at the lower layers of the protocol stack. With the 802.11b standard wired equivalent protocol (WEP) a basic authentication and encryption method was being introduced, which was upgraded to Wi-Fi protected access (WPA) in the 2003 release of 802.11g, and to WPA2 in the 2004 release of 802.11j. This j-release is dedicated to improving security and includes the extensible authentication protocol as a framework to provide firewall protection, remote authentication and other security related services. Additionally, the more powerful advanced encryption standard will replace the WEP encryption method.

The increasing use of laptops, the introduction of the Internet and the ensuing requirement for broadband access has pushed the need for more advanced home networking. While small Ethernet-based networks provided for the needs in the early days, Wi-Fi has become the flexible solution, obviating the need for rewiring and hence avoiding the related costs and inconvenience. Moreover these wireless networks have become essentially self-install.

The application of Wi-Fi in the public domain implies the introduction of an alternative means of access to the public infrastructure and in particular the Internet. This access can be considered complementary as well as competitive to both fixed and mobile access. The perception depends on the starting position of the operator and the type of customer being targeted. For a fixed network operator, Wi-Fi extends the reach of its wired network, on the one hand, and it facilitates the sharing of the wire-line access, on the other. For a mobile operator it adds broadband capabilities; but it is also a substitute for existing narrowband services. Moreover it can compete very effectively with mobile broadband services, such as 3G in semi-stationary situations. Figure 6.6 provides an overview of the positioning of the various wireless technologies against the dimensions of data rate and the degree of mobility.[27]

In moving from a corporate domain to the public domain the Wi-Fi technology does not change. What is changing is the way the equipment is being used in providing a commercial service. This relates to the way access is being provided and authorized, in the charging and billing for the service provided, and in the addition of sales and marketing of the public service. The distinction between licensed and unlicensed service becomes apparent in the price-setting, derived from very different cost structures, and in the quality of service that can be provided by the different technologies (Lehr and McKnight 2003).

From the infrastructure development model we may conclude that we have arrived at stage 3 of network modernization: the old system is encouraging the new technological developments as a feeder system. An alternative development could result from the advancement of mesh-networking, whereby each and every Wi-Fi enabled computer becomes a hub in a nomadic network. The rapid growth of Wi-Fi enabled devices would support this perspective; however, up-scaling the system becomes an issue. This applies to the large-scale use of private devices for public use, the additional functionality required at the private device, and the related consequences of resource and capacity utilization, as well as the availability of sufficient spectrum. This scenario also raises questions of an institutional nature in relation to sharing rights. In this modernization scenario a tragedy of the commons may be in the making, albeit, recent developments with respect to open source and open content suggest that new avenues can be entered successfully and alternative nontraditional approaches can expand beyond our initial expectations.

This concludes a detailed appreciative account of a unique recent case of technological development and telecom network modernization, describing for the first time the lifeline of Wi-Fi. The account exceeds the standard technology life-cycle analysis by including the role of the institutional environment, and provides an interesting perspective on how innovations emerge, which is interesting for policy-makers and regulators in encouraging entrepreneurship and economic development.

ACKNOWLEDGMENTS

This chapter has drawn extensively upon the research executed in the context of the Wi-Fi research program within the section Economics of

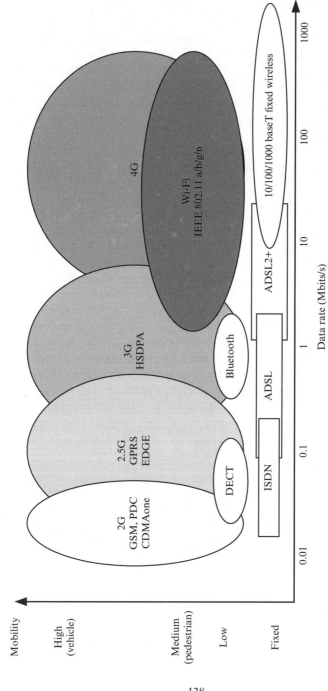

Source: Adapted from Briso et al. (2004).

Figure 6.6 Mobility and data rate for wireless technologies

Infrastructures, Delft University of Technology, Delft, the Netherlands. The authors acknowledge the contributions made by Diman Kamp, Gerd-Jan de Leeuw, Zhi Lu, Martijn Meijering, Paul Komboi and Wouter Ram. The authors also acknowledge the critical review and inputs provided by Bruce Tuch, who has been responsible for technology and standardization at NCR from the inception, William Lehr, director of the MIT Program on Internet and Telecom Convergence, and Marten Vijn, one of the initiators of Wireless Leiden.

NOTES

1. Robert Metcalfe is being recognized as the inventor of Ethernet while being associated with the Xerox Palo Alto Research Centre in 1976. Metcalfe had left Xerox PARC in 1979 to establish 3Com. In a joint effort with, in particular, DEC, Intel and Xerox the Ethernet standard was developed (Von Burg 2001).
2. The Philips Elcoma Division was the precursor of the Philips Semiconductor Division. The radio frequency expertise resided in the Applications Lab where leading edge product development took place.
3. One of the first large scale applications of the NCR–AT&T WLAN was the Wireless Andrew Project at Carnegie Mellon University in 1993 (Hills 2006).
4. For a discussion of the strategic paradox of compliance and choice, see De Wit and Meyer (2005). Bruce Tuch, Head of Development at NCR–Nieuwegein, and Vic Hayes, Senior Consultant Standards and Regulations, were assigned to this task.
5. The Institute of Electrical and Electronics Engineers (IEEE) had a strong tradition in facilitating the development of standards in the computer communication arena such as the Ethernet protocol.
6. Vic Hayes was elected as the first chairperson of workgroup IEEE 802.11 in 1990 and led the group until 2000, when his maximum term had elapsed.
7. In the first four years, major contributions were submitted by Apple Computer, HNS, IBM, KII, Lace, Motorola, NCR, Spectrix, Symbionics, Symbol Technologies and Xircom.
8. For the PHY three options were included: direct sequence spread spectrum (DSSS), infrared and frequency hopping spread spectrum. The DSSS was based on a proposal by NCR. For the MAC the distributed foundation wireless medium access control was adopted, based on a combined proposal by NCR, Symbol Technologies and Xircom.
9. Before the IEEE Standards Board considers a proposed standard for ratification, the proposal has to be approved in two stages. The first stage is a workgroup ballot, where only workgroup members can vote, the second stage is a sponsor ballot. The members of the sponsor ballot group are composed of individuals from the IEEE membership. Both are letter ballots and negative votes have to be accompanied with comments that indicate how the workgroup could change the draft so that the member could change his vote to positive. The ballot result is valid when more than 50 percent of the members have submitted their vote and passes when more than 75 percent of those voting have approved the draft.
10. For an in-depth description of Wi-Fi standards see O'Hara and Petrick (2005). For the understanding of the technology and the building of Wi-Fi networks see Ohrtman and Roeder (2003).
11. Although the standardization process can be influenced through participation and contributions, the IEEE assigns only one vote per individual who has deserved membership status through a participation requirement. In other standardization bodies membership is normally granted to a company or organization only.

12. ETSI evolved from the collaboration between telecom operators organized in the Conférence des administrations européennes des postes et télécommunications and includes the administrations, the telecommunication operators and the telecommunication industry.

13. The main difference of type 2 was in the PHY layer where OFDM instead of GMSK signals were being used.

14. The CEPT, an Association of European Postal and Telecommunications Administrations (PTTs). After the establishment of ETSI, CEPT was only responsible for the harmonization of the radio spectrum in Europe and other countries that ratified a Memorandum of Understanding (MoU). Administrations that signed the MoU agreed to implement the Recommendations of the CEPT.

15. The World Radio Conference is a UN Treaty Organization and convenes a plenary assembly every two to four years in which major agreements are being endorsed. Members of the WRC are the national states, which are represented through government officials.

16. The creation of a common market for telecommunication in Europe is an explicit objective of the reform process initiated by the European Union. The GSM project is a prime example of this policy.

17. GPRS, General Packet Radio Service, as an enhancement of the 2G mobile networks, implied a first step in the direction of packet-mode communication. For a description and assessment of the implication of the shift from circuit-mode to packet-mode communications see Lemstra (2006).

18. Apple had some early developments on WLAN technology, but this activity was stopped. When Steve Jobs returned to Apple, he recognized the value of WLAN technology and made it a strategic priority. Even before the development of the IEEE 802.11b technology was finished Lucent Technologies, under the leadership of Bruce Tuch, and Apple closely collaborated to drive the development, in particular the integration of the radio, towards the right cost points. The PC-card would be priced at US$99.95 and the access point at US$299.95.

19. The sharing of Internet access is by most operators considered as an unintended use of the fixed network access facilities. Many operators have adjusted their supply contracts to make access sharing illegal. However, enforcement is a totally different matter.

20. Trials executed by the Wireless Leiden organization using appropriate antennas have demonstrated connectivity over 9 km with throughput of up to 2 Mb/s (Wireless Leiden 2006a).

21. See the IEEE 802.11 architecture descriptions in Orhtman and Roeder (2003). The Wi-Fi standard includes also a so-called ad hoc mode, whereby Wi-Fi client stations communicate directly with each other (Wireless Leiden 2006b).

22. A provider of multi-hopping software MeshNetworks was acquired by Motorola in 2004 (Sutherland 2004). The initial functionality had been derived from the original nomadic application within the military domain.

23. Independently Sawhney (2003) has applied the IDM model to Wi-Fi with an emphasis on the US in 2003. He emphasizes the important role of incumbents in constraining the deployment of new infrastructure technologies. Moreover, 'inter-modal compatibility could be a factor that potentially deflects the evolution of the wireline–wireless relationship away from the IDM pattern'.

24. The IEEE for instance uses Robert's rules of order (Robert 2000).

25. Other areas in the wireless domain where the Dutch have been leading are Bluetooth and Lofar. Bluetooth development was triggered in 1994 by the desire to replace the wires between mobile phones and auxiliary devices with a radio connection. Jaap Haartsen, working at Ericsson at the time, led the development.

26. The term 'public' is used to denote the national network infrastructure that was once built as a public utility by government organizations or by private organizations under tight government regulation. These national networks are now more or less in private hands.

27. The characteristics of 11a and 11g are the same, 11a has only a slightly lower span. Meanwhile, ADSL capacity has been expanded to 6 Mb/s, even 20 Mb/s is being claimed, thereby transitioning into the space denoted as HDSL.

REFERENCES

Abernathy, W.J. and J. M. Utterback (1978), 'Patterns of industrial innovation', *Technology Review*, **80** (7): 40–7.

Arthur, W.B. (1996), 'Increasing returns and the new world of business', *Harvard Business Review*, **74** (4): 100–9.

Bar, F. and H. Galperin (2004), 'Building the wireless internet infrastructure: from cordless Ethernet archipelagos to wireless grids', *Communications & Strategies*, **54** (2): 45–68.

Briso, C., J.I. Alonso and R. M. Bayona (2004), '4G networks: global vision, reference architecture and applications', *Communication Networks*, **3** (3): 89–92.

De Leeuw, G.J. (2006), 'Wi-Fi in the Netherlands', paper presented at the 9th Annual International Conference on the Economics of Infrastructures, Delft, the Netherlands, 15–16 June.

De Wit, B. and R. Meyer (2005), *Strategy Synthesis: Resolving Strategy Paradoxes to Create Competitive Advantage*, London: Thomson Learning.

Fransman, M. (2002), *Telecoms in the Internet Age: From Boom to Bust to . . .?* Oxford: Oxford University Press.

Hills, A. (2006), personal communication, Pittsburg.

International Telecommunication Union (ITU) (1998), *Radio Regulations*, Geneva: International Telecommunication Union.

International Telecommunication Union (ITU) (2002a), *Trends in Telecommunications Reform 2002*, Geneva: International Telecommunication Union.

International Telecommunication Union (ITU) (2002b), *World Telecommunications Economic Indicators, 2001*, Geneva: International Telecommunication Union.

Kamp, D. (2005), 'Analysis of the Emergence of Wi-Fi', bachelor thesis, Delft University of Technology.

Katz, M.L. and C. Shapiro (1985), 'Network externalities, competition, and compatibility', *American Economic Review*, **75** (3): 424–40.

Katz, M.L. and C. Shapiro (1994), 'Systems competition and network effects', *Journal of Economic Perspectives*, **40** (2): 93–115.

Kharif, O. (2006), 'Microsoft's municipal Wi-Fi push', *BusinessWeek*, 17 November.

Lehr, W. and L. W. McKnight (2003), 'Wireless internet access: 3G vs. WiFi?', *Telecommunications Policy*, **27** (5): 351–70.

Lehr, W.H., M.F. Merino Artalejo and S.E. Gillett (2003), 'Software radio: implications for wireless services, industry structure, and public policy', *Communication & Strategies*, (49): 15–42.

Lemstra, W. (2006), 'The Internet bubble and the impact on the development path of the telecommunication sector', doctoral dissertation, Delft University of Technology.

Libecap, G.D. (2005), 'State regulation of open-access common-pool resources', in C. Ménard and M.M. Shirley, *Handbook of New Institutional Economics*, Dordrecht: Springer, pp. 545–72.

Lu, Z. (2006), '*A framework to assess the addition of value in the Wi-Fi industry*', master thesis, Delft University of Technology.

MeshNetworks (2002), *MeshLAN: Software for 802.11 Networks*, Maitland, FL: MeshNetworks.

Moore, G.A. (1991), *Crossing the Chasm*, New York: Harper Business.

Moore, G.A. (1995), *Inside the Tornado*, New York: Harper Business.

National Telecommunications and Information Administration (NTIA) (2003), 'Agreement reached regarding US position on 5 GHz wireless access devices', http://www.ntia.doc.gov/ntiahome/press/2003/5ghzagreement.htm (accessed 9 October 2007).

Nelson, R.R. and S.G. Winter (1977), 'In search of a useful theory of innovation', *Research Policy*, **6** (1): 36–76.

Nelson, R.R. and S.G. Winter (1982), *An Evolutionary Theory of Economic Change*, Cambridge, MA: Belknap Press of Harvard University Press.

O'Hara, B. and A. Petrick (2005), *IEEE 802.11 Handbook: A Designer's Companion*, New York: IEEE Press.

Ohrtman, F. and K. Roeder (2003), *Wi-Fi Handbook: Building 802.11b Wireless Networks*, New York: McGraw-Hill.

Organisation for Economic Co-operation and Development (OECD) (2005), *OECD Communications Outlook 2005*, Paris: OECD.

Ostrom, E. (1990), *Governing the Commons*, Cambridge: Cambridge University Press.

Ricketts, M. (2002), *The Economics of Business Enterprise: An Introduction to Economic Organisation and the Theory of the Firm*, Cheltenham, UK and Northampton, MA, USA: Edward Elgar.

Robert, H.M. (2000), *Robert's Rules of Order: Newly Revised*, Cambridge, MA: DaCapo Press.

Sawhney, H. (1992), 'The public telephone network: stages in infrastructure development', *Telecommunications Policy*, **16** (7): 538–52.

Sawhney, H. (2003), 'Wi-Fi networks and the rerun of the cycle', *Info*, **5** (6): 25–33.

Sutherland, E. (2004), 'Motorola snaps up MeshNetworks', http://www.wi-fiplanet.com/news/article.php/3436581 (accessed 9 October 2007).

Van Damme, E. (2001), *The Dutch UMTS Auction in Retrospect*, The Hague: CPB.

Van der Steen, M. (1999), *Evolutionary Systems of Innovation: A Veblian-Oriented Study into the Role of the Government Factor*, Assen: Van Gorcum.

Van Nee, R. (2006), 'Current status of Wi-Fi standardization', paper presented at the 9th Annual International Conference on the Economics of Infrastructures, Delft, Delft University of Technology, 15–16 June.

Von Burg, U. (2001), *The Triumph of Ethernet*, Stanford, CA: Stanford University Press.

Wi-Fi Alliance (2006), 'Get to know the alliance', http://www.wi-fi.org/about_overview.php (accessed 9 October 2007).

Wikipedia (2006), 'Wi-Fi', http://nl.wikipedia.org/w/index.php?title-Wi-Fi (accessed 9 October 2007).

Wilber, C.K. and Harrison, R. S. (1978), 'The methodological basis of institutional economics: pattern model, storytelling and holism', *Journal of Economic Issues*, **12** (1): 61–89.

Wireless Leiden (2006a), 'Techniek', http://www.wirelessleiden.nl/techniek/ (accessed 9 October 2007).
Wireless Leiden (2006b), 'Wi-Fi', http://wiki.wirelessleiden.nl/wcl/cgi-bin/moin. cgi/WiFi (accessed 9 October 2007).

7. Changing paradigms in electric energy systems

Maria Ilić and Mariann Jelinek[1]

INTRODUCTION

The electric power industry is facing a problem that, if it is not solved, will become worse over time and generate huge difficulties. The specifics of the problem are as yet unclear. The problem is suffused with ambiguity, multiple different definitions and numerous insistent stakeholders pushing their particular viewpoints. In fact, the industry faces a difficult problem or, more accurately, a difficult environment. This problem is simultaneously more complex than the existing technical paradigm can manage; more complex than the existing regulatory regime can comprehend; and now includes many former externalities that must be embraced.

Externalities refer to factors formerly ignored or excluded from the paradigm-in-use, by which those concerned with the industry made sense of their environment. Among the former externalities that can no longer be simply ignored are questions such as capacity levels and growth plans, energy use and environmental sustainability, allocation of resources to use, environmental pollution concerns, and the temporal and locational questions of power supply.

Externalities gain prominence only rarely in an industry, typically in the context of some crisis that forces a shift in attention, such as a major disaster like Three Mile Island or poorly functioning deregulation.[2] Deregulation removes the rigid barriers or requirements of the past, undercutting the dominance of long stable technologies and analytical techniques. Political forces or technologies once safely ignored rise to critical prominence, and new potential competitors appear. Because they were excluded from prior understanding of the relevant factors affecting industry, such externalities often act as huge and unexpected surprises. They throw the industry and its long-held assumptions into disarray and make obsolete formerly unexceptionable best practices for understanding, analysis and effective response to problems.

In short, the old ways of looking at problems and responding to them no longer work here. To understand the difficult problems of the changing regulatory environment of electric energy industry requires more complex and sophisticated perspectives that include what was formerly ignored (Linstone and Mitroff 1994). Without this understanding, there will be no systematic innovations in this industry. Further, individual actors concerned with only their portions of a much larger system, perform to a lower standard. However, what is of interest to us here is the evolution of the system itself. We see potential for system evolution from a rigid, hierarchically controlled entity—dominated by what we shall call the 'N-1 prevention paradigm'—to a far more dynamic, real-time optimized and information-driven entity of greater long-term robustness and efficiency.

This chapter first sketches the nature of the original, regulated industry and its challenges. Next it touches upon new challenges and opportunities already visible in the transitional energy system. Finally, it profiles the new dynamic system whose outlines can already be discerned. Its characteristics are a function of changes in technology, regulations, and system interconnectedness and their financial implications. It is also an information technology-enabled system, where information rules.

A TEMPLATE FOR A SOCIOTECHNICAL INDUSTRY ANALYSIS

Take a snapshot of an industry. At any instant the industry's configuration reflects the existing technology and institutional structure. Over time, this arrangement favors some industry structures, while at the same time impeding on others. What is practical or what is economically feasible is governed by this structure, and choices embodied at any point in time do not always exhaust the set of what is possible. Changes in any of a number of factors can affect the balance, making feasible or profitable what formerly did not make economic sense. So it is with the electric energy industry. Several factors affect the electric energy industry (see Figure 7.1).

Available technology and the present institutional structure, including regulation, rules regarding pollution and clean-up and recoverable costs, are clearly factors behind the rise of the United States (US) power grid in the particular shape it has taken. This structure is characterized by central, relatively large generating facilities connected into a network by transmission lines connecting major population centers. It embodies prior assumptions and economic decisions based on technology and institutions at a particular point in time. Investments in large-scale capital facilities such as generating capacity are not readily shifted overnight. Technology choices, once made, are exceedingly difficult to remake, as underlined by the case of

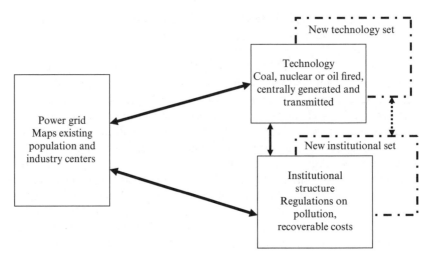

Figure 7.1   An overview of factors affecting the electric energy industry

utility companies' experiences with nuclear power. Regulations are set up to facilitate a particular vision of what is needed, and to protect against the hazards envisioned at any one moment. But which technologies and which institutions matter? New technologies can call for new institutions; new institutions can favor different technologies than those favored in the past. What seems relevant at a particular time is considered; what seems more distant is dismissed from the equation. Past experience and long-enduring trends seem appropriate guides for the future. Yet even longstanding trends can disappear.

Deregulation, driven in part by changing technology and in part by a changing political environment, changes the sets that matter, destroying old trends. By changing what may be done and by whom, deregulation creates possibilities and opportunities hitherto nonexistent, or only now practical because of technological changes, or perhaps simply invisible in the past. At the same time, technological evolution also affects what is possible—even whether or not deregulation itself makes sense. Any snapshot of what *is* captures a time-anchored complex—one that will become inadequate to a changing environment over time. Thus population growth in general, accelerating computer technology and its demands for cleaner power, new must-have appliances, and population growth in particular new places all contribute to a growing misfit between today's needs and yesterday's arrangements. Capacity needs offer a case in point.

Capacity for years was added according to a rough rule of expectation that around 20 percent buffer capacity above usual peak needs was

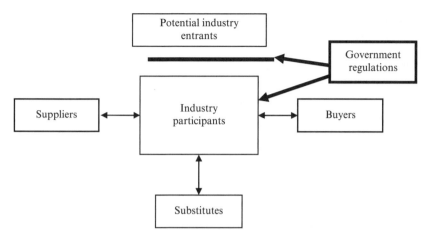

Figure 7.2   Competitive forces map for the regulated electric energy industry

required. In the regulated environment of the past, such a rule governed building new plants, and was generally predictable against well-understood characteristics of usage, usage growth and population growth projections. From an energy company's perspective, capacity needs were a function of peak usage, storage capacity and options for buying additional peak-load capacity. The current paradigm is constituted by centrally generated power, the range of viable alternative energy sources, transmission structure and the economics of the existing power grid. It is embodied on the ground; widely shared within the industry, where experience verifies its standing; and privileged by the previously existing regulatory structure. But such a paradigm is neither inevitable nor permanent.

What happens when we include new sources of power, new maps for locus of generation versus use? Updated generator technology, photovoltaic shingles, solar power, wind power, geothermal power and temperature differentials create possibilities. Information technology applied to point-of-use monitoring and switching also affects what may be technically possible; perhaps facilitating distributed generation or some hybrid of central-distributed generation. A host of possibilities begin to emerge. A modified form of Michael Porter's (1980) competitive forces map will help to organize this variety (see Figure 7.2).

In the regulated industry, government rules preclude or limit new entrants into the industry, dramatically affect participants and structure competition. Essentially, industry participants hold regional monopolies, while technical considerations control the degree to which a given generating plant can access alternative fuel supplies, for instance, as well as the degree of competition among participants, if any. Industry structure evolves in response to the regulatory environment as well as the technology first established as the industry standard.

For example, industry structure can evolve in a particular infrastructure of transmission, a particular locus of power generating facilities, perhaps dependent upon proximity to an energy source such as hydro-power. Regulations must reflect what a given technology makes possible. Costs are passed through to buyers, with limits on the profit potential for industry participants and for suppliers.

Because of high capital costs and the difficulty of retooling an extensive network of in-place capital equipment, such as the existing electrical power grid in the United States, once in place, industry configuration endures. Consequently, as change accumulates in the environment or as the pace of technological change intensifies, the degree of fit between existing industry structure and demands of the environment around it erodes over time. Change can come from any element in the picture—change in power generation technology, for instance, or transmission technology, in the physical location of industry, or in the size or nature of industry or consumer demands for power. Regardless of where change comes from, as fit diminishes, problems arise: different demands are likely over time; but their source and nature are uncertain. Where factors from the environment hitherto ignored become noticeable, the problem becomes difficult. The very models for understanding are inadequate, and what we have always known may no longer be true or even relevant.

Deregulation, one potential response to such misfit, creates dramatic revisions in the relative power of the players, putting substantial pressure on prices and costs as new claims for portions of available margin arise (see Figure 7.2). Consumers want lower prices. Yet suppliers may demand higher prices, while substitute products may undercut the industry's position. Ideally the hoped-for outcome is increased competition among rivals in the interests of lower prices for customers.

TOWARD A NEW REGULATORY AND TECHNOLOGICAL PARADIGM

Transition in the electricity sector is difficult and slow. There is a high degree of path dependency fostered by large economies of scale with a very few large, fuel-efficient power plants, among other factors. Swings and mismatches in supply–demand balance can be seen, and the electric energy industry and its customers have been vulnerable to the major shifts in fuel costs.[3] Electric utilities have been wrong in the past in forecasting much larger load demand growth than has actually occurred. This has resulted in overdesign and, consequently, in overcapacity of the system, characterized at least in some areas by very large power plants, strong transmission network and overly high costs. More recently, forecasts have erred in predicting less demand than was actually experienced. As computer usage has grown—particularly for high-reliability, high-capital cost applications like computer-controlled manufacturing—complaints about what is called 'dirty power' and unreliability have grown.[4] Where population and demand have surged, prices have soared and supplies have been tight. Meanwhile technology has progressed to offer new choices for fuel-efficient and sustainable, but smaller, generating options. Such new energy resources are not necessarily traditional competitors; but they can provide partial substitutes for mainstream power.

These changes have triggered a first phase of electric energy industry restructuring. Typically transmission-related barriers to new entrants have resulted in rather slow integration of new energy sources into the existing power industry. Even in utilities where the functional or corporate separation of the energy supply business from the power delivery entities has taken place, much remains to be done. The old paradigm of structure around existing, traditional-source power continues to dominate. Thus far, deregulation is at best partial.

Separation of vertically integrated utilities into competitive energy supply businesses has begun; but transmission and distribution businesses are still fully regulated. Managing the interface between these different worlds requires much rethinking. Among the issues are change of technical standards, new regulations and incentives to these newly formed businesses to promote most effective solutions on customers' behalf.

Potential exists for substantial new investment—in new, more efficient and cleaner generating capacity, and in transmission infrastructure as well—that promises substantial restructuring within the industry, and possibly significant new entry, perhaps driven by new technology. Not surprisingly, in the midst of this experiment in deregulation, many companies have consolidated through mergers and acquisitions. Few of them appear to be broadly analyzing the technological threats and opportunities. As a consequence, the current energy markets look like loose oligopolies more than truly competitive businesses. This situation may constitute a significant entry opportunity, if an alternative business model based on the new technological possibilities can be developed.

Other changes in practice reflect these uncertainties and opportunities. More and more small power plants are being built closer to the customers in order to avoid the cost and uncertainties related to power delivery.

This change shifts the electric power industry's longstanding geographic paradigm, while the economics reflecting the relative geography of power plants, customers and their sizes is played out. In addition, information technology (IT) is beginning to play a much larger role. Broadly distributed and more readily available IT may support much more dynamic response to demand, invisibly reconfiguring the industry. Electricity rate management on a real-time basis may improve margins for those able to take advantage of it. The trading of electricity is likely to become more widespread and actively supported by distributed IT. Depending on the dominant changes in regulatory, technical and pricing mechanisms, the electric power industry is likely to evolve into qualitatively different architectures from those of today. In what follows, we briefly describe three such possible new industry paradigms, emphasizing how IT may drive new industry configurations.

Architectures for Electric Energy Systems in the Future

Opportunities exist to make strides in all areas affecting the future electric energy industry (see Figures 7.3 and 7.4). On the technological dimension, serious research and development (R & D) offers potential for new types of energy sources, energy storage, and technologies for cost-effective customer choice, as well as a new systematic understanding of the role of transmission providers. So, too, does the promise of flexibility in power

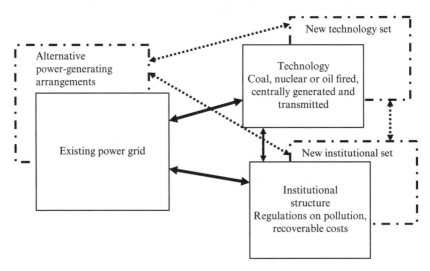

Figure 7.3   Opportunities for alternative architectures for the electrical power industry

delivery to facilitate the needs of the competitive supply–demand markets. IT deployment affects all these forces, by offering new ways of providing products and services under competition, reacting to information instantaneously. Temporal and locational aspects of demand and supply make this effort particularly challenging. In what follows, we highlight both such challenges and some emerging alternative solutions.

Before we do so, however, we make a summary of the shortcomings of the existing technologically based paradigm of today's power industry. The existing paradigm fails under several increasingly frequent conditions. The new environment is more complex and more complexly linked than in the past. The old regulatory regime fails to address urgent questions that arise. Technological possibilities not hitherto envisioned undercut the old regime. In addition former externalities demand attention. We argue that all of these conditions hold today. Such a constellation transforms the electric power industry's environment from benign to difficult. How difficult? Figure 7.4 outlines a few of the potential sources for change, noting potential shifts against a contemporary schematic value chain for the electric energy industry. Changes to smaller, cleaner and more efficient generation for instance, or alternative and most especially automated management of hybrid systems, all pose substantial potential threats to the existing industry configuration.

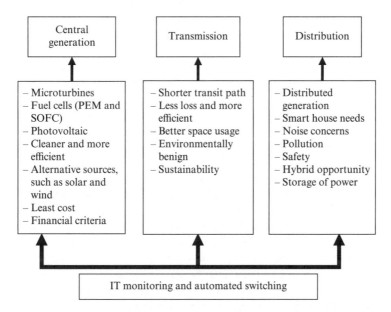

Figure 7.4   Points of potential change in the existing energy value chain

Widespread IT capability—for system management and automated switching—enormously enhances the potential of hybrid arrangements. IT creates the potential for substituting many smaller alternatives for any single element that may be out of service for scheduled maintenance—or for hot-swapping in real time, as the alternative grid's elements are put into place over time. In short, it offers an emerging migration path from the current industry configuration and paradigm to a vastly different one.

The New Sociotechnical Environment of the Electric Energy Industry

The electric energy industry's environment has traditionally been defined in purely technical terms, with little acknowledged need to attend to external factors. In the past, the regulated energy industry was guaranteed pass-through on any increase in costs. Capacity decisions were tied to economic growth in what decades of experience said was a virtually immutable algorithm: add capacity when peak demand approaches within 20 percent of total available capacity. Now a new environment insists on taking into account not only the fairly evident factors of business, economic growth and engineering technology, but also a host of new factors. Many options have been foreclosed by the syndrome of 'Not in my back yard,' and growing public resistance to dams, no less than outright intransigence on nuclear power and even its clean-up and shut-down costs. These factors have also dramatically shifted financial risk.

But the complexities do not stop with political fallout or financial stringency. New technologies, potential new entrants and externalities not hitherto considered important all play potentially disruptive roles. New entrants can be new companies, including substantial rivals created by mergers and acquisitions among hitherto noncompeting firms; but also new sources of energy from alternative generation sources, like photovoltaic shingles, distributed generators, wind or solar power. None were considered rivals to mainstream generation in the past, and, even now, they are difficult to assess, since they do not generally substitute for all power needs. Still, the potential for IT to knit these elements into new virtual power grids cannot be dismissed (Awerbuch and Preston 1997).

Of particular interest here is the emerging reality of complex, computer-controlled hybrid systems. Thus partial systems that could easily be dismissed as inadequate not long ago, can now be managed in concert to substitute for much or even all of a consumer's needs, at least some of the time.[5] In the same fashion, energy storage capacity has been evolving, making partial solutions more attractive for some customers at least, while consumer-size generation equipment has substantially improved in quality even as it dropped in cost. Thus it was long believed that electricity could essentially not be stored, particularly for consumer use. Yet advances in battery technology have made many consumers familiar with uninterruptible power supplies for their computers – and a few with the potential for battery storage as a bridge to automatically started home generation. Commercial installations are already in use.

Similarly wind and solar power can be used as available, even where neither alone might be a viable alternative to traditionally distributed power, if IT manages shifts between the different power sources. Photovoltaics, fuel cells and microturbines are already nearing the kilowatt-hour cost of industrial gas turbines, for much smaller-output units. Still newer technologies, like flywheels for energy storage, are also under development, with initial commercial installations for uninterruptable power supplies (Platt 2000).

In strategic terms, the threat here is that what was formerly dismissed as irrelevant can emerge as a viable substitute for the existing arrangements. Thus industrial customers or even homeowners can become self-supplying, wholly or partially. Further with legislation requiring buy-back, such self-suppliers can in effect integrate backwards. The significance of such possibilities is by no means entirely clear; such customers may be threats to existing suppliers of electric energy, or they may be potential allies in the effort to create a more robust, survivable electric power network. Threats may be opportunities in disguise. It is to these possibilities that we turn next.

A Possible Framework for Solving Energy's Difficult Problems

The existing industry paradigm is generally characterized as a fully centralized, large-scale system—a century-old model. The transitional industry is seeing aggregation across nontraditional boundaries: the new factors are unlikely partnerships, participants who neither own generation nor transmission facilities, and vastly different groupings of power sources. Finally, the likely end-state industry architecture will become very much more distributed, with a large number of relatively small actors, as is already the case in some developing countries.

The evolution process is slow, inconsistent and heavily dependent on regulatory uncertainties, pricing mechanisms as well as on the actual technology transfer process. Major questions remain concerning the technology transfer of fuel-efficient and environmentally acceptable energy resources, the evolution of appropriately distributed architectures, and the development of IT to support customer choice. The interplay and interdependencies among these factors is also uncertain at present.

Through a concept of homeostatic control, Schweppe predicted one likely end-state paradigm for the electric power industry in 1978. Homeostatic control is based on distributed, automatic usage adjustments by individual users in response to local frequency and voltage changes (Schweppe et al. 1980). The technology and regulatory setup of 1978 was not ready to support this vision, but contemporary developments render the ideas once again relevant. It is only very recently that commercially cost-effective distributed technologies on customer and generation sides, as well as in flexible control of wires, have begun to emerge. Only with the coming of micro power has Schweppe's vision at last begun to materialize (see Dunn 2000): micro power refers to widely distributed, smaller local generation nodes often by small-scale fuel cells and gas turbines that reduce or eliminate the need to transmit power over long distances, while also providing on-demand supply capability for load-leveling.

The R & D achievements needed to support the evolution of the electric power industry into these new architectures are substantial. Yet what is necessary is not so much one immediate solution as removal of a series of related bottlenecks. Moreover, as the system evolves, the value of each component will change, revealing new possibilities for the whole. Thus even now microturbines, or fast switching, create alternatives that were impractical not long ago.[6] Small-scale, stand-alone generating capacity for home use has little apparent value in a contemporary urban setting. Yet if a reliable switching system permitted many such small generators to respond to partial system outages elsewhere or sudden demands, the system as a whole could acquire valuable surge capacity.

A given technology may have a completely different value, depending on the overall industry paradigm and the state of evolution of other elements in the system. Moreover, managers need to develop operating, maintenance and planning tools for various possible paradigms. Even the old industry is no longer the same, since deregulation has introduced competition in the supply business. Thinking through paradigms helps to envision new scenarios.

A typical schematic for an electric power system as it has been is shown in Figure 7.5. Contemporary systems are generally characterized as having very large power plants, often distant from the load centers being served. Power delivery from these plants to the control centers is carried out by means of a high-voltage transmission system designed by utilities or groups of utilities within each region. Moreover, the regional or national grids are interconnected via even higher voltage transmission lines, so-called tie lines. The longer the transmission lines, the greater the power loss between transmission point and eventual delivery to customers. Until very recently, each region or country planned enough generation to serve its native load: the inter-regional or international level planned to supply

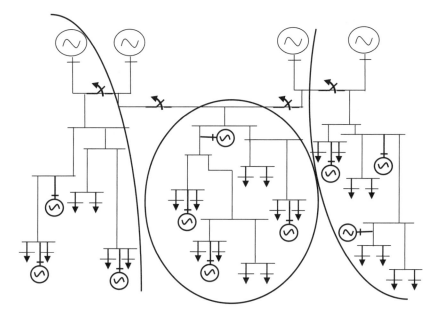

Figure 7.5   Hybrid paradigm in electricity distribution

native customers and share the burden of reliable service among the regions and countries when any very large component fails. Both achieved reliability by anticipating likely failures or service outages equivalent to the largest component of their own systems.

Present-day systems operation relies on passive additional capacity, that is, standby production and network capacity. There is little attention to flexible decision-making; a far more robust response that would be possible if available reserves could be used more effectively. To start with, present-day knowledge of various system parameters, whether equipment or wires, including the settings of protective relays used in different software, is quite unreliable. Because such data is recorded, database update and error become problems. The software tools in place—such as state estimation, load flow studies, contingency ranking methods and the like—are used as ancillary information for a system operator assumed to be intimately familiar with its own system. This has led to the industry-wide approach of preventive, rather than corrective systems operation. That is, the system is normally operated in a sufficiently conservative way so that if any of the single critical equipment outage occurs, customers are unaffected, at least for some reasonable time. Conservative assumptions and rigid forecasts are used in place of real information about the system.

At the high-voltage transmission level, this so-called N-1 contingency criterion calls for the system provider to have operating generation reserve equivalent to the largest power plant in the area, typically around 20 percent of total generation. Utilities have over time become more interconnected in order to share the burden of this reserve. Tie line dimensioning of the connections between different utilities has been done primarily with this in mind. However, these tie lines have not been designed for economical active transfers under normal conditions, but for emergency sharing. Yet over time, the divide between the economy transfers and reliability has become less pronounced. In the US, for instance, utilities have cooperated in a bilateral way to schedule energy imports–exports in and out of their areas without affecting inter-regional reliability. For example, there is a pre-agreed limit on how much one could import from Canada into New England in order not to affect the reliable service in Pennsylvania. These limits are derived from studies generally done offline for most likely outage scenarios; no online coordination exists for ensuring that, as these schedules vary, the interconnection operates reliably.

Often there is insufficient coordination between the distribution systems and the high-voltage transmission grid. Historically, most failures have occurred at the distribution level; therefore, meeting the N-1 criteria at the high-voltage transmission level is by no means a guarantee that continuity of service will be as expected at the user's level (Ilić et al. 2001). This turns out to be a very critical disjuncture when it comes to incentives for small power sources at the distribution level, customer choice and the reinforcement of the distribution grid as a survivable system.

Similarly planning is done quite conservatively for assumed load growth. Most of the transmission and generation redundancy comes from the anticipated need to cope with critical equipment outages. These are very low probability, high-impact events, which are hard to guard against using deterministic decision-making, such as the N-1 security criterion. In the US, some argue that the industry has consequently opted for over-design under the old regulatory setup. Others, pointing to California, note the systematic underdesign in the face of dramatic growth in demand.

The current industry transition in the US is characterized by new processes. Energy supply has now been made competitive, at least at a wholesale level. At least functional, if not corporate, unbundling of the transmission, distribution and generation businesses is under way, although far from complete. In some states, retail competition at the customer level has already begun. And wire companies are required to allow power delivery to all suppliers. Each of these processes creates new opportunities, multiple sources of business uncertainty—and calls for different technology development for its full exploitation. Meanwhile residual regulation based on the older configuration endures to affect expectations and financial outcomes. The parallels to earlier deregulation of telecommunication is striking; once AT&T was required to allow others to attach equipment to its lines, substantial competition followed rapidly.

The electric energy industry is caught in a hybrid system, in more than one sense of the word. The system is partly regulated for transmission and distribution, partly competitive for supply. There is still much large-scale generation, although this is gradually being supplemented by smaller, more numerous power plants. Yet the technology to exploit this potential is not yet in place, most particularly an integrated IT management system. While the physical processes of balancing supply and demand are continuous, at present various switching and decision-making signals are discrete time signals (switches in Figure 7.5). Today's system is exposed to an inconsistent mix of regulatory and technical constraints. And the regulatory constraints do not reflect either existing technical possibilities or desirable technical development paths.

System users are likely to begin to respond to market signals, when they have genuine choices at a retail level—much as with telecom services or the airline industry, for instance. This process is likely to be facilitated through the energy service providers, load-serving entities and alike-load aggregators, who might enter into different longer-term agreements with the users to provide them electricity at mutually agreeable terms. Yet the process of effective load aggregation, including creation of consumer syndicates, is vulnerable to the regulatory rules relating to wholesale electricity markets and transmission provision, particularly with respect to reliability-related risks. Who bears responsibility—and thus financial liability—for system reliability at any given point? The financial consequences are important.

Today, for example, costs for massive system outages due to weather or overload are borne by users, while the utility repairs its equipment. In the US no account is taken for losses or damage to consumers, such as frozen pipes or loss of foodstuffs in refrigerators. The price of electricity is generally high to assure extra capacity in generation and stronger transmission lines, in case some equipment fails or goes out of operation for scheduled maintenance.[7] The regulatory and market rules will have to be designed to carefully support unbundling of reliability-related risks under open access. Some customers could potentially opt for a contractually determined level of outage risk, an hour per week or month, for a given price, or for a much higher or lower outage risk for another price. Most of the hedging instruments address regional transmission uncertainties, such as transmission congestion contracts (Hogan 1990) or flowgate-based approaches (Cazelet 2000)[8] that seek effectively to make the owner of these instruments risk-neutral: shifting the risk to the transmission provider and ultimately the load-carrying entity. Yet the system as presently configured has not been structured for maximum survivability or for dynamic robustness.

OPPORTUNITIES FOR TECHNOLOGICAL INNOVATION

Hardware

Technological innovations can be identified at three levels, that is, the hardware, the system and software. About hardware, advances in various components in the recent past offer potential for new systems reconfiguration and dramatically improved robustness. Most notably there has been significant progress in the development of a variety of near-cost effective new power sources, ranging from smaller-scale combined cycle gas turbines (CCGTs) through micro diesel engines, microturbines, wind power, solar power and very small hydro, and so on. Similarly there has been significant movement toward technologies for consumer choice and price-responsive use of electricity, ranging from automatic meter readings, through one-way and two-way wireless communications between the users and providers of electricity. A variety of household automatic controllers have appeared to help implement price-elastic demand use (Black 2000). Moreover, at both transmission and distribution levels, there have been major theoretical breakthroughs in the area of direct power flow control, ranging from electronically switched reactive devices through efficient direct current transmission (Hingorani and Gyugyi 1999).

Some of these technologies are primarily sustaining in their intended impact, facilitating existing industry operating and planning methods. Others are more disruptive of the current practices and strategies. Thus widespread economical distributed generation could make obsolete existing large-scale generating and transmission facilities. In general, methods supporting an active customer response to the price of electricity over various time horizons as well as small-scale distributed generation (negative, varying load) are likely to be disruptive to existing industry paradigms (and perhaps to existing participants).

Systems

One of the major R & D challenges for the electric power industry comes from the system-wide interactions of various components, at various levels of hierarchies and varying degrees of aggregation, through a variety of technical, regulatory and price feed-forward and feedback signals. The time horizons, over which these signals feed the actual physical process, ranges from seconds (primary feedback on generators, flexible alternative current transmission systems) through minutes (automatic generation and voltage feedback schemes at each control area level). Their form ranges further, including open-loop (feed-forward signal) scheduling for the anticipated system level demand so that technical constraints are not violated (constrained economic dispatch, optimal power flow and unit commitment). Various, much slower, planning and system design approaches to facilitate the long-term load growth trends have been typical in the existing industry.

These feedback and feed-forward signals are designed in today's industry, with present-day economics in mind. However, actual price feedback is not a precise signal, although contemporary planning approaches often assume it is. Instead the price has been averaged over all customers within each utility, both temporally and spatially. Potential consumer choice creates potential for differentiating prices. In the same way, the regulatory signal is very straightforward and parametric, reflected only through the rate at which return is ensured (yet such a metric ignores quality of service as well as potential differentiation).

Actual progress in systems research has been much harder, slower to show results, and less focused in comparison to the progress in research and new technologies for individual component designs, despite much effort over the past three decades. Systems research literally started following the power grid blackouts in northeastern US in the 1960s and 1970s, and accelerated whenever this type of problem reoccurred, most recently in California.

The power systems research community has done much detailed system modeling and analysis for short-term operations, assuming coordinated, centralized decision-making. Models range from methods for stationary analysis, through understanding system dynamics under small perturbations and, to a lesser extent, transient dynamics in response to large equipment outages. Decision-making tools that facilitate system operation in near real-time range from state estimators, to static deterministic scheduling of generation, to minimizing operating costs for the estimated demand, and so on.

Given the complexity of large-scale power systems dynamics, most of the approaches for operating under large equipment outages have been based on offline scenario analyses of one kind or the other (Ilić and Zaborszky 2000). This area remains loaded with the theoretical challenges seen in any complex dynamical systems, as typical models are high-order differential algebraic equations rich in phenomena hard to simulate in an online environment. Nevertheless progress has been made toward dynamic security assessment, which would mean near online stability analysis as operating conditions change, by exploiting unique structural properties of power systems dynamics. Much less work has been done toward systematic control design methods for individual components, utility or interconnection levels (Ilić and Zaborszky 2000).

The situation is much worse when it comes to modeling, analysis and decision-making for planning under uncertainties. In general, tools are entirely static; very few effective stochastic methods exist for dynamic decision-making to optimize long-term actions, such as investments into generation or transmission capacity, in response to unforeseeable uncertainties. Yet clearly such dynamic modeling capability is increasingly needed, because long-term commitments must necessarily be made in the face of uncertainties. Particularly in an era characterized by rapid technological development, long-established technology configurations seem almost certain to be beset by substantial change.

The underlying theoretical problems are those of complex, large-scale dynamic systems, which exhibit many nonlinear phenomena under large equipment outages, including chaos and bifurcations (Ilić and Zaborszky 2000). In contrast, the available decision-making tools are hierarchical and coordinated at various levels of the existing hierarchies. The technical standards supporting the system operations and planning are closely dependent on these underlying hierarchies (NERC Interconnected Operations Services Working Group 1997). In short, the tools we have are compromises intended to approximate acceptable responses to mathematically intractable problems, even though we know that complex non-linear systems are not predictable by deterministic methods. Research efforts have been generally stronger in the analysis and weaker in the decision-making–design aspects for the electric power industry.

As with the individual component hardware at component level, systems-related approaches and challenges can be identified. Some approaches aim to improve the performance of the system in order to sustain the industry architecture as it is, while other disruptive technologies would instead facilitate the transition of the industry into what it might become. As with components, disruptive systems approaches do not necessarily favor existing configurations, older technology or incumbent participants.

Software

IT tools play an increasing role in the present industry; but they need much improvement to make the system as a whole more efficient and flexible. There are some obvious values to IT tools in moving the industry from its current passive prevention perspective to corrective, online decision-making. If done right, IT tools could ensure more robust operation with less generation and transmission reserve while maintaining the same or even higher levels of reliability. Such robustness in the face of perturbation is derived from real-time response to outages or demand surges, and by active creation of virtual networks (to work around outages, or call up additional supplies) on the fly.

Yet long before such a real-time system emerges, IT tools can play an important role. Thinking in terms of decision-making as a switching process within a hybrid system, switches will have to be very fast, very smart and act upon much online information to achieve their coordination. Research on this subject is worthwhile, even if one assumes that the industry will stay as it is. IT offers the promise of substituting information and response capability for capacity to achieve dynamic response to uncertainty. The ultimate benefit would be more efficiency and robustness, obtained through clever IT tools. Customers could benefit from guaranteed standards of technical performance and price differential choices. Such systems appear essential for genuine customer choice in a deregulated environment. They may also benefit providers by lessening required assets and enhancing operational efficiency.

THE NEED FOR REGULATORY REFORM

The regulated power industry in the US has until recently been based entirely on a guaranteed rate of return. For its part, the utility has been obliged to serve all customers in its geographical area (circled in Figure 7.5). The regulatory performance standards for checking whether the service has been provided accordingly are averaged over time and geographically. In addition, standards generally relate to the allowable number of interruptions in the electricity service as seen by a customer. The price of electricity has, therefore, been a result of lumped costs encountered for operations, maintenance and capital investments; all averaged within any given utility. Utilities have managed to negotiate the actual rate of return, depreciation rates, and so on, and currently have nonuniform rates of return.

This type of regulation does not allow for either differentiated quality of service or any customer choice of quality. It is a macro approach in which all that utility does, over the entire year and all of its customers, get averaged out. More specifically, there are no temporal or special distinctions in regulatory rules for today's industry, although it is fairly straightforward to show locational and temporal cost differences when meeting the same quality of service to different groups of customers. This hiatus in regulations reflects older technology where differentiation was difficult or impossible (see Figure 7.1). A second critical aspect of guaranteed rate of return regulation is its lack of effective incentives favoring the most adequate technologies, particularly in an environment of technological change. Transfer of new technology from the laboratory to commercial use has been slow, particularly in the area of systems software and control designs.

Some exceptions to these limitations are visible in special arrangements for larger users. Industrial users with special needs for reliability may pay lower prices depending on continuity of service, the amount of energy and the time of use agreed upon. Of course, larger users can often credibly threaten to self-generate, strengthening their bargaining power with energy providers. Emerging technology, particularly IT for active switching combined with distributed small-scale generation, suggests the potential for democratizing this adjusted bargaining power. However, it is apparent that new regulations, such as buy-back provisions, affect both bargaining power and technology deployment.

The Emerging Electricity Industry of the Future

In sharp contrast to the present operating paradigm of the electric power industry described above, a likely end state and a new paradigm for the electric power industry as it might be have begun to emerge. The new technologies shaping the very structure of the industry are already here. Many of these technologies are disruptive to current practices. The most profound and disruptive change is likely to occur in moving from a few very large power plants to literally thousands of much smaller power sources, amounting to the same or, more likely, greater total capacity. These new smaller sources could be new commercial or domestic usage plants, in addition to existing private power plants supplying some larger industrial users. Buy-back power arrangements are likely to be routinely available for self-generating users, and will impact on the remaining demand and technological needs.

There are many other new technologies in the making which would make even small users of electricity much more responsive to their actual needs. These range from long-available set-back thermostats, through to automatically balanced demand and adjustable-speed motors, all supported by various metering and switching devices. Some users may desire more environmentally sustainable green power than currently provided by existing power plants. Others may prefer lower cost, greater control over power availability, or the potential for lowering pay out by selling cheaply generated solar or wind power back into the grid.

On the wire side, we can predict a huge number of often independently controlled switches, many of these being located closer to users. More

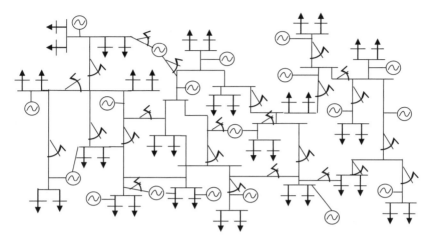

Figure 7.6   The electricity industry of the future

localized storage of energy, particularly of locally generated solar or wind power, also appears likely. Such storage will have the fundamental value of enabling the users to acquire energy at lower price, for use when regular utility power is more expensive. At present, storage is large, heavy and expensive. It is generally used to assure uninterruptible power, such as for critical users like hospitals or computer systems. With more effective, lower-cost devices, storage could become routine, and potentially very widely distributed. The old belief that electric power systems are without storage is likely to crumble soon.

IT has clear potential for changing patterns of energy use by end consumers, as well as for changing the locus of generation. In addition, IT can promote changing work and residence patterns toward broader distribution. Telecommuting, including very long distance telecommuting from remote or rural locations, is one possibility. All these technologies, if adopted, would lead toward a new electric power industry paradigm (see Figure 7.6). The implications of such changes in usage, generation, work and residence patterns for R&D needs are huge.

Possibly the biggest technological challenge facing the industry is actual implementation of supply–demand entities based on homeostatic control. Such implementation would be decentralized, at least to the level of coalitions of users or electricity providers. Systemic formation of sufficiently adaptive coalitions for customer choice, portfolios of distributed generation to sell electricity, and mini grids within the existing interconnected system to serve groups of customers, all require research to establish clear objectives for these entities and for their optimization. The optimization criteria of interest are typically long-term benefits to customer coalitions, long-term profits for the portfolios of producers of electricity and profits for the designers of mini grids. Other criteria may also be desirable, such as system robustness or reduced carbon footprint.

In addition manufacturers will have to develop adequate hardware to support the flexible response of these coalitions to changes in operating conditions, as well as to electricity prices, such as automatic meter reading; or to changes in fuel prices, which would shift the prices offered by different providers. Internet links with embedded software are likely; but they carry with them the need for hacker-resistance, anti-virus and worm programs and the like. Switching at various locations in any such system will again utilize embedded IT for simplicity, in comparison to the existing switching in today's power system architecture. Embedded IT switching also results in a highly reconfigurable network architecture. The higher the number of automated decision-makers, the simpler the switching logic is likely to become. In consequence, involved control, such as sliding mode control, is likely to be replaced by a swarm-type distributed intelligence, embodied in various simple decision-makers. Swarm decision-makers adopt over time by learning through a distributed or hybrid internet.

Reliability in the new industry configuration becomes a differentiable factor, nonuniform and provided in response to the specific demands of individual users for a particular quality of service. Its management is effectively based on contractual agreements among the affected parties. This is fundamentally different from the current paradigm, under which the interconnection was built in response to the need to share and dilute the large impact of equipment failures. In the new architecture with many small participants, the reserve needed in case any single piece of equipment fails will be drastically reduced. Possibly the hardest technological implementation will be the last resort implementation by the remnants of today's utilities, for those customers who do not have a chosen provider. This problem is very difficult because the entire interconnection must be operated as one, despite various uncertainties created by network users who only use the network for backup service when their contracts are not met. This generally creates great uncertainty for planning and operation of the interconnection. Differential reliability offers a pricing mechanism to allocate reliability, charge for perturbations created by unusual demand, and call on surge capacity to maintain system integrity.

Challenges for the Future Regulatory Regime

To implement differentiated reliability service many regulatory questions must be resolved. Some believe that electricity should remain a basic public good to which all are entitled, independent of their ability to pay. However, if a certain level of socially acceptable service is to be provided, it is necessary to establish regulatory and pricing rules to enable this under competitive power production. Others prefer an end state in which the entire industry rests on simple, value-based competitive incentives, possibly with very little regulation and perhaps none in pricing—and no guarantees of service without payment.

Systemic regulatory and pricing mechanisms for minimizing problems during the transitional from current industry practices to whatever end state is envisioned, create more major R & D challenges. These problems are further emphasized by the regulatory asymmetries between competitive supply and demand, and, what has long been seen as a natural monopoly, the transmission industry. The wire business is characterized by lumpiness in investments, very long depreciation time, as well as both economies of scale and economies of scope. Temporal and geographical aspects of power delivery also make delivery pricing quite complex. Since the existing infrastructure is designed and operated according to best effort, rather than guaranteed performance outcomes, it is highly unlikely that guaranteed reliability can be provided to all for quite some time to come. Systematic R & D is needed on performance-based regulation for socially acceptable service reliability and its valuation, under conditions of pronounced temporal and geographical differences in products. How, in such a system, should regulations be crafted to assure reliable service?

Decision-making uncertainty—and robustness-reliability risks under uncertainty—must be reflected in regulatory arrangements. Further, to be effective for the future, regulations must provide incentives for ongoing technology development and transfer into use. Supply side, wire and user-side technology, feedback and feedforward technology, and further IT development must all be encouraged to facilitate system robustness. Three types of uncertainty are involved: long-term load growth trend uncertainty; long-term substitution potential, which results from actors' independent discoveries and actions (for example, independent decisions to add self-generation capacity affects the need for transmission lines); and contingencies and equipment status on a moment-by-moment basis. Each form of uncertainty requires a somewhat different regulatory perspective. How will the system know of user needs, growth potential and projected capacity? The old regulatory system centralized decisions in regional monopoly providers. A completely decentralized system, with no coordination, appears to be in place at present, if the California power crisis is any indication. Public dissatisfaction with the crisis demands some form of coordination.

The Role of Information Technologies in the New Electricity Industry

The technological, regulatory and pricing aspects of a new electric power industry are further complicated by the opportunities created through IT. A future decentralized system might provide coordination through information requirements—any device attached to the power grid might be required to announce itself and its characteristics (for example, how much power it uses or might generate). In any event, regulations will have to assure that the necessary information is provided as needed to coordinate the system, preferably in some automated, non-intrusive way.

Markets, users and groups can be reaggregated and reconfigured virtually, via IT. Such reconfiguration will depend on patterns of use or demand, and the quality required, defined in terms of characteristics such as reliability, noninterruptibility and amount of power. Given multiple sources for power and multiple markets (reconfigurable on the fly, at least potentially), a viable new industry structure might center on brokers who buy and sell contracts and obligations for power provision by others to make profits or get advantages, owning no assets for generation or transmission themselves, but servicing the IT-reconfiguration demand.[9] Such brokers are already present in the industry under transition, but often with poorly defined market rules, particularly in relation to the reliability risks.

IT also affects the electric power system's dynamic characteristics in another way. Information is not perfect, and externalities like weather intervene; information asymmetries are worth money. Pervasive IT creates the potential for profiting from such asymmetries. Simultaneously, however, the Internet and pervasive computer penetration raise the potential for a much more equal balance of information between energy users and energy vendors at all levels, including both industry users and consumers. The ability to use information is not homogeneous, however, and the ability to change or reconfigure in response to demand shifts and opportunities is also worth money. Inter-temporal information and need asymmetries translate to noncoincidental peaks: thus information can be used as a substitute for capacity, convenience, demand and time.

IT's impact on the structure of the system as a whole, no less than on possible configurations of the system that may emerge over time, can scarcely be overstated. Indeed real-time information offers the single most powerful response to systemic difficulties: response capability can respond to what is, at any given moment, rather than seeking to forecast a complex, nonlinear system. By operating on fact and rapidly readjusting, rather than on forecasts which will surely be wrong, dynamic IT-enabled system response will diminish the perception of difficulty. But how?

A SPECULATIVE VIEW ON TRANSCENDING PROBLEMS

The technological and institutional challenges outlined above, both for the industry in transition and for an emergent industry as it might be, do not instantly offer us a well-defined approach. As we have suggested (see Figures 7.3, 7.4 and 7.6), successful solutions for dealing with the difficult problems at hand must recognize the interdependence of technological, regulatory and pricing elements to any eventual solutions, if overall industry performance is to approach socially optimal or even economically sustainable performance. Also, under competition, it is important to shape these incentives through signals from the environment. Signals must come from other parts of the context, including regulators, customers, suppliers and society at large, so that overall system performance is best for the society as a whole. This is a very difficult task. Only systemic R & D can generate the fuller understanding of interdependencies and designs, the technical, regulatory and pricing signals needed, and the system-level modeling to help identify where major payoffs may reside. It is already quite obvious from difficult transitional experiences that lack of such a full picture is disruptive to a smooth evolution from the current practices to an effectively deregulated industry.

A key element in transcending difficult problems is to comprehend the character of the shift in paradigm. It is not simple. In sharp distinction to analytical models and approaches, the needed new paradigm is synthetic. The nature of the change can be highlighted from a predominantly static perspective, in which excess capacity and centralized planning seek to respond to forecast needs; to a predominantly dynamic perspective, in which information serves effective interaction and buffering in dynamic, real-time reoptimization of the system, moment by moment (see Figure 7.7).

Both the transition and the end state of a dynamic system are IT enabled (see Figure 7.8). There will be system-level challenges, whether or not major developments occur in components or regulations. Information technology will be critical even in such a case. However, it is equally clear that without substantial further development in IT penetration and integration at the system level, neither incumbent industry participants nor the system as a whole will achieve the flexibility and survivability needed for the future. Figure 7.8 highlights the desired direction of system evolution: toward greater dynamism, flexibility and responsiveness, along with greater robustness and capability for self-healing from various perturbations.

Competition brings changed incentives—some negative, some positive,

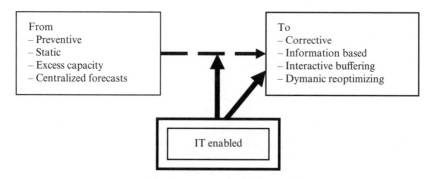

Figure 7.7   System paradigm change in the electricity sector

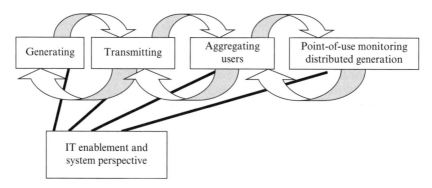

Figure 7.8   Information technologies' role in the emerging dynamic energy systems

from incumbents' points of view. Individual actors may find profit from R & D servicing their specific, individual needs. Yet the system itself must not be ignored: this is the major role for government R & D, to assure that dynamic signals are generated to guide system-level benefits. Laying out the desiderata—dynamism, flexibility, information-enabled system robustness and survivability—underlines the gap between today's system and the need.

The barriers to progress are many. To start with, current US academic structure is not well positioned to support aggressive progress on the R & D agenda outlined above. Primarily because of strict divisions between engineering, policy, and business and economics research, much academic research is simply too narrow in scope. The R & D needed here involves the active collaboration of experts in all these multiple areas. Only interdisciplinary perspectives can support the progress essential for overcoming the current status quo and transcending the difficult problems inherent in disruptive developments that cross disciplinary boundaries.

Beyond these disciplinary boundaries, it is essential to comprehend the pervasive impact of IT in marrying technology to strategic potential. New businesses, as well as seismic shifts in existing industry standings, are likely as a result of information technology applications. Certainly the changing environment, technology and IT already pose dramatic changes in information asymmetries long assumed immutable. Thus change will also occur in the power and dominance that formerly flowed from old asymmetries, but are now called into question. Surely, too, this will call forth changes in the potentials and externalities with which managers must contend. Above all, here too it should be evident that not only are the pieces evolving— components, elements, rivals and regulation—but also the system itself will be changed in its most fundamental dimensions. Smart switches, broadly distributed on the wire side and at the point of use, create feedback potential as a function of their embedded IT. Thus IT serves as a connection mechanism to enable a dynamic adaptive system.

Contemporary IT tools require substantial development before they will be adequate to these needs, however. Financial analysis of the risks to system reliability requires a far more dynamic understanding of how and where failures occur, and of how alternative configurations affect reliability at multiple levels, in different aggregates. The information needed by users, and thus by their presumably automated decision-makers, will include dynamic price adjustments to reflect moment-by-moment power availability, so that equipment outages instantly raise prices to alert users. Dynamic, performance-based information is needed to recognize and facilitate the role of price spikes, whether instantaneous, as with equipment outages; or more enduring, as with fuel-cost adjustments. Information technology can create liquid forward markets, to support appropriate investment decisions. In the medium term, demand incentives to encourage use response, turning on self-generating capacity or improvements in efficiency of use, are also likely to be IT driven.

Yet at present, performance information for power providers is minimal and not provided in a form useful for consumers. Information to fuel forward markets or medium-term demand responses is equally lacking, as is effective information on trends. Both hardware and software developments are needed to support these information challenges. All trend toward system flexibility, dynamism and robustness.

The biggest challenge is system reconfiguration. What kind of reconfiguration? The required new organization of the system will be a function of technology, especially IT, and of regulations, particularly those that foster new technologies for generation, transmission, switching, monitoring and virtual aggregation. Because each of these factors drives profit dollars, each will presumably drive research dollars as well. But research on the system per se, and its best organization in light of accelerating IT capabilities, will very likely remain a government responsibility, for at present the system as a whole is nobody's business, so no single actor takes responsibility, and no incentives to do so are in view.

The potential IT offers is nothing less than a new paradigm for robustness, at the system level, based upon dynamic optimization in real time, and using active information exchange (on price, demand and capacity); and between multiple levels, to substitute for the passive and centralized control of the past. Total system reliability must be maintained, despite changing virtual aggregates, mini-grids and even neighborhood associations for power generation, down to individual-level decisions to acquire generating capability. Dynamic interconnections and system-wide links can potentially provide substantial equifinality across this range by creating potential additional generating capacity, available on a contract basis. From an information-based perspective, such equifinality, which substitutes aggregates of many smaller users' local generating capability to buffer the system from surges, suggests that information about capacity supports economies of scope in an electric power system. Both additional capacity and temporal and geographical distribution are dimensions of system scope.

CONCLUSIONS

The electric power system at any moment is the outcome of complex interactions among existing technology, perceived needs and possibilities, regulations and institutional structures. Any given configuration reflects best efforts and compromises among different interests of the past, so that at best the system is a function of assumptions, technology and regulations of a moment. Over time, any configuration becomes less well suited to the demands placed on it as technology, needs and possibilities change. But both the in-place technical system and the institutional structure of regulations and economic profit endure, changing only slowly. Deregulation promises huge changes, yet the old framework of technology, institutions and regulations offers insufficient guidance for decisions going forward. Decision-makers in business, government and environment, and consumers need a new framework for understanding what is possible, and for evaluating alternatives. We have described some of the opportunities posed by IT, from a system perspective: without the larger perspective (and without understanding the limits of the old paradigm) it is difficult, if not impossible, to transcend the old paradigm's constraints.

Restructuring the electric power industry creates change, along with new, strong incentives to form new companies, create alternative business models and exploit hitherto unseen opportunities. These incentives could be either good or bad; they can encourage more efficient technology, or create opportunities for huge individual profits based on the exclusion or exploitation of others. As in other network industries, like telecom or aviation, deregulation can give rise to unanticipated problems, unless a broad systems view is taken. Proactive R & D, both with respect to policy and regulation, can help to predict these problems and thus avoid them.

The difficult problems described here for the electric energy industry are real. They arise out of the inadequacy of older paradigms-in-use that have long dominated industry thinking. Our description addresses them from the perspective of this industry. However, the phenomenon of difficult problems is far more general. For example, it can be said today that there is no genuine long-term storage for electrical power. A broader perspective suggests that there may merely have been insufficient incentives until now to develop appropriate technology. At present both the incentives and the technical state of the art are rapidly changing. For instance, industry is actively developing flywheel technology for energy storage for various use contexts, including hybrid automobiles and their plug-in batteries for private homes. Moreover the notion that electric energy is uniquely ephemeral is not persuasive; the airline industry's seats on any given flight are capacity that exists and is available to sell only until the plane takes off.

The difficult problem faced by the electric energy industry demands a multidisciplinary approach. The issues simultaneously involve IT, organizational and managerial matters, social and political concerns and, of course, industrial economics, no less than a broad array of relevant technologies. Above all, the interrelated complex of technology, economics and finance and regulatory policies transcends disciplinary silos. We argue that any unidimensional approach is necessarily partial and thereby limited in its insight as well as potentially misleading or even dangerous in its advice.

Key national and international research agencies could play a critical role in taking the lead by aggressively nurturing multidisciplinary R & D. They ought to be involved in creating an inter-agency agenda for forward-looking R & D directed at the evolving electric power industry, for the problems also cross national borders. Moreover, the regulatory bodies on a regional, national and supranational level can support the innovation through meaningful regulatory designs. The potential benefits from such R & D are higher than ever before. On the other hand, if the difficult problems of the electric power industry are not addressed, society is likely to see major problems in the area of electricity use.

NOTES

1. This chapter derives from many discussions by the two authors during their service at the US National Science Foundation. Professor Jelinek served as a program director for Innovation and Organizational Change in the Social Behavioral Economic Directorate. Professor Ilić served as a program director for Control, Networks and Computational Intelligence in the Directorate of Engineering, National Science Foundation, Arlington, Vermont.
2. Three Mile Island drove nuclear accident risks into dramatic prominence, as did Chernobyl some years later. The net result of these incidents was a solidification of resistance to nuclear power in the United States and elsewhere. Note that the issue is simultaneously political, environmental and perceptual, and not purely technical.
3. These developments are quite similar to the airline industry, nowadays deregulated to a quite high degree; but, like the energy sector, the airline industry has not adapted its business models to new realities, as continuing losses testify.
4. 'Dirty' power refers to electric power supply that deviates from the expected technical quality, for instance, with respect to the voltage level or frequency.
5. These systems could not substitute previously for all a household's power needs during a lengthy spell of cold, cloudy weather for instance, or because manufacturing costs were too high (see Dunn 2000; Economist 2000).
6. Micro turbines are small turbine units intended for one or a few customers, in contrast to huge production-size turbines employed by electric utilities. Fast switching makes use of rapid-response automatic shifting from one power source to another or for rapid load-shedding.
7. Rolling blackouts in California and soaring wholesale energy costs on the West Coast in early 2001 underline the issues, as does the consequent slowdown in the California economy, the world's sixth largest.
8. Flowgate-based congestion-management approaches rely on widely distributed gates that automatically control electricity flow, responding to changes in supply or demand.
9. Such brokers already exist. The Williams Company, a major power broker servicing the Western US, has experienced record profits in the current California power crisis, due principally to energy trading according to company statements reported in the *Wall Street Journal* (26 December 2000).

REFERENCES

Awerbuch, S. and A. Preston (eds) (1997), *Virtual Utility: Accounting, Technology and Competitive Aspects of Emerging Industry*, Dordrecht: Kluwer Academic.

Black, J. (2000), 'Survey of technologies and cost estimates for residential electric services', MIT working paper series EL 00-009 WP, December.

Cazalet, E. (2000), 'Automated power exchange', *IEEE 2000 Power Engineering Society Summer Meeting*, 1: 64.

Dunn, S. (2000), *Micropower: The Next Electrical Era*, Washington, DC: Worldwatch Institute.

Economist (2000), 'The dawn of micropower', *The Economist*, **346**: 75–7.

Hingorani, N.G. and L. Gyugyi (1999), *Understanding Facts: Concepts and Technology of Flexible AC Transmission Systems*, New York: IEEE Press.

Hogan, W. (1990), 'Contract networks for electric power transmission: technical reference', working paper, Boston, John Kennedy School of Management, Harvard University.

Ilić, M. and J. Zaborszky (2000), *Dynamics and Control in Large Electric Power Systems*, New York: John Wiley & Sons.

Ilić, M., J.R. Arce, Y. Yoon and E. Fumagali (2001), 'Assessing reliability as the electric power industry restructures', *Electricity Journal*, **14** (2): 55–67.

Linstone, H.A. and Mitroff, W.I. (1994), *The Challenge of the 21st Century: Managing Technology and Ourselves in a Shrinking World*, Albany, NY: State University of New York Press.

NERC Interconnected Operations Services Working Group (1997), 'Defining interconnected operations services under open access', NERC Interconnected Operations Services Working Group, March.

Platt, C. (2000), 'Re-energizer', *Wired*, **8:05**: 1–6.

Porter, M.E. (1980), *Competitive Strategy: Techniques for Analyzing Industries and Competitors*, New York: Free Press.

Schweppe, F., R.D. Tabors, J.L. Kirtley, H.R. Outhred, F.H. Pickel and A.J. Cox (1980), 'Homeostatic utility control', *IEEE Transactions on Power Apparatus and Systems*, **PAS-99** (3): 1151–63.

PART III

Policies

8. Public values versus private interests: an empirical comparison of business strategies in liberalized infrastructures

Casper van der Veen, Peer Ederer, Fabienne Fortanier, Alexandra Rotileanu and Bob de Wit

INTRODUCTION

The provision of infrastructure services to an economy is today dominated by private companies. It results from the privatization of many former state-owned companies, utilities and even state functions in the infrastructure sector. Public values, therefore, can no longer be achieved by direct action of the state as their guardian, but must be achieved through the market behavior of private companies. However, private companies are by definition not in the business of providing public value. Indeed, their task is to maximize their value to their private owner, a function which is deeply rooted in and protected by the property law system of any modern industrial economy.

A conflict will therefore inevitably arise: whereas the public is dependent on, and interested in, the achievement of public values from infrastructure, the private companies that must provide such public values are not. That sets the fundamental basis for regulating market behavior of private infrastructure companies, such that their business conduct is forced within certain frameworks of action, which shall ensure the achievement of public values. Hence the notion arises that any achievement of public value comes more or less at the expense of the achievement of private value. As a result, there is intensive research and experimentation into which regulatory framework is best suited to make private companies forgo their native profit maximizing behavior and behave instead toward certain goals.

The achievement of public and private values need not be a zero-sum game. It can be observed that a win-win situation is achievable, where both private and public values are being maximized, without being at each other's expense. This results from the fact that companies do not exhibit the uniform competitive behavior that macroeconomic models typically assume. Instead, companies can and do draw from a large variety of decision-making patterns for choosing how to compete in the market to maximize their private value. The research question, therefore, is which patterns of decision-making behavior concur with which types of public values in a win-win mode.

This question is answered by analyzing the strategic decision-making patterns or biases of different infrastructure companies, as well as the achievement of public values in different countries where these companies operate, and determine whether and what type of relationship there is.

The outcomes of the analysis are relevant in two ways. First, in such instances where a relationship between strategic bias and public value maximization could be established, regulators should be interested in and favoring certain strategic choices inside companies through regulatory action, if public values shall be maximized. Such relationships could be established in three cases: when network strategy bias toward coopera-tion increases the public value of reliability; when corporate strategy bias toward synergy increases the public value of overall quality; and when the purpose strategy bias toward responsibility increases the public value of access.

Secondly, in such instances where such a relationship could not be established, regulators should in fact not be interested in favoring corre-sponding strategic choices. For instance, there does not seem to be a rela-tionship between corporate strategy bias toward market responsiveness and any public value achievement, even though this is often implied by regulatory behavior, for instance in the unbundling debate in the electric-ity or the railway sector.

There are some additional, incidental findings yielded from the follow-ing analysis. Strategic biases in decision-making differs enough across the sample, such that it can be shown that the strategic stance of a company is a choice of the company's management, not a result of the industry condi-tion. In addition, the biases are neither significantly related to the country of origin of the company, nor the industry in which it operates. Therefore, there are no self-fulfilling mechanisms of regulatory ambition operating which would account for the above results. Finally, in the sample ana-lyzed, there is no trade-off observable in the achievement between public values, that is, the maximization of the one having to be at the expense of the other.

STRATEGY BIAS AND PERSPECTIVES

Top managers are often required to anticipate, define and solve difficult problems (Schweiger et al. 1986). Rittel and Webber (1973) introduced the complexity of modern-day problems, classifying societal, policy and strategy issues as difficult. In order to make sense of the world around us, companies often simplify reality into polarized distinctions that conceal complex interrelationships (Lewis 2000). These polarized distinctions are represented in the strategy perspectives or strategy biases that firms have. Companies start from different assumptions about the nature of each strategic issue, and, therefore, arrive at a different perspective on how to solve strategy problems. At the heart of every strategy issue a fundamental tension between apparent opposites can be identified, without implying that merely one of these is correct. Each pair of opposite perspectives creates a tension, as they seem to be inconsistent, or even compatible with one another. These opposites confront companies with conflicting pressures, forcing them to deal with these contradictory forces simultaneously (De Wit and Meyer 2004).

The issues that we assume to be the highest on the corporate agenda of infrastructure companies are corporate-level strategy, network-level strategy and organizational purpose. Corporate-level strategy is the strategy a firm develops for a range of businesses. Key questions are which businesses the firm should be in, and how they should be managed and aligned. Network-level strategy is the strategy a firm develops together with other firms. The key question here is what type of relationship should be maintained between organizations. When discussing organizational purpose, the reason for an organization's existence is being identified. Here the key question is whose interests the organization should serve (see de Wit and Meyer 2004).

Corporate-level Strategy

Firms seeking growth have a number of directions in which to expand. Of course, they can pursue many growth options while staying within the boundaries of a single business. However, firms often broaden their scope further, venturing into other lines of business—into multi-business corporations. The corporate strategist may choose to enhance the scope of his or her company for general environment reasons, that is, the milieu in which the firm operates; industry environment reasons such as market structure; and firm specific reasons or internal company motives, such as the dissemination of management skills (Miles 1982; Ramanujam and Varadarajan 1989). A typical example is the cable industry, where the current trend is to venture into the triple-play of Internet, television and telephony. The challenge is to select an optimal portfolio of businesses and to determine how they should be integrated into the corporate whole, in what is usually called corporate strategy (De Wit and Meyer 2004). Which businesses should the firm be in and how should the corporation be managed?

It has become a widespread policy to organize multi-business firms into strategic business units (Rumelt 1974; Whittington and Mayer 1999). Each strategic business unit is given the responsibility to serve the particular demands of one business area. The complicated issue is how to bring together the separate parts into a cohesive whole (De Wit and Meyer 2004). When firms decide to apply a high degree of centralization, resources and activities are physically brought together into one organizational unit. In this case, headquarters plays a central and active role. Even when resources, activities and product offerings have been split along business lines, integration can be achieved by ensuring that coordination is carried out between business units. But integration is also being realized by standardizing resources and activities across business unit boundaries. This creates the opportunity for economies of scale and rapid competence development without the need to physically centralize or continuously coordinate. The extent to which these solutions are being applied depends on the demand for synergy or the demand for responsiveness (De Wit and Meyer 2004).

Synergies arise by aligning business units to work together into a cohesive whole, creating value higher than stand-alone value—coordinating the activities of various business units into a larger whole to capitalize on the potential benefits of working together. The cable industry largely benefits from leveraged resources, as Internet, television and telephony can all make use of cable connections. In the same way, in the railway industry, both passenger transport and transport of goods make use of the same rails. Another source of synergy, aligning positions, plays a role when not resources but product offerings of diverse business units are related to one another. The cable industry is again an example, improving the company's bargaining position toward customers and competitive positions toward one another in all triple-play markets.

Responsiveness signifies reacting quickly to demands of the environment, having the autonomy to respond to the specific circumstances in each individual business area. Here the focus is on stand-alone value of each strategic business unit, in order to maximize flexibility and speed to answer to dynamic market demands (De Wit and Meyer 2004). A company can hardly neglect to be responsive at all, with the danger of having a competitive disadvantage compared to rivals that better match the conditions of the environment. Therefore, business responsiveness is a key demand for successful corporate-level strategy. However, it is under constant pressure of high governance costs, slower decision-making, strategy incongruence, control and misaligned incentives (De Wit and Meyer 2004). To which of these two conflicting demands—synergy or responsiveness—companies are giving priority, depends on the strategy perspective that they adopt.

Network-level Strategy

As a recent trend, governments have decided to stimulate competition in countries' most important infrastructural industries. They believe that competition would enlarge the possibility to realize certain public values. For instance, UNIFE, the association of the European Railway industry, has stated that the encouragement of competitiveness of rail transport contributes to economic growth and support of the internal market, promoting safe and sustainable mobility and reducing public expenditure by inducing better rail performance. Deregulation policies in infrastructural industries have significantly increased competition; however, at the same time, companies seek to embed themselves in cooperation to be able to withstand this fierce competition. It is clear that different companies have different perspectives concerning the need for either autonomy or embeddedness (De Wit and Meyer 2004).

No firm is purely autonomous. All firms must necessarily interact with other organizations in their environment and therefore have interorganizational relationships. These relationships can evolve without any clear strategic intent or tactical calculation; but most companies agree that actively determining the nature of their external relations is a significant part of what strategizing is about. Even avoiding relations with some external parties can be an important strategic choice.

How organizations deal with one another is strongly influenced by what they hope to achieve (Preece 1995; Dyer and Singh 1998). When two or more companies seek to cooperate, they generally do so because they expect some added value—assuming to obtain more benefit from the interaction than on their own. The same sources of synergy as discussed in the previous section apply when examining the objectives for interorganizational cooperation. Two firms can work together to leverage their resources: by putting their stocks of assets together, their quality and/or quantity increases. This can happen either via learning from each other (Doz and Hamel 1988; Shapiro and Varian 1998), or via lending each other's resources. Other partnerships are oriented toward integrating activities. The linking of activities in the vertical chain is the most common form of integrating activities. Lumping occurs when companies integrate similar activities to achieve economies of scale. Lastly, firms can align their positions, matching their product offerings in order to improve their bargaining position. This can take the form of leaning, when done with industry actors, or of lobbying, when done with contextual actors (De Wit and Meyer 2004).

It is clear that a lot can be gained by cooperation and embeddedness. Yet a company also puts a lot at stake when doing so. It is for this reason that many firms decide to remain autonomous and minimize their interaction with, and dependence on, other parties. Firms will experience a constant tension between the pressures for competing, thus remaining autonomous, and cooperating. Companies inherently need to work with others, while simultaneously they need to pursue their own interest. Organizations need to be competitive in their relationship with others, as the interests of different companies are often mutually exclusive, leading to a zero-sum game. Companies should be assertive in pursuing their own agenda. To a certain extent companies should take an autonomous stand and minimize their dependence on others, while trying to maximize others' dependence on themselves. Just as with corporate-level strategy, here, as well, to which of these two conflicting demands—embeddedness or autonomy—companies are giving priority in their networking behavior depends on the strategy perspective that they adopt.

Organizational Purpose Strategy

Because the infrastructure industry supplies some of the primary needs of society, many different stakeholders are involved. Most citizens cannot live without the products or services provided by the industry and are very much dependent on them. At the same time, infrastructure companies have to pursue growth and profit, possibly at the expense of other stakeholders, such as its suppliers or buyers, but also governments, local communities and activist groups. In the electricity and railway industries, this ambiguity is also prominent due to environmental issues. These sectors especially lose trust easily from the community as soon as evidence suggests that profitability is given priority over social responsibility. Companies and individuals differ in their perspective on which of the two should be the preferred strategy. There is an obvious pressure for profitability in order to survive, foremost as a privatized company without funding from government. However, when this is the sole objective of a company, this could lead to decreased trust and employee commitment, which in the long run could offset initial profitability. Because of this dynamic between the interests of the various stakeholders inside a company, the importance of a purpose strategy cannot be neglected.

Companies constantly make choices and seek solutions based on an understanding of what the organization is intended to achieve (De Wit and Meyer 2004). Companies are confronted with many different claimants who believe that the firm exists to serve their interest. Demands are placed on the firm by shareholders, employees, suppliers, customers, governments and communities, forcing companies to weigh whose interests should receive priority over others. In the telecommunication industry, customers want the provision of good, reliable and affordable service to be what their provider has been founded for; shareholders see the company more as a cash cow to serve their interests; and governments feel that the company should contribute to the country's broader objectives.

The enormous impact of corporations on the functioning of society is widely recognized. Political parties, labor unions, community representatives, environmentalists, the media and the general public all take a certain perspective on the role that organizations should play within society. For example, the European Union (EU) stated many objectives for the electricity sector:

> Europe needs an energy industry that is dependable, in terms of security and continuity of supply; sustainable, in terms of its environmental performance; and competitive, delivering an efficient service to households and businesses and thus contributing to the competitiveness of the European Economy and the quality of life of its citizens. (European Union Commission 2003, pp. 739–42)

It appears to be almost an impossible task to fulfill all these wishes.

In countries with a market economy, it is generally agreed that companies should pursue strategies that ensure economic profitability, but that they have certain social responsibilities as well. But this is where the consensus ends. Organizations take on opposite perspectives with regard to the relative importance of profitability and social responsibility. When companies strive toward profit maximization, shareholders will be delighted; but this will raise a conflict with the optimization of benefits for other stakeholders. Again there is a conflict between two seeming opposites, profitability and social responsibility. Ultimately companies will develop different perspectives on which objectives to give priority and develop their own ways to integrate the two opposite demands, which then becomes their purpose strategy bias.

PUBLIC VALUES

The notion of public interest remains indistinct and uncertain, even though it has been part of philosophical or political dialogues for centuries. Defining the concept of public values has been and still is an ambitious goal. Various academic disciplines have expressed their interest in the matter: political science, public administration, administrative law, policy analysis, economics, to name but a few (Moore 1996). However, there is hardly any stand-alone literature on this topic: rather than focusing on public value and defining the concept, most authors make reference to it in a marginal way or cite it as an ideal, standard or criterion (Beck Jørgensen and Bozeman 2007).

By the end of the twentieth century, democracy, as ideology and as regime, was firmly established, and so was the idea that it was the duty of the government to serve the public interest (Manent 2001). The welfare state pushed this belief even further: the state should not only defend the public interest, but should create public value. This idea assumed far more responsibility and a much more active role of the state in public affairs. Yet the last decades have modified the way of thinking over public value. Whereas traditionally the achievement of public value was assumed to be the responsibility of the public sector, lately public value has become increasingly associated with private actors as well (Moore 2003).

The concept of public value has been intensely disputed in the debates around liberalization and privatization. What arrangement of actors, private or public, is ideal to serve public value (Bozeman 2003)? In the past decades, the notion that business organizations should also create value for the society—aside from achieving their own private value—has gained popularity. The tendency toward deregulation and globalization in general has increased the pressure on companies, especially large companies, to do business in a socially responsible manner (Moore and Khagram 2004). Over the last years, public value has been subjected to heated debates on policy-making and policy evaluation, and is a focal point throughout various scientific disciplines. In due course the meaning of the concept has shifted and broadened, according to the debates in which it was invoked. The study of public values has left an abundance of explanations, definitions and boundaries.

A Universe of Public Values

Bozeman and Beck Jørgensen (2007) conducted an extensive study of the literature on public value, in which all values or principles referred to as public values are gathered and classified. The result is 'a universe of public values' (72 values in total), to quote their expression, out of which the most often quoted are professional standards, the rule of law, effectiveness, use orientation and democracy. Their taxonomy is preceded by an introduction to the concept and to the existing taxonomies. The authors define public values not as the output of public policy (which is typical for how public administration literature had been written), but more as considerations that should be taken into account, or principles to be followed, when taking decisions of public relevance. Public values are not immutable, universal truths, but rather culture or time-bound. They may be formulated by politicians and policy-makers, but are not 'owned by them' (Beck Jørgensen and Bozeman 2007). Rather policy-makers translate values from politics to society, within the current public context.

Before Bozeman's and Beck Jørgensen's works, a frequently used classification of public values was a hierarchy, which has dominated the discussion so far. In the hierarchy public values are said to be either primary ultimate, that is, intrinsic values, ends in themselves or goals subject only to philosophical and moral inquiry, or instrumental, that is, means to reach goals, derived ends, subject to causal inquiry (Dahl and Lindblom 1953). Improving on this hierarchical classification, Bozeman and Beck Jørgensen propose a classification in function of proximity or vicinity of meaning, which results in eight major clusters of values around eight nodal values. Nodal values are fundamental values with a relatively high number of values with a similar meaning.

Bozeman's (2003) and his and Beck Jørgensen's work (2007) provide the most appropriate theoretical framework. It provides a mid-range conceptualization of public values—neither too philosophical, nor too instrumental. Moreover, the authors not only define public values; they also make an inventory and classification of public values. The outcome is, as mentioned above, a universe of public values, which are grouped in function of proximity or vicinity of meaning, resulting further in eight major clusters of nodal values. The advantage of this inventory is to provide an overall impression of the entire universe of public values, comprising a very large number of values, whereas most public value authors typically focus on a limited number of values. In addition values are placed next to each other and extracted from the heated debates in which they were deadlocked. This generates possibilities to craft new constructs based on values, to identify relationships among values, and to think of new groups and classifications. The disadvantages are closely related to the latter argument: taking the values out of their context raises the dangers of confusion and loss of meaning. Even if they can still be understood, a large part of the message, of the ideology they carried can be lost. However, this loss of context actually served the purpose of this study very well.

As a non-normative study that is separated from any public value ideology, we needed a theoretical basis that is also non-normative. Moreover the large overview of public values allowed a proper selection of the values or variables to measure. Bozeman's and Beck Jørgensen's large pool of values ensured that no essential values are missed or misinterpreted. This framework provided the bridge between theory and operationalization. With the public values universe in mind, industry-related policies were screened in a search for the relevant public values in each infrastructure sector.

Five Public Values Relevant in Infrastructure Industries

Five public values have been identified that nowadays are of specific relevance for infrastructure industries: sustainability, reliability, quality, price and access. While this inevitably involves some arbitrary judgment, the selection process shall be illustrated with one public value in the electricity sector. A frequently cited public value in this sector is choice, that is, the ability of customers to make a choice between different suppliers and/or product qualities. However, choice in itself does not create either public or private value. Neither the consumer nor the state is per se any richer by being allowed a choice as to the provider or product. Choice turns out to be only an enabler, or an instrumental value, toward achieving the principal targets of price and quality. Price in this case stands for lowest possible cost per kilowatt-hour delivered, and quality mostly stands for the ease and user-friendliness of access to the network.

These five public values can have different expressions in the four sectors observed. For instance, quality is largely influenced by ease of access in the electricity sector, but more influenced by the rate of innovation in the cable sector. The selection of the five public values was thus depending on a set of criteria. Public values should be observable among most of the four sectors that were analyzed. They were prominent in the public debate of each sector. They seemed to be final values, for instance worthwhile for their own sake, rather than instrumental for other goals. The final value could be expressed in a tangible wealth achievement, for instance reliability translates into cost reductions for industry. The five values had to be reasonably independent of each other. Finally, empirical data are available for quantifying the achievement of the public value across five countries.

Hypotheses on Public Values and Corporate Strategy

Combining the three strategy perspectives and the five public values elaborated in the previous paragraphs, we can develop a series of hypotheses on how these may be related, building on general economic and strategic reasoning as well as recent policy developments.

First to be considered is the relationship between corporate strategy and public value creation. Corporate strategies toward synergy reflect the extent to which various phases of the product chain, as well as related products, are integrated—vertically and horizontally—within one firm in order to take advantage of economies of scale and scope. In contrast, a corporate strategy toward responsiveness is reflected in a focus on building and exploiting specialized competences for producing a single product or engaging in a clearly demarcated activity. It may be argued that a strategy toward synergy allows firms to reduce production costs due to economies of scale, hereby resulting in lower-priced products; to engage in cross-subsidization, thus being able to guarantee wider access; and benefit from intra-firm knowledge transfers, ensuring overall higher quality, reliability and sustainability. This would imply a positive relationship between corporate strategy biased toward synergy and public value creation. However, strategies toward synergy are also coupled with high coordination costs. In addition, large and integrated firms often result in (internal) monopolies that experience no competitive pressures to create higher public or private value. The latter concern has been a prime driver of many of the EU's policies toward unbundling and liberalization in many of the sectors we study. Therefore we hypothesize:

H_1 A corporate strategy toward synergy is negatively related to the creation of public value, as measured by sustainability, reliability, quality, price, access and PVmean.[1]

Second to be considered is the relationship between network strategy and public value creation. Firms with network strategy biased toward embeddedness are engaged in a wide range of cooperative relationships with competitors, suppliers and buyers, but also governments, and non-governmental organizations. These relationships may range from strategic alliances on research and development, or shared product development, to engaging in industry associations. At the other extreme, firms with network strategies biased toward autonomy have, in fact, no network strategy at all. Such firms prefer to go it alone, in order to protect firm-specific knowledge and technologies from competitors for instance. In line with the first hypothesis, it may be expected that strategies toward autonomy are most conducive to public value creation, as increased cooperation may result in collusion. However, network strategies are often considered to be the optimal combination of markets (competitive pressures) and hierarchies (coordination and economies of scale). Therefore we hypothesize:

H_2 A network strategy toward cooperation is positively related to the creation of public value, as measured by sustainability, reliability, quality, price, access and PVmean.

Finally to be considered is the relationship between purpose strategy and public value as perhaps the most self-evident of the three. Firms with purpose strategies biased toward profitability tend to be primarily concerned with their bottom line and financial health. Firms with purpose strategies biased toward responsibility show great awareness of their public goals and function, including many dimensions of corporate social responsibility. While such greater awareness may partly reflect window-dressing, it is generally assumed that greater awareness of public goals is also reflected in greater action toward creating public value. Therefore we hypothesize:

H_3 *A purpose strategy toward responsibility is positively related to the creation of public value, as measured by sustainability, reliability, quality, price, access and PVmean.*

AN EMPIRICAL RESEARCH ON STRATEGY PERSPECTIVES AND PUBLIC VALUES

Data were collected for a total of 42 firms from four sectors across five countries. Information has also been gathered on the five dimensions of public value that is created in each sector in each country. This implies that we have a data set that combines two different levels of aggregation: first, the firm level and, secondly, the country-sector level. In our analyses, we used the data sets at both levels of aggregation in order to explore the relationships between strategy perspectives and public values. The data set at the company level with 42 observations enables us to explore in detail the various strategy perspectives of firms, and to relate these to sector level outcomes.

However, since there are differences across the sectors and countries as to how many firms are present in each sector—ranging from one firm in Belgium's telecom sector, to five firms in Britain's railway industry — such an approach may lead to unintentional weights in the data. To correct for the potential biases in our findings that this may cause, we also worked with the second data set at the country-sector level. Here we only have 20 observations, linking the average strategy perspectives as well as the diversity in strategy perspectives within a sector to a sector's performance on public value. Without showing the details here, the result of this analysis was that the findings between country-level analysis and company-level analysis do not differ significantly. We therefore concentrate the discussion on the company level analysis.

The empirical research is based on a comparison of two sets of data: one set of data describing the strategic decision-making behavior of companies; and another set of data describing the achievement of public values. If a statistical correlation between these two sets could be established, then these are believed to be caused by decision-making patterns of companies creating the achievement of public value.

The key challenge of the research was to create these two data sets in such a way that they would become accessible for statistical analysis, as neither of them is readily provided in regular reporting structures, let alone cross-industry and cross-country. The way this has been done is by comparing 42 different companies from five adjacent European countries in four infrastructure sectors, in order to achieve a representative sample for the analysis, which would be unbiased by either infrastructure or country models.

The 42 companies were investigated along three different arenas of company decision-making patterns, and then related to the achievement of five different public values in the countries where they operate. In each infrastructure sector all major companies were investigated, representing in each sector around 60 to 90 percent of the total turnover in sales. The total set of observations for strategic behavior impacting the achievement of public values amounted thus to close to 500 data points.

Five countries were chosen—Germany, France, the United Kingdom, the Netherlands and Belgium. They form an area of northwestern Europe that exhibits a spread of large and small countries. Moreover they represent countries typically believed to be following different regulatory paradigms and with different regulatory traditions toward the achievement of public values. With this spread of regulatory framework and size, these five countries are well suited to represent the overall universe of possible country versus public policy choices for achievement of private versus public values.

Four subsectors were chosen to represent one sector each from the major infrastructure networks: electricity for energy, telecommunication fixed lines for communication, cable operators for media network, railways and passenger services for transportation. Originally a subsector from the water network was supposed to be included as well; but technical issues in data provision and company selection led to dropping this fifth sector from the analysis.

Each of the four sectors exhibit different industry models of vertical integration in the countries. In each case, the company selection followed the criterion of choosing the companies which are operating downstream toward the final customer, and which together represent the large majority of customer's experience for the particular infrastructure sector in each country. This selection criterion was chosen, as it is assumed that

Table 8.1   Selected firms by sector, subsector and number of companies

Sector	Subsector	Selected firms	No. of companies
Energy	Electricity	Electrabel, EDF, ENBW, RWE, E.on, Vattenfall, NUON, Essent, ENECO, Powergen, National Grid, Scottish Power and Scottish & Southern Energy	13
Communication	Telecommuni-cations (fixed lines)	France Telecom, Deutsche Telekom, KPN, Belgacom and British Telecom	5
Media network	Cable	France Telecom, UPC Broadband, KDG, Tele Columbus, Primacom, UPC, Essent, Casema, Telenet, Brutélé, ALE-Teledis, NTL and Telewest	13
Transportation	Railway	SNCF, RFF, Deutsche Bahn, ProRail, NS, SNCB, Arriva, National Express, First Group, Translink and Virgin	6

companies operating downstream toward customers are also those that determine largely the achievement of public values. Table 8.1 summarizes the firms and sectors selected for the empirical research.

Measuring Strategic Bias

The decision-making patterns or biases at companies were measured in two stages: a desk research concerning the strategic bias of the companies; and a validation of the desk research results by interviews with high-ranking strategy officers of each company. For the desk research phase, the externally oriented communication of the companies was screened for indicators or typical expressions of a particular strategic bias. The typical communication material reviewed were websites, annual reports, newsletters and analyst presentations. The indicators that were looked for are typical expressions for what type of strategic bias a company has. For instance, an organization which is functionally organized is typical for synergy-driven companies, whereas business unit organizations are typical for responsiveness-driven companies. The more typical indicators for any given strategic bias a company accumulated during the review, the higher a score it received for this particular bias. The strategic biases are measured on an either/or basis, that means a company could either be synergistic or responsive or somewhere in between; but it could not be both at the same time.

The scores thus derived for each company, and where this company stands relative to its competitors in the industry, were then presented during interviews with high-ranking strategy officers of each of the companies. These strategy officers could then provide additional evidence that might lead to an adjustment of the score in either direction. For the most part, the interview results confirmed the scores of the desk research phase.

Measuring Public Values

The particular challenge for measuring public value achievement lies in creating a measure that would be comparable across the different industries. For instance, a 99 percent reliability might be an excellent achievement for railways, but would be unacceptable for electricity and unworldly for telecommunications. Measures of quality might not be directly comparable at all between sectors. Furthermore, measures also needed to be chosen which are consistently taken across all five countries.

The way this was achieved was by utilizing the EU's measures and translating them into ranking achievements within the EU 15 countries. For each sector, several of the EU's data series and documents were utilized. Typically these were either White Papers by the Directorate General TREN in the EU Commission, particular studies commissioned and published by the EU, or periodical benchmarking reports as part of the EU Lisbon Agenda. The achieved ordinal ranks could then be compared between the industries. For instance, instead of comparing a 99 percent reliability rate, railways in France achieve the fourth rank of the five EU countries in terms of accessibility and electricity achieves the first rank within the EU in terms of reliability, and so on. By comparing the relative rankings, the industries in the countries and their different values become comparable with each other.

DATA PRESENTATION

For the statistical analysis, the three strategic biases were given numerical values. In corporate strategy, the bias toward responsiveness carries the value of 1, while the bias toward synergy, 6. If a group of companies in an industry or in a country has the value of, say, 4.5, then most companies in that group have a rather synergy-oriented strategic bias. However, these numerical values do not imply a qualitative evaluation of the strategy. The higher value for synergy orientation does not mean that this is a better strategy. In network strategy, the bias toward autonomy carries the value of 1, while the bias toward cooperation carries 6. In purpose strategy, the bias toward profitability carries the value of 1, while the bias toward responsibility carries 6.

The achievement of public values is also expressed in numerical values of 1 to 6. In this case, however, the higher the score is, the better is the achievement of the public value. The construction was derived such that the worst-performing EU 15 country received a score of 1, while the best received 6. The performance of the five countries of this study was then respectively placed in between that numerical band. If one of the countries was the best performing, it received a score of 6, or if it was exactly in the middle of all EU countries it would have received a score of 3.5.

For the public values, also a summary construct was developed, called the PVmean, which is the simple arithmetic mean of the respective public values per sector. The measure is mostly valuable for the statistical analysis, less for any content meaning.

FINDINGS

Differences between Sectors and Countries

Tables 8.2 to 8.4 describe the data, examining the extent to which potential industry or country differences are present in the data. Table 8.3, differences by country, and Table 8.4, differences across industries, have a similar layout: they display both the means for the selected variables across country or industry categories and the number of observations (n) included in each category. So Table 8.3 indicates that the six French firms in the sample score an average of 4.25 on corporate strategy, meaning they tend to be synergy oriented. For each variable, F-tests (ANOVA) have been conducted to explore the extent to which the means across the countries or sectors also differ significantly from each other.

The results in Table 8.3 indicate few significant differences across countries for both the corporate strategy variables and the public value variables. However, as these tests are relatively sensitive to the number of observations, and since we cover virtually the entire population of firms in the sectors and countries that were selected, some interesting observations can be made.

For the strategy variables, we find the strongest differences across countries regarding the corporate strategy and purpose strategy. French and

Table 8.2   Descriptive statistics at company level by public values

	n	m	Sd	Min.	Max.
Corporate	42	3.71	1.13	1.4	5.5
Network	42	3.44	0.80	2.2	5.0
Purpose	42	3.88	0.90	2.0	5.5
Sustainability	13	2.04	0.63	1.5	4.0
Reliability	24	3.13	1.26	2.0	6.0
Quality	42	4.24	0.91	2.3	6.0
Price	42	3.53	1.46	1.0	6.0
Access	29	3.10	1.38	1.0	5.5
PVmean	31	3.50	0.64	2.3	4.7

Note: Corporate strategy: 1 = responsiveness; 6 = synergy. Network strategy: 1 = autonomy; 6 = cooperation. Purpose strategy: 1 = Profitability; 6 = Responsibility. Public values of sustainability, reliability, quality, price and access: 1 = lowest relative rank; 6 = highest relative rank of EU 15.

Table 8.3   Descriptive statistics at firm level by country and public values

	FRA	n	DEU	N	NLD	n	BEL	n	GBR	n	F (Anova)	Sig.
Corporate	4.25	6	3.80	9	4.23	9	3.22	6	3.22	12	1.85	0.1395
Network	3.88	6	3.40	9	3.33	9	3.43	6	3.34	12	0.53	0.7127
Purpose	4.17	6	3.37	9	4.39	9	3.75	6	3.79	12	1.81	0.1474
Sustainability	4.00	1	2.00	4	1.50	3	2.00	1	2.00	4	n.a.	n.a.
Reliability	3.00	3	4.00	5	2.80	5	4.00	2	2.67	9	1.20	0.3088
Quality	4.33	6	4.24	9	3.73	9	3.77	6	4.80	12	2.64	0.0488
Price	2.42	6	3.39	9	3.89	9	3.83	6	3.75	12	1.19	0.3317
Access	2.40	5	2.40	5	3.00	6	3.60	5	3.75	8	1.32	0.2911
PVmean	2.98	4	3.43	8	3.31	7	3.36	5	4.19	7	4.05	0.0111

Note: Corporate strategy: 1 = responsiveness; 6 = synergy. Network strategy: 1 = autonomy; 6 = cooperation. Purpose strategy: 1 = Profitability; 6 = Responsibility. Public values of sustainability, reliability, quality, price and access: 1 = lowest relative rank; 6 = highest relative rank of EU 15.

Dutch firms appear to have a stronger tendency toward synergy, while the other countries are rather midway between the two biases. French firms also appear to have a stronger focus on cooperation than firms from other countries. As for purpose strategy, again the French and the Dutch score more—toward more responsibility—while the Germans appear most leaning to a profitability bias.

It is important to note that, while these differences may be substantial,

Table 8.4   Descriptive statistics at company level by industry and public values

	Electricity	n	Cable	n	Telecom	n	Railway	n	F (Anova)	Sig.
Corporate	4.31	13	3.41	13	3.32	5	3.53	11	1.96	0.1365
Network	3.41	13	3.35	13	3.32	5	3.65	11	0.32	0.8083
Purpose	3.62	13	3.76	13	3.94	5	4.29	11	1.26	0.3035
Sustainability	2.04	13		0		0		0	n.a.	n.a.
Reliability	3.15	13		0		0	3.09	11	0.10	0.9063
Quality	4.69	13	4.04	13	4.40	5	3.86	11	2.15	0.1101
Price	3.46	13	4.15	13	3.40	5	2.91	11	1.54	0.2192
Access		0	2.35	13	4.00	5	3.59	11	4.68	0.0183
PVmean	3.35	13	3.49	13	3.92	5		0	1.44	0.2542

Note: Corporate strategy: 1 = responsiveness; 6 = synergy. Network strategy: 1 = autonomy; 6 = cooperation. Purpose strategy: 1 = Profitability; 6 = Responsibility. Public values of sustainability, reliability, quality, price and access: 1 = lowest relative rank; 6 = highest relative rank of EU 15.

they are not significant. We do find significant differences across countries with respect to some of the public value variables—in particular quality, and PVmean. The British firms score far higher on quality than the others, while the Dutch and Belgians perform much worse on quality. Also for the PVmean, we find that British firms appear to create the most public value on average, though here the French score particularly low—primarily due to poor scores on price and access.

The differences across industries for the strategy variables are—as in the case of country differences—not significant. Most differences can be found for the corporate strategy variable (highest F-value among the three). Particularly electricity firms tend to have a strategy that is more oriented toward synergy than firms from other sectors. Railway firms score relatively high on purpose strategy, indicating an orientation toward responsibility.

As for the public value variables, in particular access differs significantly across the various sectors; but it is not measured in the electricity sector. Telecommunication firms score high, while cable firms score low on this variable. And here too, as with differences across country, firms differ almost significantly across industries as regards quality. Electricity firms perform relatively well, while cable and especially railway firms lag behind. Interestingly, PVmean does not differ significantly across industries.

The following conclusions can be drawn from the data description.[2] First, differences across firms for strategy variables are generally not explained by country or industry effects. Interesting and almost significant differences have been found for corporate strategy (French, Dutch and electricity firms tend toward synergy, while Belgian, British and telecommunication firms toward responsiveness) and purpose strategy (French, Dutch and railway firms tend toward responsibility, while German and electricity firms are more profit oriented). Secondly, differences across firms for the public value they create are not strongly explained by country or industry effects. Interesting and significant differences have been found for quality (British and electricity firms perform well, while Dutch, Belgian and railway firms score low), access (telecommunication firms perform well, cable firms score low), and PVmean (British firms perform well, French score low). Finally, weighting of the data due to different number of firms across sectors and countries appears not to be a problem.

STRATEGY PERSPECTIVE AND THE CREATION OF PUBLIC VALUES

Bivariate relationships provide the key step toward testing our hypotheses concerning the relationship between strategy perspectives of firms and the public value created by the sector in which they operate. For that purpose, we identified the correlation coefficients. The coefficients will not only help in exploring relationships between strategy perspectives and public value; but they can also help to assess the extent to which strategy perspectives are related among each other. And similarly, for public values, whether high scores on one public value is generally associated with high scores on other public values as well, or whether there are potential trade-offs, for example between price and quality. Table 8.5 first displays the correlation coefficients among the variables measured at the firm level.

In Table 8.5, the boldfaced correlation coefficients between the strategy biases and the public values are of primary interest. There we find four significant relationships, three of which will be explained in more detail below. The most significant relationship between sustainability and network, has been discarded for content reason. It is primarily influenced by the high sustainability score of the French electricity sector, which in turn is primarily caused by their high usage of nuclear power. Since it does not seem useful to investigate a particular link in the usage of nuclear power and the network orientation of French EDF, this relationship is not further considered.

There are some significant correlation coefficients between different strategy biases; for instance, one bias in corporate strategy appears to be related to another bias in purpose strategy. From a theoretical point of

Table 8.5 Correlation coefficients between public values at firm level

	Corporate	Network	Purpose	Sustainable	Reliability	Quality	Price	Access
3 Corporate	1 [42]							
4 Network	0.05 [42]	1 [42]						
5 Purpose	0.38** [42]	0.38** [42]	1 [42]					
6 Sustainability	−0.09 [13]	0.78*** [13]	0.28 [13]	1 [13]				
7 Reliability	0.20 [24]	0.39* [24]	0.10 [24]	0.80*** [13]	1 [24]			
8 Quality	0.31** [42]	−0.04 [42]	−0.02 [42]	−0.05 [13]	−0.13 [24]	1 [42]		
9 Price	−0.25 [42]	0.11 [42]	−0.20 [42]	0.29 [13]	−0.04 [24]	−0.22 [42]	1 [42]	
10 Access	0.18 [29]	0.11 [29]	0.44** [29]	0 [0]	0.87*** [11]	0.26 [29]	−0.44** [29]	1 [29]
11 PVmean	−0.19 [31]	0.24 [31]	0.18 [31]	0.72*** [13]	0.74*** [13]	0.28 [31]	0.50*** [31]	0.64*** [18]

Note: *** $p < 0.01$; ** $p < 0.05$; * $p < 0.10$.

186

view, such clustering of strategic bias is to be expected in the form of temporary strategy recipes, and therefore does not harm the analysis further.

Likewise, there are a few public values which appear to be related. However, at close look, this is true only for reliability and sustainability in the electricity industry, and access and reliability in the railway sector. Rather, the absence of more relationships between the public values would indicate that there are no trade-offs in the achievement of one value at the expense of the other, at least as far as this analysis can tell. This is surprising. From judging the public debate, we would expect such potential trade-offs in particular between price and the other public values. But we only find a significantly negative relationship between price and access. The strong correlations between PVmean and other public values indicate that PVmean captures all dimensions relatively well. This is further confirmed by scale analysis of the three public values that are measured for the majority of the firms (Cronbach's alpha is 0.57).

SIGNIFICANT CORRELATIONS

With the data in Table 8.5 we can test the hypotheses formulated in the introduction, by examining the correlation coefficients between the various dimensions of public value and the strategy perspectives. We find four significant correlations.

First, there is a correlation between network strategy and reliability. This indicates that firms that are more inclined toward cooperation create higher public value in terms of reliability than those inclined toward autonomy. This finding applies to the electricity and railway sectors and supports hypothesis H_2. It can be illustrated with the case of SNCB, the Belgian railway firm. In the railway sector Belgium shares the highest score for reliability with Germany. But it is Belgium, represented here by SNCB, who achieves this through extensive cooperation. As SNCB enjoys a monopoly position in Belgium, it hardly has any exposure to competition. In addition, as a state-owned company, its strategy will inherently be more aligned with its country's public values. Most partnerships are international: with NS and SNCF for the operation of Thalys, with some international players in freight such as Rheinkraft and IFB. Some local partnerships include the Movibilites and Telenet, with electronic communication and information technologies providers. The group also cooperates with other transport providers in order to be able to offer integrated and reliable mobility solutions.

We find a second important positive correlation between corporate strategy and overall quality. This indicates that firms that are more inclined toward a strategy of synergy create higher public value in terms of quality than those with a strategy toward responsiveness. This finding applies for the entire sample of firms. This is a particularly striking finding. It is indeed the reverse of hypothesis H_1, which expected a relationship between responsiveness orientation and the achievement of public values. This relationship can be illustrated with the example of Casema, the Dutch cable firm. Casema has moved to a more flexible systems architecture and process harmonization across business units, employee functions and technology in order to create synergies. This included reducing the number of systems in operation; maximizing reuse of existing human and technological resources; introducing an effective customer value management program; offering expanded channel management; and reducing time to market for new value-added services. Casema's business units are separated according to function, whereas human resources, legal and regulatory affairs, and communications and public affairs are organized at a central level. This policy is supposed to increase the quality as employees are rewarded according to total company performance.

The third significant relationship is established between purpose strategy and access. Firms that are more inclined toward a strategy of responsibility create higher public value in terms of access than those with a strategy toward profitability. This finding is based on the entire sample of firms excluding the electricity sector, and supports hypothesis H_3. This significant relationship can be illustrated with the case example of KPN, the Dutch telecommunications firm. KPN plays an active role in education and in developing adapted services such as text telephone service. This shows their willingness to act in the interest of a broad group of stakeholders and is attached to the values of access and inclusive information society. KPN also cooperates with the National Fund for Help to Elderly People by supporting the helpdesk where elderly people can go with all sorts of general questions. In general the Netherlands score very well on access.

INSIGNIFICANT CORRELATIONS

The remainder of the correlation coefficients is not significant. They do not support any of the hypotheses we identified in the introduction. Some particularly interesting correlations that we expected to find, but that do not hold up to empirical scrutiny, are for instance that there is no relationship between corporate strategy biased toward synergy and price or PVmean, while we hypothesized a negative relationship (H_1). This means that firms that are integrated are not worse at creating public value for these dimensions—including low prices—than firms that have a strategic bias toward responsiveness. We also find no relationships between network strategy biased toward embeddedness with price, quality or access. This means that firms that tend to cooperate with other firms or other organizations generally create neither more nor less public value on these dimensions than firms that remain relatively autonomous.

This puts into doubt a pervasive preference of regulators to unbundle value chains and inhibit cooperation between industry players. For instance, the European Telecommunication Network Operators Association, that represents telecommunication industry players in European policy and regulatory issues, expresses its strong belief in autonomous competition as a basis for improved services and innovation in the region. However, this relationship is not supported by our data.

We also cannot observe a correlation between a purpose strategy toward responsibility with quality, price or access. This means that some firms do not practice what they preach. On the other hand, it also means that firms that are very profit oriented also do not create more or less public value— not even lower prices—than those that are not. For instance, the railway sector is very public value oriented. Therefore government policy seemed to think that they would safeguard values such as price and quality. In practice, however, this seems not to be the case.

CONCLUSIONS

There are three observed significant bivariate relationships or correlations between strategy perspectives and the dimensions of public value: network strategy biased toward embeddedness and reliability; corporate strategy biased toward synergy, and overall quality (this is particularly interesting as we hypothesized negative relationship); and purpose strategy biased toward responsibility and access.

We find that while the three different strategy perspectives reflect distinct dimensions of corporate strategy, some of these perspectives are correlated. Firms that are biased toward responsibility in their purpose strategy, also tend to be biased toward synergy in their corporate strategy and biased toward embeddedness in their network strategy. Theory would predict such a pattern to emerge, which is confirmed by this analysis. We do not find strong evidence of trade-offs between different public values, either in the correlation coefficients or in the F-tests.

The research set out to explore the relationship between strategy perspectives and public value. We developed three main hypotheses that guided the quantitative analysis: we expected a negative relationship between corporate strategy biased toward synergy and public value creation; and a positive relationship between public value creation and the other two strategy perspectives (network biased toward embeddedness and purpose biased toward responsibility).

As explained in the methodological part, measuring these concepts is difficult. Still we were able to compile a data set of 42 companies, across five countries and four sectors, which could be analyzed at two levels of aggregation, thus yielding additional insights. The descriptive statistics indicated that the variables are normally distributed. Differences across firms for strategy variables or public value are generally not explained by country or industry effects. At the same time, weighting of the data due to different number of firms across sectors and countries appears not to be a problem. In addition to links among strategy perspectives, we studied the relationships among the individual public values. We do not find strong evidence of trade-offs between different public values, either in the correlation coefficients, or in the F-tests.

The findings from our bivariate analysis of the relationships between strategy perspectives and public value generally support H_2. We find a positive relation between network strategy biased toward embeddedness and public value. Findings also support H_3. In this case we find a positive relation between purpose strategy biased toward responsibility and public value. However the findings reject H_1. We find a positive rather than negative relation between corporate strategy biased toward responsiveness and public value. The correlation coefficients among the individual variables indicated positive relationships between all strategy perspectives and public value creation. Furthermore, firms that score high on all three strategy variables at once are indeed the ones that create most public value, both overall (PVmean) as well as on the majority of individual dimensions.

The analysis yielded insights on three levels. First, there are relationships observable between strategic orientation of companies and the achievement of public values. That fact in itself merits that such relationships should be better investigated. This seems all the more prescient, as the observed relationships in this analysis are not conforming to the implicit assumptions often pursued by regulatory practice, for instance in the typical preference for unbundled services, privatized companies or induced competition between providers.

Secondly, the analysis was made additionally difficult, as much of the comparative methodology for assessing public values needed to be developed from scratch. Since the infrastructure industry is so heavily influenced by public value achievement, it might be a fruitful field to develop more methodologies to operationalize public values also for empirical cross-comparative purposes.

Lastly, to the degree that the observed relationships in this analysis hold true, further investigation is required to establish the causal mechanism between these three strategic orientations and the respective achievement of public values. Only a detailed understanding of this causal mechanism is likely to lead to a regulatory practice that can fully leverage the available resources for the maximization of both private and public gain.

NOTES

1. PVmean is the simple arithmetic mean of the respective public values per sector. Pvmean should be interpreted as follows: the higher the value, the better public values are safeguarded.
2. For the statistical analysis it is important to note the values found for the various variables are normally distributed and can therefore be used in subsequent calculations without problems.

REFERENCES

Beck Jørgensen, T. and B. Bozeman (2007), 'The public values universe: an inventory', *Administration & Society*, **39** (3): 354–81.
Bozeman, B. (2003), 'Public value failure: when efficient markets may not do', *Public Administration Review*, **62** (2): 145–61.
Dahl, R. and C. Lindblom (1953) *Politics, Economics, and Welfare*, New York: Harper Torchbooks.
De Wit, B. and R. Meyer (2004), *Strategy Synthesis: Resolving Strategy Paradoxes to Create Competitive Advantage*, 2nd edn, London: Thomson.
Doz, Y. and G. Hamel (1988), *The Alliance Advantage: The Art of Creating Value Through Partnering*, Boston, MA: HBS Press.
Dyer, J.H. and H. Singh (1998), 'The relational view: cooperative strategy and sources of interorganizational competitive advantage', *Academy of Management Review*, **23** (4): 660–79.
European Union Commission (2003), 'Energy infrastructures and security of supply', *Communications from the Commission of the European Parliament and the Council*, pp. 739–42.
Lewis, M.L. (2000), 'Exploring paradox: towards a more comprehensive guide', *Academy of Management Review*, **25**: 760–76.
Manent, P. (2001), *Cours familier de philosophie politique*, Paris: Fayard.
Miles, R.H. (1982), *Coffin Nails and Corporate Strategies*, Englewood Cliffs, NJ: Prentice-Hall.
Moore, M.H. (1996), *Creating Public Value: Strategic Management in Government*, Harvard, MA: Harvard University Press.
Moore, M.H. (2003), 'The public values scorecard: a rejoinder and an alternative to "Strategic Performance Measurement and Management in Non-Profit Organizations" by Robert Kaplan', Harvard University, working paper no. 18, Hauser Center for Nonprofit Organizations.

Moore, M.H. and S. Khagram (2004), On creating public values: what business might learn from government about strategic management, working paper, Harvard University, John F. Kennedy School of Government.

Preece, S.B. (1995), 'Incorporating international strategic alliances into overall firm strategy: a typology of six managerial objectives', *International Executive*, **37** (3): 261–77.

Ramanujam, V. and P. Varadarajan (1989), 'Research on corporate diversification: a synthesis', *Strategic Management Journal*, **10** (6): 523–51.

Rittel, H.W.J. and M.M. Webber (1973), 'Dilemmas in a general theory of planning', *Policy Sciences*, **4**: 155–69.

Rumelt, R.P. (1974), *Strategy, Structure and Economic Performance*, Cambridge, MA: Harvard University Press.

Schweiger, D.M., W.R. Sandberg and J.W. Ragan (1986), 'Group approaches for improving strategic decision making: a comparative analysis of dialectical inquiry, devil's advocacy, and consensus', *Academy of Management Journal*, **29** (1): 51–71.

Shapiro, C. and H. Varian, (1998), *Information Rules: A Strategic Guide to the Network Economy*, Boston, MA: HBS Press.

Whittington, R. and M. Mayer, (1999), *The European Corporation: Strategy, Structure, and Social Science*, Oxford: Oxford University Press.

9. Disruptive technologies in communications: observations from an entrepreneur

Malcolm Matson

INTRODUCTION

This contribution is not from an academic, but rather an entrepreneur who, for the past 25 years, has been focused on the local deployment of the disruptive digital technologies that are marking out the information age. There is no claim that the observations, comments and conclusions made below are the result of exhaustive and rigorous research and analysis—they are not. Rather they result from personal empirical and anecdotal evidence gained at ground level, in the hurly-burly of the marketplace. They have been tempered and tested by a fair amount of commonsense reasoning; but they make no claim to being more than that. Therefore, there will be gaps and errors of omission and commission in what is presented which, hopefully, will spur others to more rigorous and deeper analysis, scrutiny and argument. However, the fundamental, underlying hypothesis is stark and simple.

Never before in history has the extent, nature and pace of the impact of technological innovation been dictated primarily by the vested interests that stand to be negatively disrupted by it, rather than by the anonymous mass of end users who will discover and create new uses for, and benefits from, these new technologies. The relatively recent human-made tools by which vested interests achieve this artificial shaping and slowing of history are their compelling influence on public policy formulation and the subsequent framing of sector-specific regulation which assumes and assures them of maintaining a place in tomorrow's landscape.

WAVES OF TECHNOLOGICAL REVOLUTIONS

It is worth starting with some well-researched facts. Talk of our being in the midst of a revolution in information technology (IT) is now commonplace. There is a general understanding that somehow or other, this is a revolution. Something special is happening in our world as a result of IT. In her important book on technological revolutions, Carlota Perez (2002) provides a well-documented account of how such periodic waves of technological innovation are the very stuff of history. Taking the mid-eighteenth century as a starting point, she identifies five technological revolutions between then and the present day. She argues very persuasively that there is a distinct rhythm and timing to the emergence of each of these technological revolutions, and the form and pace with which they develop. Moreover, her research has identified that, '[e]ach technological revolution results from the synergistic interdependence of a group of industries with one or more infrastructural networks' (Perez 2002, p. 13). This development and deployment of an enabling and underpinning new infrastructure specific to each of these new ages is foundational to Perez's subsequent conclusions relating to the delivery of a 'golden age' of untold benefit and wealth creation (see Figure 9.1).

What strikes me as being particularly significant about these waves of industrial revolution is that none of the previous industrial revolutions has ever been deliberately planned or delivered by those responsible for the infrastructural network of the prevailing age. My question is therefore, what is the philosophical, political, economic or rational basis for departing from this with the current IT revolution? Or, to be more specific, why is the telecommunications (telecoms) industry, born in the nineteenth century, the inevitable heir to the new broadband digital infrastructure of the twenty-first century and the IT revolution? Why have we decided to anoint the telecoms industry with the unique task and responsibility of developing the infrastructure which will herald the new 'golden age' which, if history is anything to go by, will replace and subsume the paradigm in which the sector was born, grew up and flourished? For that is just what we appear to have tried to do, and persist with.

A cursory contemplation of the five technological revolutions identified in Figure 9.1 might lead one to make several hypotheses. First, paradigm-changing technological innovation giving rise to new infrastructures is always created by entrepreneurs outside the infrastructure industry(s) upon which it will have prime impact. Secondly, the infrastructure industry(s) upon which it will have prime impact can never embrace and deploy such paradigm-changing technological innovation in a timescale that meets market demand and the implicit impetus of the technology. Thirdly, left to themselves—they usually do not even try—and hence the paradigm-changing technological innovation pervades the market, creating the golden age, often subsuming the previous infrastructure.

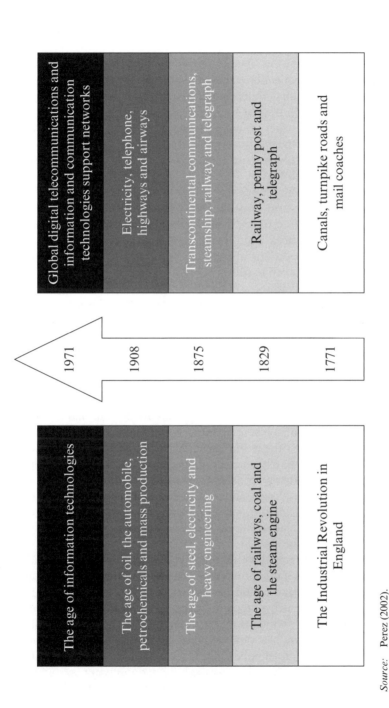

The age of information technologies — Global digital telecommunications and information and communication technologies support networks

1971

The age of oil, the automobile, petrochemicals and mass production — Electricity, telephone, highways and airways

1908

The age of steel, electricity and heavy engineering — Transcontinental communications, steamship, railway and telegraph

1875

The age of railways, coal and the steam engine — Railway, penny post and telegraph

1829

The Industrial Revolution in England — Canals, turnpike roads and mail coaches

1771

Source: Perez (2002).

Figure 9.1   Technological revolutions and ages of infrastructure development

A TALE OF THE REGULATION OF DISRUPTIVE TECHNOLOGIES

To illustrate the above mentioned hypotheses, consider the canal industry in the UK as it was when it underpinned the original industrial revolution. The first canal was built in 1761 by an entrepreneur, Francis Egerton, the Third Duke of Bridgewater. It worked with sensational effect—carrying coal from his mines to the mill markets of Manchester, and everyone prospered. That exemplar set fire to an explosion of canal infrastructure development in the UK such that by 1825, there were more than 4500 miles of canal. Canals were, by that time, the transport industry.

Then, against this world of canal transportation, spot on time at the dawn of the nineteenth century, a number of engineering entrepreneurs such as Richard Trevithick and George Stephenson delivered the disruptive technological innovations of steam locomotion and rail track which would eventually give birth to railways.

Imagine a political and regulatory environment pertaining at that time as it does today. There would undoubtedly have been a minister in some government department who had specific responsibility for the canal industry—seen as a strategic sector of the UK economy—indeed, it may well have been state owned. If privatization-enlightenment prevailed, then there would no doubt have been a regulator, a sort of Office of Canal Operations and Management (OCOM). Sector-specific policy and regulation would abound—all in the name of promoting competition and protecting users' interests. Then, out of the English mechanical engineer George Stephenson's inventive mind, the technologically innovative steam engine arrives on the world stage. What happens? First, the canal industry, which immediately perceives the significance of this potentially highly disruptive technology, proclaims its potential value and benefit and urges their minister and regulator to take stock of this new technological innovation. It considers framing appropriate legislation and regulation to promote its deployment potential in a manner that benefits all stakeholders of the time.

Secondly, the government would then appoint experts and consultants to prepare the analysis and reports on which any promoting and enabling legislation and regulation would be framed. The appointed consultants would obviously have relevant special expertise, knowledge and reputation in transportation—which would be evidenced by an impressive client base in the canal sector. This poisoned cocktail of vested interests, politicians, regulators and public policy pundits would no doubt have resulted in a well-argued report. This report would have undoubtedly come up with several conclusions. This new railway technology undoubtedly had great potential. It should be deployed as soon as possible to maintain Britain's economic and military power. However, substantial potential dangers and issues in the technology require regulation. For instance, the regulation should consider the threat of boiler explosions, runaway trains, frightened animals, and so on. In addition, steam locomotive technology should be deployed by licensed operators who have a proven what we call today a track record. Finally, OCOM's light-touch regulation should bring all this into being.

The undoubted solution implementation would have been the laying of railway track up and down every towpath beside every canal in the country, with locomotives running on this track to pull the barges. But the frightening fact is that such an incumbent driven deployment of the disruptive technology would have looked like a win-win situation for all concerned. For instance, there would be faster movement of coal and other materials; a greater utilization of canal capacity; a minimized public risk through licensed regulatory regime; the birth of a new engine manufacturing industry; the massive growth of steel and rail output; and so on.

In the absence of any sector-specific regulation and public deployment policy, the reality was very different. It was a totally unimagined or unplanned golden age of new wealth creating opportunities, industries and social benefits. These benefits were diverse and extensive and included the birth of a world-beating shipbuilding industry on the banks of the river Clyde; a new industry of leisure as the seaside at places like Blackpool could became temporary host to the working classes; the development of street lighting as the visitors in Blackpool wanted to wander the streets at night in light; standard time as a replacement for sun-based time related to longitude; and, finally, better dental health in the cities as fresh milk with its calcium could now be transported there rapidly from far-off farms. All this was the result of the unfettered disruptive technology of the steam locomotive in the hands of entrepreneurs with the market of end users being the primary, if not sole, arbiter of its value, use and mode of development. And the canal industry? Dead and buried within 20 years.

It is not hard to see similar examples of these facts from earlier ages. When, in the middle of the fifteenth century, Johannes Gutenberg deployed the disruptive technology of movable type—the world took a giant leap forward. The vested interests of the document production world it changed (the scribes and quill-makers) were left dead in their tracks. Had they been afforded special public policy or regulatory protection, would the scribes have deployed movable type? The answer is undoubtedly positive, but only in a manner to ensure their own survival, such as in their back office as a means to produce their invoices more quickly.

I would suggest that this natural Darwinian-like cycle of death and resurrection brought about by disruptive technology is what has marked the progress of humankind during the last centuries. In the 1980s, for no examined or specifically argued reason, governments around the world decided to try to change the rules in the domain of information communications technology (ICT). Let us examine the futility and damaging impact for society at large of this attempt to intervene in technological development.

DISRUPTIVE TECHNOLOGIES AND STRANGLING SECTOR SPECIFIC REGULATION

Since the establishment of the telephone industry in the 1870s, the fundamentals of the underlying telephone technology has dictated a business model which prevails throughout the now mature global cartel of telecom operators. The model's characteristics can be summarized thus: first, to charge end users on a noncost-related basis for the exclusive use of a pair of copper wires to the local exchange (plus selling and renting them a telephone handset where possible); secondly, to charge end users for the orderly allocation of a scarce resource—trunk and international network capacity or bandwidth capacity—and doing so on a time and distance related tariff; and thirdly, developing and selling network-embedded value-added services and content.

This business model is rooted in the fundamental topography of the technology (see Figure 9.2). The latter consists of telephone handsets linked by a dedicated pair of copper wires to an intelligent local central office or exchange, which in turn can be connected to other local and international central offices around the world over a network of a limited number of copper wires, with final connection to the party being called mirroring a similar topography at the far end. This vertically integrated business model generates well in excess of $1000 billion dollars a year (International Telecommunication Union 2007).

This business model, framed around a vertical integration of network and services, was, and largely still is, the model that underpins the world of telecommunications. It resides deep in the fundamentals of every telecoms operator, their management and shareholders—both state-owned or privatized incumbent and all the new entrants brought into being since the mid-1980s. It was supposed that the introduction of competition between these old and new vertically integrated businesses, which were developed around the vertically integrated business model of the telephone era, would deliver benefit to end users. However, at the very moment this politically motivated privatization and competition-promoting public

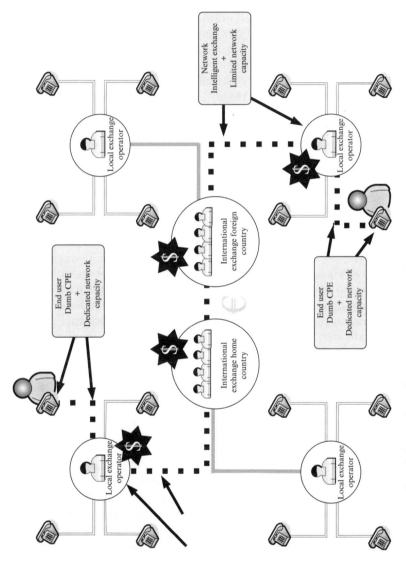

Figure 9.2   Topography of the analog telecommunications technology

199

policy was beginning to take hold around the world, disruptive technology suddenly bursts upon the scene.

There are three seminal disruptive digital technology innovations of the latter half of the twentieth century. They have the potential of becoming to the telecoms sector what the steam engine was to canals. The silicon chip dramatically entered intelligent and low-cost consumer devices such as personal computers and organizers, music players and gaming consoles. Optical fiber has become the medium for the transmission of information. The last disruptive technology is the software-controlled radio.

Like all others before them, these fundamental technology innovations held the implicit power to change the world completely and not just to annihilate the operators of the old paradigm, but to render obsolete and powerless the very business model on which they have prospered for over a century. These disruptive technological innovations, as they combine together, created a new technological context. Scarcity is replaced by abundance with developments in optic fibers. Traffic routing and control migrates away from the network to the control of end users. The passage of time confirms Moore's law, the empirical observation that the complexity of integrated circuits, with respect to minimum component cost, doubles every 24 months.

First, nobody has yet determined a finite upper limit for the capacity of a single strand of optical fiber, which is the size of a human hair. Indeed, ingenious engineers push the limit ever higher with every passing year. In 2004 a team of physicists, computer scientists and network engineers led by the California Institute of Technology transmitted 101 gigabits per second through optic fiber.

> [The] data transfer speed is equivalent to downloading three full DVD movies per second, or transmitting all of the content of the Library of Congress in 15 minutes. It also has been estimated to be approximately 5% of the total rate of production of new content on Earth during the test. (Cal tech press release 24 November 2004)

It seems that the bandwidth capacity of fiber is effectively infinite. The open-market value of anything in infinite supply is zero.

Secondly, in the world of telephony, the routing of traffic was embedded in, and under the control of, the intelligent central offices of the telecom operators. End users in the world of Alexander Graham Bell had to talk to the operator of the phone company, and, only on the payment of a toll would any connectivity beyond that point be opened up to them. Just as in a railway, in the world of voice telephony the routing of the trains is controlled by the signalman working for the track authority and not the train driver, so it was in the analog world of voice telephony. In the digital world brought about by the disruptive technologies listed above, the opposite pertains. The network becomes like a motorway, where the intelligence and control necessary to route the traffic is in the hands and head of the vehicle driver. The control of motorways is passive with signs indicating whether a particular destination is in this direction or that, but utterly powerless to control, or even know, the intended destination of any particular vehicle—until that vehicle routes itself to one place or another. So it is with the intelligent packets of bits that we create with our keystrokes on the computer—each knowing its purpose and destination and simply looking for a big fat pipe to traverse the world—being guided toward its intended destination by interrogating effectively passive routers embedded in the network. The global telephone network and the Internet are both communication systems and interface with humans; but that is about all they have in common.

Thirdly the impact of Moore's law adds massive impact to the society changing power of disruptive digital technologies. In 1976 a hard disk drive with the capacity of 1 billion bytes would have cost $560000. Today it costs 56 cents, that is, one millionth of the cost. End users around the world can now purchase digital hardware and software from their local supply store or over the Internet, which is the match of that available to the mightiest telecom company. The bedroom of any teenager in the developed world can readily be crammed with powerful, cheap equipment that only a few years ago was the privileged domain of broadcasters, Hollywood and mass media newspapers. Digital technologies offering outrageous abundance at minimal cost are available to all, and so real scarcity is eliminated.

The telecoms industry, protected by sector-specific legislation and regulation which it had significantly helped to frame, was able to deploy these three disruptive technologies in a manner that supported and sustained their original business model (see Figure 9.3). Abundant fiber capacity replaced the limited number of copper wires connecting central offices, that is, the trunk and international networks. Digital computers replaced the human operator and subsequent, electro-mechanical switches in the central office. Mobile operators acquired spectrum rights to mimic the same business model on a wireless basis.

What the telecoms industry failed to grasp was the earth-changing impact of end users at the periphery also being empowered by digital technology. Whether it has been the explosive growth of personal computers, networking and, more recently, access to license-exempt wireless spectrum which has triggered massive investment in new wireless networking devices and mind-blowing innovation that has enabled low-cost, user-driven mesh networking to become a reality, users are discovering that they can build

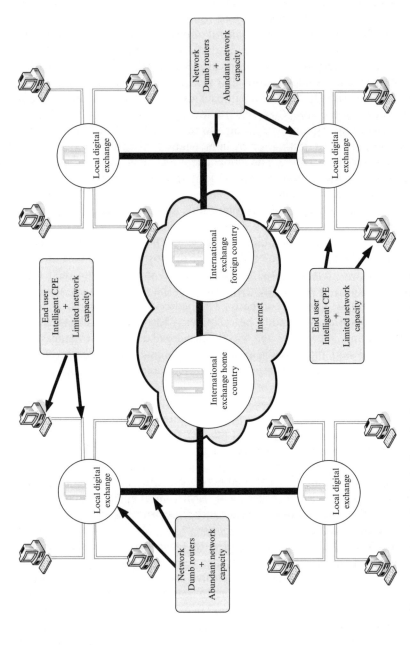

Figure 9.3   Topology of today's digital telecommunications technology

their own home and office networks and use them on a zero-cost marginal basis. Couple this with the astounding growth of the Internet as an open access digital network where, once access is obtained, then bits travel to and from around the world at zero cost regardless of their decoded form, that is, voice, video or data.

The digital content and intelligence is increasingly seen to reside at the periphery in the hands and minds of the individuals and companies that create them. They are the very people who consume the creative services and output of others elsewhere at the periphery. Yet a world of would-be peer-to-peer connectivity demands symmetrical open access. We have, for instance, the telecommunication software Skype, which powerfully demonstrates this. It has shown that, in this new digital world, even basic telephony is simply a small application that sits on an end user's computer, rather than a service provided by a network operator. Access to oceans of unused fiber capacity in the trunk and international networks is deliberately restricted as the owners, incumbent and competing operators desperately try to sustain obsolete business models by artificially creating bandwidth scarcity.

This absurdity only persists thanks to the fact that governments, public policy-makers and politicians with well-intentioned but misguided intentions to modernize the world have mistakenly taken to looking to yesterday's powerful vested interests to map a smooth, migratory path to the future deployment of these digital disruptive technologies. Why on earth governments should have expected the telecoms industry of yesteryear to bring in the new age and deploy the disruptive technologies which have the inherent ability to make obsolete their very business model is for others to study. For now it is important to recognize that this is precisely what has been happening and to consider the negative consequences for end users.

LESSONS TO BE LEARNED

When the telecoms sector was privatized, it is my contention that we should have permitted the emerging disruptive digital technologies alone to erode the monopoly status of the local incumbent. Leaving enterprising entrepreneurs free in the marketplace to adopt, adapt and deploy new technological innovations around new business models, with the market of end users alone determining the ultimate fate of these disruptive technologies, is the lesson we should learn.

It is this unfettered power of disruptive technology which fuels the progress and wealth creation that occasionally delivers a golden age. Instead of realizing this back in the early 1980s, as our politicians and public policy-makers around the world quite rightly sought to unhitch the telecoms sector from stifling state control, they listened and looked to vested interests rather than to history, for the guiding principles by which it should be done. In many places, this situation persists to this day. In the UK, there is a self-created and perpetuated Broadband Stakeholders Group which provides the UK government with advice on broadband. They gather several organizations involved in broadband to influence policy, regulatory and commercial issues.

The result is that we have created a regulatory behemoth that thinks that it, and it alone, can create a market whereby the new disruptive technologies are deployed to everyone's benefit. This flawed approach to progress has delayed the full flood of benefits inherent in these disruptive digital technologies being enjoyed by the world's users and thereby triggering the golden age that Perez suggests should be around the corner.

However, I believe that it is no more than a delay. The opening of the floodgates is as inevitable as was the wheel. There are, emerging around the world, hundreds if not thousands of examples of what are becoming known as open public local access networks. They are resulting from citizens, cities and municipalities beginning to appreciate that they need to exercise initiative to deploy these disruptive technologies in a manner which results in their primary value and benefit residing with themselves and not being sucked out of the community by absent third-party owners and operators.

There are some hopeful signs. Take Estonia for example. The capital city, Tallin, had three Wi-Fi hotspots in 2000; eight years later, it has over 300. Estonia openly embraces the disruptive technology of software-controlled wireless, which is being seen almost as a democratic right. This presents a perfect example of what happens when private enterprise is free from overbearing government sector-specific regulatory policy. Estonia's citizens appear to see the link between easy or free access to information made possible by these disruptive technologies, on the one hand, and their new democracy, on the other. When the country won its independence from the Soviet Union in 1991, a forward-thinking government looked to IT, the Internet and the underpinning digital technologies as central pillars of Estonia's future economy. At relatively little cost, Estonia leapfrogged into a place among Europe's cyber elite—and gave the world Skype. Since then wireless has taken hold as nowhere else in Europe. Seventy-five percent of the population own mobile phones from which they can pay for anything from a glass of beer to space in a parking lot which will also call the phone when time is nearly up. Government ministers conduct weekly cabinet sessions online. It is freely admitted that the key to the success of wireless in Estonia has as much to do with a hands-off approach from government as with deliberate strategy. From the start, an independent Estonia pursued a ruthless free-market line: no state monopoly for telecoms, minimal regulation and healthy competition among commercial players. 'The government sees no need to regulate,' says Tex Vertmann, an IT advisor to Prime Minister Juhan Parts. 'In Estonia cyberspace belongs to all. That's democracy'. (Underhill 2004).

There is also surely a strong free trade argument. Adam Smith famously wrote, 'People of the same trade seldom meet together, even for merriment and diversion, but the conversation ends in a conspiracy against the public, or in some contrivance to raise prices' (Smith 1776 [1976], p. 175). One should leave aside the claim that many would make, that nothing exemplifies better Smith's quote than the telecommunications industry and the International Telecommunication Union. It is now widely understood and accepted that the world is best served if raw materials and physical products pass freely through the sea and air ports of the world, without undue restriction or the imposition of special tariffs or tolls. A question therefore needs to be asked: why in the information age is not the world best served by the bits of value and information being assured free passage to and from every computer port, without restriction and the imposition of special tariffs or tolls? For that, in effect, is what we have allowed to emerge by erecting public policy and regulation that has to date anointed the telecoms sector and its obsolete business model with the right to control the information highway and impose a toll on every item of passing traffic. Rather, the innately free and open nature implicit in the disruptive technologies of digital abundance should be allowed to have market sway and to dictate the form and mode of operation of their deployment. Sector-specific public policy intervention and regulation is the very tool which incumbent vested interests have successfully adopted over recent decades to help them mitigate the impact of disruptive technologies and thereby to extend their life beyond that which a free market would naturally grant.

The emerging reality of open public local access networks is increasingly being regarded as great news for the world and for anyone making digital hardware or software or content. It is bad news for any country that is seeking a smooth, telecom company-driven migratory route to the future. Disruptive technologies do precisely what they say they do—they disrupt. Let them do it!

REFERENCES

International Telecommunication Union (2007), *Key Global Telecom Indicators for the World Telecommunication Service Sector*, http://www.itu.int/ITU-D/ict/statistics/at_glance/KeyTelecom99.html (accessed 1 October 2007).

Perez, C. (2002), *Technological Revolutions and Financial Capital: The Dynamics of Bubbles and Golden Ages*, Cheltenham, UK and Northampton, MA, USA: Edward Elgar.

Smith, A. (1776), *An Inquiry into the Nature and Causes of the Wealth of Nations*, reprinted in W.B. Todd (ed.) (1976), *Glasgow Edition of the Works and Correspondence of Adam Smith*, vol. I, Oxford: Oxford University Press.

Underhill, W. (2004), 'Freedom in the air waves', *Newsweek*, 7–14 June, http: www.newsweek.com/id/53926 (accessed 1 October 2007).

Index

Titles of publications are in *italics*.